Kago, Kastom and *Kalja*:
the Study of Indigenous Movements in Melanesia Today

edited by
Marc Tabani and Marcellin Abong

Cover photo:
© Credo/Marc Tabani

© pacific-credo Publications, 2013
ISBN 978-2-9537485-1-2

Aix-Marseille Université - CNRS - EHESS
CREDO UMR 7308, Marseilles

Kago, Kastom and *Kalja*:
the study of Indigenous Movements in Melanesia Today

edited by
Marc Tabani and Marcellin Abong

pacific-credo **Publications**

Contents

Chapter I

What's the Matter with Cargo Cults Today?

Marc Tabani

Complex Movements in Contemporary Melanesian Anthropology

What has happened to those indigenous movements in Melanesia that, over six decades, have been categorized – somewhat imprecisely – as "cargo cults"? Have they simply vanished in the wake of modernization, globalization or nation-building? Have they disappeared without passing on any tangible contemporary legacy to the peoples of countries such as Papua New Guinea, the Solomon Islands or the Republic of Vanuatu? Or do they persist, not as a matter of fact, but merely as a post-modern metaphor of desire? According to Lindstrom, the answer to both questions depends on what precisely we are talking about: the "real thing" in its "ethnographic accuracy" or "the stories we tell about [them]" (1993: 12-13). Indigenous social movements are still occurring in southwest Oceania – where their precursors have been observed for decades – even though some anthropologists now consider that it reduces their social complexity to call such movements "cargo cults".

A recent trend in anthropology has been for specialists to embrace a deconstructionist perspective in reaction to the wide public fascination and appetite for "Western writings on cargo cults". In this approach, ethnographic data are subordinated to a main theoretical goal to treat cargo stories as mere archives of past colonial hegemony. Jebens observes that, according to some current critical appraisals, cargo cults "even do not exist as an identifiable object of study" (Jebens 2004a: 2). It is difficult in this perspective to imagine any persistence or continuity in these movements, or any future. Here, cargo cult stories are examined to study the Western Self: why and how did We create Them? Cargo cults or millenarian movements are seen as Western popular and academic reifications – "neither Cargo nor cults" (Kaplan 1995) – even if they do exist as Western phantasmagorias (Kaplan 2004). Cargo cult writings are assumed mostly to be intended to pathologise Melanesians' cultures to better repress them. However, despite their "uncertain and confusing ethnographic reality [they]…

after all, cannot be claimed to exist in the minds of Western observers alone" (Jebens 2004a: 10).

Attendees and participants in our ASAO session[1] "*Kago, Kastom, Kalja*: Old Theories and New Realities in the Study of Melanesian Movements" (meeting in Santa Cruz 2009 and Alexandria 2010), took a different approach. Most were convinced that classic cargo cult studies have been quite heuristic and useful for a comparative understanding of culture contact, Christianisation and social change in Pacific societies. Despite its derogatory and colonial connotations, however, there was less consensus on whether the concept still efficiently serves analytic and descriptive functions. The participants debated the validity of the concept, since this appears as a necessary stage for discussing the continuity of these phenomena. Like former cargo cults, most indigenous movements flourishing in Melanesia today are responses to disturbing cross-cultural challenges, and continue to involve ritual organization. All these movements take place in context of and in relation with an embracing globalization, especially since "cargo" has become historically "a symbol of the breach between whites and natives" (Keesing nd.). According to late Keesing, the Kwaio's *kastomu* in Malaita provides a key to better scrutinize the complexity of the concept of cargo as expression of hostility towards the colonial whites and not just of simple materialism. To relate the study of Melanesian movements with the more recent issues of *kastom* and *kalja* is an innovative analytical strategy. It also helps solve what Keesing, in his posthumous writing, considered as "remaining problems" in the study of these movements: "Why are they so similar, why do they appear in certain places and not in others, how to turn their creative energy in a more constructive direction?" (Keesing *ibid.*).

This volume was inspired by a desire to establish the past and present status of "cargo cults", or whatever label or expression we choose to apply to such movements in order to emphasize in their factuality the material manifestations of ongoing beliefs, via things – stuff, objects, matter – that are evident in their particular social and ritual processes. The question of materiality is embraced in many of the papers (Dalton Ch. 2, Biersack Ch. 4, and Lindstrom Ch. 7). These beliefs, often fraught with millenarian ideas, intermingled with neo-traditional cosmological knowledge, gave rise to complex social movements and continue to do so. Sometimes they may persist as outdated beliefs, harking back to the colonial period, now waiting to be

---

1. Participatians included Joshua Bell, Terry Brown, James Clifford, Rick Feinberg, Christine Jourdan, Eben Kirksey, Maria Lepowski, Michael Scott, Joel Robbins, the eight contributors to this volume and many more observers.

incorporated in, or discarded from, emerging regional or national popular narratives, even though in every case numerous field reports over a long period attest to their "ethnographic accuracy".

Indeed, on the island of Tanna (Vanuatu), for example, it is "true" that people built airstrips in the 1950s to await the landing of planes loaded with Western commodities promised to them by a spiritual guide, prophet or spirit called John Frum. Those expectations involve complex aspirations that extend beyond coveting fridges or cars, but their material manifestation is undeniable, even if not sufficient at all. In regards to globalization process the factuality of past and present movements once labeled as cargo cult "should be understood as an encounter between materialism and something beyond materialism which might be called 'religious' but which probably needs another name, since that term doesn't make much sense anymore because, for so many people, it isn't a matter of 'belief' but instead of knowledge" (Dalton Ch. 2).

The Continuity of John Frum Beliefs and Practices

To illustrate this from my own experience, when I started to study millenarian ideologies on Tanna at the beginning of the 1990s, I thought that the beliefs surrounding them had already been consigned to the past. My first field observations led me to conclude that the enduring elements of the so-called "John Frum movement" were undergoing a process of folkloricization; that symbols of John Frum peoples' historical struggle, like the protection of *kastom*, had been appropriated by state ideology as a precursory nationalist claim. I had to wait until events in 2000, and those of the following year, changed my mind.

After a natural disaster on the island and in the wake of many church sermons about the "end of the world" that was to occur in 2000, a new John Frum prophet arose. Prophet Fred predicted the immediate end of the world. He insisted that people must climb the mythical hill of Yenkahi and rebuild Noah's Ark, proclaiming that all the followers of the movement would be safe, while the non-believers would perish. Faithful supporters would win eternal life, regaining their youthful selves – they would change their skin like crabs. A few weeks later, the bush in Yenkahi had been cleared. Houses were built and for some years the village became the largest on the island. Over 3000 people lived there, without working gardens, because an abundance of supplies was expected. Hundreds of pigs were killed in a day, for sacrificial purposes, without being consumed. Every day the prophet Fred reported new signs and visions. Among the followers, many were educated ni-Vanuatu citizens, teachers, nurses and other public servants who had resigned from their jobs, some of them coming from the capital Port-Vila and even from other islands.

The movement gradually declined after strong action by the government of Vanuatu, which sent armed forces to suppress its activities. The "ethnographic accuracy" of some tangible aspects of the *muvmen blong Fred* has also been recorded on film. This documentary (Tabani 2005) is based on real events. It shows real people expressing their intimate thoughts and heartfelt beliefs. It reveals how they organized into social movements that manifested many similarities with classic, old-school "cargo cults". The birth, the development and the repression of the movement bears many similarities to the initial emergence of the John Frum movement in the 1930s, even though nobody invoked the "cargo cult" label to describe this revival. Several offshoots of this recent movement arose, bidding against each other with different millenarian promises: the impending arrival of billions of dollars (movement of Joe Keydu, middle bush Tanna); the resurrection of the dead (movement of Karis, north Tanna); the renewal of the "true *kastom*" (in all the John Frum movement's different branches).

Persisting Divergence in the Use of a Classic Label

Several papers delivered at the Santa Cruz 2009 and Alexandria 2010 session retraced movements that expressed quite similar beliefs, accompanied in some cases by profound social consequences. However, the strongest expansion in the field of cargo cult studies is occurring in the realm of cargo stories and images, where a strand of contemporary anthropological argument contests the label "cargo cult" as an analytic category (McDowell 1988; Hermann Ch. 6) and even sometimes challenges its factual accuracy or ignores regular warnings to preserve "an ethnographically grounded anthropology" (Robbins 2004: 258; see also Tabani 2007). Today there are a wide range of Melanesian voices who themselves, whether they use the expression (*kago kalt*) pejoratively in relation to their fellow citizens (Sullivan 2005, Jebens 2007) or adopt it as a criticism of Western consumerist practices (sometimes called *kago kalja* in Vanuatu), also contribute to the burgeoning literature and scholarly debate on the topic. Indeed, it became evident in the sessions that "Cargo cults won't die quietly" (Lindstrom 1993a: 163; see also Dalton Ch. 2, Biersak Ch. 4, Macintyre Ch.5), either narratively or factually.

Despite the diverse characteristics and multiple orientations of all these movements, since their birth in colonial times in the wake of Christianization processes, significant family resemblances have prompted the need to categorize them by means of an encompassing label (see Dalton Ch. 2). Although semantically weak or vague, the strength of the "cargo cult" label has been its propensity to become familiar, if not famous, and occasionally notorious (Lindstrom Ch. 7). The "Western fascination" with cargo cults is as old as the interest shown in them by academic anthropology and Pacific Studies; but "their presence in popular, pre-Internet media accounts and texts (journalism, music lyrics, art, novels, and the like)" (Lindstrom *ibid.*) has been given a new platform through the blogosphere. Previously a synonym for economic and political irrationality in liberal ideologies, the notion of cargo cult has now become part of a post-modern spiritualist movement – lying somewhere between virtual global voodoo and New Age sustainability.

As Clifford observed during a 2009 ASAO session, when the papers which make up this volume were first discussed, among critical anthropologists, it is still the case that "even if different participants disagree about the use of the term, nevertheless everybody who hears 'cargo cult' immediately knows what we are speaking about". Scott too, even though he rejected the label in his analysis of Makiran stories, reminds us that:

> "Readers familiar with the literature on so-called 'cargo cults' in Melanesia will immediately recognize elements from a well known repertoire: an underground town full of modern infra-structure and technology controlled by autochthonous powers or the dead; claims to be in communication with this realm; Americans as ancestor-like liberators bringing development; and expectations of imminent transformation from relative poverty to prosperity, from relative obscurity to centrality" (Scott 2010b).

Nevertheless, he adds, "even if the concept of 'cargo cult' had not been under critique for several decades, the term would not accurately describe the data. I found no evidence of any cultic activity or movement relating to the Makiran underground" (Scott *ibid.*). Abong (Ch. 3), like Scott, does not make use of the "cargo cult" label to examine the history of the Nagriamel movement in Santo and in the Northern Islands of the former New Hebrides. However, even in Abong's account, the reference to America – associated with movements or mythologies influenced by World War II experiences that appear to be founded on rational apprehension of material differences – also frequently invokes supernatural sources for the disparity:

> "On Ambae, people shared the story of Anqa Tagaro, a tradition of a civilization that existed in a previous time. This was identified as 'Bali Hai' in the novel *Tales of the South Pacific* by the American writer James Michener. These myths are connected to beliefs about the [Ambae] island's Manaro volcano. They tell the story of the kidnapping of the guardian of wisdom and knowledge, someone by the name of Moltare. Moltare was later said to be kidnapped by

the Americans during World War II. He was taken to America and it was thanks to his knowledge that the United States succeeded in becoming the world's most powerful nation" (Abong Ch. 3).

It is the coupling of the fantastic and mythical elements with the mundane realities of economic disparity that remains a source of interest – both for participants and for anthropologists.

However vague and imperfect the notion of cargo cult is, our longstanding familiarity with it should at least encourage us to return to the Melanesian field and to ethnographic facts. Both cargo and associated phenomena and stories have undergone radical transformations since World War II, and especially since Melanesian countries gained independence. Accordingly, the first aim of the papers in this volume is to present different analytical approaches to the study of social movements in Melanesia with regard both to their current situation and to continuities with the past (see Abong Ch. 3 and Macintyre Ch. 5). The persistence of cargo cults, as real things, and as concepts, either "derogatory or celebratory", has remained a central theme in contemporary Pacific anthropology: "although these movements continually transform themselves at the local level, on a global scale we should consider it to be a liminoid category – a permanent state in a transformative global process of which we are a part – a kind of essential friction" (Dalton Ch. 2). This involves, paradoxically, retaining the concept at the same time as we are beginning to relinquish it; using it, even though it is "under erasure" (Hermann Ch. 6, Dalton Ch. 2), in order to break with its colonial connotations, as well as with its postmodern Western legacy.

Cargo Cult Terminologies

Even when abstracted from its connections to "cults", cargo persists as a narrative or conceptual syndrome. "Cargo", as such, is a polysemic notion, in English and also in related Melanesian pidgins. Referring both to the container (boat, *sip*) and to the content (shipment, *kago*), it provides at least two opposed but dynamically related meanings. Furthermore, cargo is also a modern concept used to describe industrial processes and goods, to refer to things produced by Western scientific rationality and political economy, in the context of liberal exchange ideologies and the development of heavy industry. However, for Melanesians in early colonial contexts these could not initially be perceived either as "modern" or "Western." They were simply the totally new and unseen part of a metaphysical and strategic secret, a part of the explanation of the essential secret of white men's wealth, of the mystery of their material abundance.

Converted into a symbol, a shared vision of the surpassing of new realities, cargo cults should be considered as total social facts (see Dalton Ch. 2). The technological specificities of the foreign goods and their incredible quantity would become evident through their massive acquisition via autonomous ritual processes. Cargo is not necessarily an imperfect notion when used in this way to signify symbolic aspects of the Melanesian desire for foreign technological goods or money. *Kago* continues to be used in Melanesian pidgins as a synonym for great quantities of imported goods and commodities.

Since contemporary Melanesians still use notions of *kago* or *kago kalt*, it is interesting to correlate present-day pidgin terminologies with former vernacular terminologies relating to traditional notions of abundance, goods and belongings, or of gaining benefits through the use of supernatural powers. In the case of Tannese society Lindstrom mentions the notion of *nauta*. He defines *nauta*, a word shared by several Tannese languages, as "possessions, goods, cargo, stored food" (1986: 96). My own informants elaborated it thus: *nauta* applies to food, but also to having a woman, children, pigs or fowls, gardens; all kinds of indigenous wealth which can be propitiated by means of Tannese ancestral magical stones (*kapier*). *Nauta* applies to "everything which makes our life easier" (even those things for which there are no stones, such as manioc, sweet potatoes and bullocks, goods that were assimilated to Tannese *nauta* through their cultural appropriation). Not simply a collection of material objects, like *kago*, *nauta* is the product of supernatural powers (*paoa*, see Lindstrom 1990). The Bible has also been classified as *nauta*, even though it is shared by Tannese and foreigners. Foreigners could also have their own *nauta*, "wealth belonging to their culture"; but since foreigners have lost most elements of their "former *kastom*," their power today is based on *kago*, on what Tannese called *sisar*.

For the Tannese, *Sisar* is every kind of wealth that lacks ancestral magical stones. *Sisar* might also be considered as a supernatural power. But today, more prosaically, it has become just a means of making money. Even new churches today, suspected of encouraging the cult of money, are considered *sisar*. This notion illuminates the power or dynamic of the "*rod blong kago*", namely maximizing profits (*kwik kas* in Bislama). In Lihir, McIntyre (Ch. 5) stresses that ideologies of "*bisnis*" and "*winmani*" are also subject to such magical control: "The use of the Tok Pisin term *pawa* (power) is significant of the relationship between knowledge, especially esoteric knowledge, and the capacity to exert control over people and things."

Indeed cargo, as a label, can hardly be suppressed as such precisely because it refers to a process of categorization, of affirming rules of conduct, applying cultural codes on to foreign or unknown things. It might be compared with using barcodes on manufactured commodities, or with using another software program to decrypt esoteric values: "There are several reasons for anthropological wariness. First is the fact that 'cult' is a term that has two meanings, one pejorative, the other not. Historians and people writing in Religious Studies have no problems with the term – it simply refers to the organised adherence to a particular set of ritual practices that people believe affect and effect temporal and material aspects of their lives. Ancient historians can write about the 'Cult of Mithras' and nobody bats an eyelid; medieval historians write of the rise of the 'Cult of Mary' and people recognise that it refers to a specific movement within broader (Catholic) Christian ritual traditions during and following the 12th century. It has acquired some of its pejorative associations in 20th century America where it is used to refer to (often bizarre) new religious movements" (Macintyre 2010). Anthropologists have always considered that the cult of the dead was the main religious set of beliefs and practices in ancient Pacific societies.

As cults, cargo movements also share many similarities with those mystery cults that existed in Hellenic and Oriental antiquity (Rohde 1925, Dodds 1959) and also with many of the nativist movements that appeared in different colonial contexts. They are mass initiatory and oppositional movements; ritual organizations that seek to assist their followers to grasp the nature of cultural shifts, face the challenges engendered by new and disturbing events and adapt to radical sociopolitical, economic or religious changes. Contemporary aspects of Melanesian neo-ritual organizations seem to conform to the same cultural model that moulded them during the colonial period and in the context of culture contact in which they arose.

In French, the word "culte" is much more neutral than in English. It simply refers to the ritual elements of any religious organization. But there is another related notion that has become clearly derogatory in French, that of "secte". The official discrimination against sects has increased since 1995, when the French Parliament began compiling an extended list of "dangerous" sects based in France. According to a parliamentary committee of enquiry, sects can be defined as posing two kinds of threat: "Threats to the individual: mental destabilization; the exorbitant nature of the financial demands; causing the individual to break with their social environment; inflicting bodily harm; the indoctrination of children. Threats to society: making pronouncements of a more or less anti-social nature; disturbances to public order; the serious nature of legal proceedings; potential bypassing of conventional economic networks; attempts to manipulate legal authorities" (*Commission d'enquête sur les sectes*, Alain Gest and Jacques Guyard, 22 December 1995). That is why I feel upset whenever I read or hear people referring to the John Frum movement as a "sect". However, if we leave the political field, setting aside its common associations, and restrict ourselves to sociological terminology, the John Frum movement is based on a cult, defined as the totality of external religious practices and observances, as well as being organized like a sect: a subdivision of a larger religious group.

The ethical and semantic problems arose, as several researchers assert, through the juxtaposition of the words "cargo" and "cult" (Hermann Ch. 6 and Dalton Ch. 2). This symbolic association has been intuitively extended and resonates with other terms such as *hocus pocus* and *mumbo jumbo*, conjuring up notions of magical nonsense formulae. The forging of the "cargo" and "cult" association quickly led to the justification of the repression of social movements by colonial powers and more generally to converting "cargo culting" into a symbol of the strangeness and inferiority of Melanesian cultures. In a context where Enlightenment notions had tied rationality to civilization, these activities came to represent archetypes of the "primitive". According to Hermann (Ch. 6), colonial discourses on cargo cults shared a "propensity for associating 'Cargo cult' with pejorative ideas, as for example when they spoke of 'madness', 'primitiveness', 'heathendom' and 'backwardness'… What none of these discourses did, however, was recognize the existence of links that might have promoted a dialogue between the indigenous people and the Europeans".

Once cult, in its association with cargo, became so heavily fraught with irrational, agonistic and primitivist ideologies, cargo cult cultures were stigmatized. They were interpreted as, and reduced to, the illusionary beliefs of Melanesians that they might assume control over the supernatural power of cargo (see Macintyre Ch. 5). By extension "cargo cults" gave birth to "cargoism"; this expression gained even more currency: "'Cargoism' is the great bugbear of Melanesian development. Having derived from 'cargo cultism' (the greater bugbear of colonial Melanesia) 'cargoism' has jumped regional boundaries to become a popular English language reference to all kinds of raised expectations, any general devotion to materialism and, most surprisingly, the slippage between investment and return for everything from environmentalism to economics" (Sullivan 2005: 1). Ritual means associated with cargoism have been identified as "cargo mentality" or "cargo thinking". All the derogatory aspects of the "cargo cult" label, with its evolutionist connotations, are the direct inheritance of the colonial period.

Classifying Melanesian Movements Today

Among scholars who still consider that ethnographic studies of cargo cults have provided a heuristic device for the comparative understanding of culture contact, Christianization and social change in Pacific societies, the attempt to provide an encompassing definition of real phenomena has not yet been abandoned. Such definitions rely strongly on the Melanesian characteristics of these movements; this is justified by the fact that, in the history of Oceanist anthropology, the concept of cargo cults has very seldom been applied to Polynesian, Australian or Indonesian cultural contexts (about the frequent and widespread occurrence of millenarian movements in Melanesia as compared to their rarity in Australian societies, see Tonkinson 2004). Indeed, during the conference, Martha Macintyre offered for discussion the following defining characteristics:

"In both places where I have encountered cargo cults they have included practices and beliefs that are characteristic of other movements that have been designated 'cargo cults' in Papua New Guinea:
• They involve ritual activities that in some way imitate or mimic actions associated with whites/Europeans.
• These activities are aimed at effecting transformations and/or reversals in status (often associated with skin colour), wealth and power for adherents.
• They involve stories of the 'loss' of skills, goods and knowledge to white people (often those who colonized them) through some moral failure or offence. Some of the rites or practices aim to redeem these failures in order to effect the transformation.
• They have (charismatic) local leaders.
• They have strong nativist elements – that is, they aim at advancing the political interests of local people by appealing to the reinstatement of specific 'traditional' practices and they see their movement as one that reclaims self-determination and independence from (white) foreign control.
• They entail beliefs in the return of ancestors bringing wealth in the form of money, European goods etc – 'cargo'.
• They include utopian and/or millenarian ideas of a future in which people will not have to labour.
• They have continued over many decades, changing slightly, but maintaining core beliefs and practices.

The cluster of attributes marks these movements out as 'cargo cults' in many respects. The blend of elements that can be considered 'political' and 'religious' is typical of similar movements in Papua New Guinea." (Macintyre 2010).

This proposal reminds us of the need to specify more precisely which set of ethnographic facts we have in mind when we refer to the notion of cargo cult, both in its geographical delimitation and in its historical continuity. I expressed the same need while presenting my findings on the long-lasting John Frum movement, which has continued to flourish since at least 1937. Even if most anthropologists studying this movement in the field have refrained from presenting it in terms of a cargo cult, their ethnographic work has nevertheless contributed to giving the John Frum movement a place in the Top Ten of the most famous cargo cults. Therefore, in order to be more precise about the past and present attributes that the John Frum movement shares with other movements that had put much emphasis on the theme of the cargo appropriation and still frequently do so, I propose the following elements of classification :

• They are mass phenomena, totalistic and federative. Their mythic and ritual features facilitate the extension of the usual limits of local collective identification processes. Their proselytism provides their followers with an individuated dimension that enables the supplantation of traditional affiliations. Different attitudes, marks and bodily signs are used to personify these transformations.

• While encouraging the emergence of prophetic figures of authority, indigenous Melanesian movements accompany and accelerate drastic changes of the pre-existing order. This overthrow ideally coincides with an upheaval of the whole world: the social landscape, political frontiers, mythical topography and environment will be totally transformed.

• They suppress or deeply modify the existing ritual organization: they can destroy or rehabilitate elements of the existing material culture; at the same time they ritualize foreign commodities or technologies. In their oppositional dimension, they accentuate the spiritual consequences of ongoing changes.

• Their syncretic and millenarian aspects attempt to redefine and validate new links between indigenous and foreign transcendent representations. In the special conjuncture effected by these cultic movements, reconnection with ancestral powers together with the suppression of foreign domination are concomitant events and could be seen as the key to immortality. Thus, the agenda of their followers is framed by a new vision of temporality (see Tabani 2008a), trying to start and accelerate a metaphysical countdown.

However imperfect and incomplete such attempts at definition or classification of family resemblances in a "well-known repertoire" might be, they express the need to pursue a comparative approach in the study of these indigenous and/or millenarian movements across geographic and cultural space as well as through time. Some participants in the *Kago, Kastom and Kalja* ASAO sessions expressed reservations about the risk of becoming diverted, where attempts at definition might be sidetracked into adopting an exclusively "typological" approach. While Scott (2010a) acknowledges that his recording of Makiran stories implicitly relies on something similar to the definition of cargo cult that Tabani and Macintyre are developing, he adds:

> "I have several reservations about explicitly foregrounding such a list in isolation. 1) I'm concerned that a typology reifies cargo cult as something that is iconic of Melanesia (creating what Appadurai [1988: 37] would term a 'metonymic prison'). 2) Such a typology risks, furthermore, holding Melanesia in the 'savage slot'. 3) Perhaps most importantly, creating a single typology in isolation privileges cargo cult as the presumed starting point for any comparative work in a way that may foster a tendency to assimilate other phenomena to cargo cult, rather than allowing differences to emerge and contribute to more nuanced theorization." (Scott 2010a)

Kago, Kastom, Kalja

A promising direction for the reanalysis of both the cargo cult concept and its underlying social facts could be to link and compare it with other similar or related notions. Leaving aside the notable *tabu*, *mana* or *big man* concepts, there is only one concept that has emerged in the history of Melanesian anthropology that has a core status on a par with the idea of the cargo cult. This is the concept of *kastom* which gained currency in the 1970s, coinciding precisely with the period when Melanesian nations gained independence. While, as Clifford commented concerning cargo cult, everybody immediately knows what we mean by the term, this can be hardly claimed for the notion of *kastom*. Nobody would disagree about the usefulness of the notion of *kastom* as a condition for understanding the genesis of contemporary Melanesian ideologies and cultures. Even so, whether we focus on the various different ways Melanesians brandish their *kastom* as a cultural symbol, or on the interpretations of foreign analysts who try to determine which kind of indigenous characteristics apply to *kastom*, it is as hard to find any agreement on the scope of its precise meanings as it is on the social practices to which it refers.

Both concepts have been integrated into Melanesian pidgins, but as related to social movements: *kago kalt* is currently fraught with negative colonial overtones, while *kastom* is more frequently praised as embodying positive aspects of post-colonial processes of collective identification. Nevertheless, both concepts have been used by anthropologists to describe theoretical and practical constructions, ideologies or social movements specifically relevant to Melanesian cultural contexts. Indeed, even when they are strictly set apart, they appear historically and culturally complementary. According to Jeben's definition, "since the cultural recognition of otherness is more central to *kago*, in the context of *kastom* we deal with the objectivation of one's own traditional culture, that is self representations" (Jebens 2007: 10). And a major project remains: to interrogate these concepts in order to determine if *kago* and *kastom* are linked to the same historical origins or whether they are distinct products from two different time periods.

Lindstrom, for example, analyzes the developments of exegesis on cargo and *kastom* as subsequent rather than as parallel, even though both concepts are ideologically connected. He proposes to seek Melanesian *kastom*'s genealogy in former "cargo cult culture" (1993b). More recently, in an article contesting acultural critiques of *kastom*, Akin tries to analyze how *kastom* has been transformed into what anthropologists used to call "culture" (2004). According to the Solomon Kwaio example studied by Akin, *kastom* is not just an ideological selection of pre-colonial cultural traits, practices and institutions turned into an identifying symbol, politically used by nationalist elites for nation-building purposes. He considers how, through a long process of revitalization, reorganization and reinvention, *kastom* has become a visceral part of community cultures. That *kastom* ideology can follow different or opposite directions is a point which has been regularly asserted. Some of these ideological constructions could of course succeed in becoming part of popular social reality and a basis for new imagined communities. *Kastom* as culture, even at a national level, is an ideological and even anthropological fiction which over time could become real.

Less clear is Akin's claim, that his "critique of acultural approaches does not of course hold for studies of Melanesian 'Cargo cults', an extensive literature notable for its invisibility in most writings about *kastom* despite much topical overlap" (2004: 318). Indeed, anthropologists have abundantly culturalized cargo cults in the past, while later, they have over-politicized *kastom* debates. Claiming that the transformation of *kastom* into culture is the consequence of the oppositional developments of the Maasina Rule movement, Akin does not seem to consider *kago* either as *kastom* or as culture.

A possible reason for Akin's reluctance to explore these connections himself is that if cargo cults are Melanesian, they have generally been considered as the hallmark of a deep cultural break with Melanesian societies' pre-colonial cultural past. Cargo movements were frequently laden with anti-traditional nihilism (the Vailala madness became the main example of the destruction of the old ceremonial complex, Williams 1923, see Tabani 2008a), while *kastom* has frequently been promoted as a clear sign of continuity, of the indigenization of modernity or of cultural revitalization. Within the semantic field of cargo cult, the metaphorical dimension of the challenge posed by drastic social change is something which persists. When cargo cults are assimilated to "indigenization of modernity processes" (Sahlins 1999), to what extent might such "developman process" (Sahlins 1993) be claimed to be similar to that of the ideological rise of *kastom*?

Lindstrom has suggested in his writings that we consider *kastom* as comparable to cargo cult: "The making of the new-culture-in-the-making necessitated a discourse of *kastom*, or at least something like 'culture' [...] The public political re-establishment of tradition, or the invention of novel ritual that occurred within cultic contexts, solidified and fortified notions of local culture and convention in general" (1993b: 501). In the John Frum movement for example, *kastom* and John Frum cultic activities have been closely associated by colonial delegates and missionaries and in turn condemned together as incompatible with the diffusion of the Christian faith and the Condominium legal order.

The John Frum movement, for example, has continued to present itself as the guardian of *kastom*, even if the cultic practices and syncretic imagery and beliefs of the movement rely on strong Christian principles and reinvented traditional patterns (see Tabani 2008, 2010). We could certainly extend this self-characterization to other post-World War II movements such as Maasina Rule, the Paliau movement or the Yali movement. Scott also insists on the link between the assignment of the supernatural dwarfs of Makira's underground and the *kastom* issue: "the kakamora are not only the source of the army's extraordinary powers, they are also the custodians of a lost true Makiran language and *kastom* which the army will one day assist them to restore" (2010b).

Cargo cults in Melanesia could be seen as the first colonial occurrences of a large-scale and intensive production of neo-traditions, in a period where the concept of *kastom* had not yet received any scientific, ideological or mass media coverage. *Kago* as *kastom* may have been the initial process of claiming the defence of local sovereignties before the official reinvention of such "cargo cult *kastom*" and the widespread use, in the 1970s, of the notion of *kastom* for political purposes in the nation-building context, up to its latest incarnation as "State *kastom*" (Tabani 2002, Babadzan 2009). Cargo cult-*kastom* was fragmentary and selective, as is modern official state *kastom* today. But while Cargo cults focused on "strange gods bearing gifts", official national *kastom* focuses today on state regulation, law and order and on politicians, technocrats and NGOs providing development help. We wonder also how far the Makira matter which Scott is proposing as an alternative to the Cargo cult explanation is also the product of such precursory "cargo cult *kastom*": a *kastom* discourse that precisely reproduces in a post-colonial Melanesian context both proto-nationalist and millenarian stances that have been assigned to classical cargo movements in colonial times (Scott 2012: 117; 121-122).

To return to Akin's analysis, we cannot forget that the question of cargo cults coincided with the very beginning of the "*kastom* as reinvented tradition" debate: "The ideologies of our time, unlike Cargo cult ideologies, are phrased in terms of 'culture' and other anthropological concepts, as they have passed into Western popular thought and intellectual discourses" (Keesing 1989:33). With the replacement of cargo cults as "developman processes" by *kastom*-sustainable development (also labelled *kastom ekonomi* in Vanuatu), we do not just acknowledge a change in the source of expected abundance, but also one that entails the replacement of different "semiologies of sovereignty" (Keesing 1989: 28). These political ruptures could have a significant influence on the process studied by Jebens in which Melanesians themselves have appropriated the negative charge of cargo cults: "'Colonial usage' [of the term 'cargo cult'] does now seem to be reproduced in indigenous discourses… to derogate opponents. Here [in Melanesia] 'Cargo cultism' continues to be an ideological weapon of exclusion: the cargo cultist is always 'the Other'" (Jebens 2004b: 157). Indeed, this reinforces the need for enquiry into the historical relationship between *kago* and *kastom*.

Today, in Vanuatu for example, many movements which in the past have been called "cargo cults" are frequently redefined by Melanesians as "*kastom* movements" or, even more neutrally, by outside observers as "indigenous or social movements". But for some neo-evangelical churches operating in the Pacific today these movements are purely and simply the products of "Satan's work". Moreover, examples from PNG show, too, that different groups sometimes adopt the label of *kago kalt* – and as one that is inherently powerful, not shameful (see Lattas 1998 and also Macintyre Ch. 5).

Kastom Movements, Globalization and Nation States

In order to provide answers to some of the questions raised in this volume, we should assess the deep implications of cargo or *kastom* movements for the agendas and governance of independent Melanesian states. It is not enough to speak about "marginal cargo cults" or "micronationalisms" if we wish to evoke the actual directions of movements like the Nagriamel, the Turaga nason or Melanesian Brotherhood, just to take examples from Vanuatu and the Solomons. The leaders of these movements denounce fraudulent schemes initiated by state rulers, or even the excesses of modern consumer society, as cargo cults or even as *kago kalja*, and oppose them to *kastom ekonomi* and indigenous governance principles. To what extent does land speculation rest on the expectation that uneducated island *man ples* or *man bush* will exhibit cargo behaviours and sell their land for insignificant sums of money?

For former anthropologists, movements like John Frum were intended to generate new forms of collective identity. From their point of view, ritual means to ascertain identity were doomed to be overtaken by new modes of pragmatic action and rational organisation. Cultic contest emanating from 'pre-rational' politico-religious movements would dissolve during the political process of decolonisation and nation-building. Peter Worsley (1957), who, with Jean Guiart (1951), was one of the main propagators of this argument, adds to his thesis that the factor of "proto-nationalism" in Melanesian post-contact societies sums up a process of integration or centralization encompassing different traditionally non-united social groups. According to Worsley, this federative process is central to the dynamics of most Melanesian pre-World War II politico-religious movements. Historically, their rationality is supposed to lie in their becoming (Kilani 1983), in their transformation into bureaucratic forms of organization and unification. This ineluctable process of secularisation, which leads from lower class religions to anti-colonialism, should also open the way to the invention of a wider identity based on shared feelings of a community of culture.

This proto-nationalist theory, formerly used to explain different sorts of indigenous movements usually classified as "cargo cults", is contradicted by the facts. It is a matter of fact that the observed direction of most of these movements since the World War II period went from immediate political reaction (disobedience to colonial and mission domination) to sophisticated religious changes. The more virulent the initial spontaneous opposition (seen as irrational by a former generation of anthropologists), the more prolific and complex the syncretistic processes that succeeded to it and extended it. Currently, in Tanna, political innovations are mostly seen as socially disintegrative, while religious innovations are generally considered integrative (Tabani 2002:121). According to the proto-nationalist theory, Melanesian millenarian movements are specific to colonial contexts; thus, their future should be examined in continuity with post-independence nationalist claims.

Movements like John Frum have generally been opposed to nationalism, to the centralisation of power and to national integration. Of course, one can find some similarities between cargo cults and manifestations of state nationalism. Lindstrom, for example, noted that:

> "Like cults, the new states organise and attempt to regulate bodily experience by means of parades, military drilling, hygienic public health and anti-Aids campaigns, and national sports competition. Like cults, the new states institute novel regularities of space and time in the form of national capitals/headquarters, flag bedecked parliament houses and other ritual centres, and state holidays. And like cults, the states demand both national harmony and unity (1993b:507)".

However, one cannot infer a sociological equivalence from symbolic similarities between the integrative scope of indigenous movements on the one hand and the nation-building assimilation model on the other, nor can a shared ideology be identified; the continuity between both models of social construction is not obvious. The amalgamation of cargo cult, *kastom* and national cultures does not present any evidence of historical continuity. Frequently, when national political leaders promote the idea of national integration and community harmony, their speeches are filled with mythological and messianic metaphors; during their electoral meetings they promise cargo symbols and then proceed to ritualized rice distributions. Producing miracles and preparing cult followers for salvation are usual activities for bush prophets, but these goals do not fit in well with modern politicians' official state-ments, nor are they a requirement for state leaders' legitimacy. Unfulfilled cargo prophesies do not weaken the faith of cultic movements' followers: the millenarian hopes they raise are just postponed, unlike false electoral promises, which are publicly denounced as political propaganda or corruption and can provoke social protest and civil riots.

A recent tendency for national politicians is to claim for themselves some oppo-sitional aspects of the legacy of former indigenous movements. It is remarkable that, if the proto-nationalist analysis of cargo cults has lost much of its explanatory effi-ciency, it is still used politically by ni-Vanuatu political leaders. Barak Sope, for example, former cofounder of the nationalist Vanuaku Pati and later of the Vanuatu Republic, was one of the most virulent opponents of cargo and indigenous movements (especially the John Frum movement in Tanna and the Nagriamel movement in the northern part of the archipelago). He largely contributed to the imprisonment of Jimmy Stevens, leader of the Nagriamel movement and instigator of a secessionist rebellion, for eleven years (Abong Ch. 3, Tabani, 2008b), though in 1991 Sope's National United Party concluded a political alliance with the Nagriamel. When he was appointed Prime Minister in 1999, Barack Sope attended the annual ceremonies of the John Frum movement in Tanna that followed. The talk he gave in the village of Sulphur Bay asserted a convergence between the rebel movement and his own political ideology:

> "The constitution of Vanuatu declares clearly that there is enough space left under the sun of Vanuatu for all of our customs, or for the John Frum movement or for the Nagriamel movement, or for any movement or organisation. And any movement has the right to go on. Everybody has the right to follow them, as well as to vote, to go to school, to use roads or to go to the hospital. The constitution is the guarantee for these rights and everybody must respect it.
> I came for the first time to Sulphur Bay when I was at the university, writing my book, to speak with Mweles and some other old leaders of the John Frum movement. In these times, the Vanuaaku Pati didn't exist and neither did the National United Party nor any other political party. No one but the John Frum and Nagriamel movements were yet present. And in those times, these old peoples had already spoken about independence, about this independence which has become our present" (personal recording 15th February 2000).

In any case, if today's nationalist representations of the nation in Melanesia use and abuse a reinterpreted tradition along with other essentialised symbols of the past, it has proved more difficult to assimilate syncretistic religious imagination inspired by millenarian movements.

If it does not make sense to speak about proto-nationalism, could movements like John Frum be characterised as micro-nationalisms instead? After all, they handle state symbols (government, flags, headquarters and uniforms), and their leaders declare themselves ready to die for their *kastom*. Nevertheless, the charismatic power that is their cement is mostly expressed in religious terms. Theirs are nativisms that largely focus on millenarian hope. Their main goal is to transcend the contradictions between Christianity and earlier pagan beliefs (Keesing 1989). A nationalist view of the state cannot furnish a key to such local and non-shared quests for identity.

The John Frum movement did not lead to any routinisation of the charismatic power of its leaders. The Tannese proclamation of a '*Tanna nason*' (Tanna nation) or references to the '*John Frum kastom pipol*' (customary people) are conceived along the lines of biblical models such as the idea of 'God's chosen people' or of the preserved spirituality of 'Israel's lost tribe'. The people of Tanna are seen by John Frum followers as a spiritual model for all nations in the world, and this spirituality (*wan speretual*) is considered to be the source of great powers (*paoa*) permitting global action.

Followers of the John Frum movement reject state *kastom* and the *kago* label for complementary reasons – unless *kago* is applied to others (in this negative sense cargo cultists are always and inevitably "others"): "*tru kago kalja i stap long Vila, long saed long politik*" (true cargo emanated from the politicians in Vila), "*Jon hemi no kago*" (John is not the cargo) is a current *leitmotiv* in the speeches of some John Frum leaders. But for Tannese, as well as for anthropologists, the less they speak about cargo the stronger the impression formed by initiated observers that nothing resembles the John Frum movement as much as other Melanesian cargo cults: "John didn't say that we would receive all goods for free, but all goods finally came." "We only believe in *kastom*, but to receive millions of dollars from our ancestors we need plastic member cards attesting to our true *kastom* filiations." If some analysts still question whether cargo cults have been anything more than mere illusions or an anthropological mirage, there can be no doubt that, through ultraliberalism and state practices, they have attained a substantial reality as well as considerable mythic force. In a globalized world, cargo cult, like *kastom*, has become a metaphor for the domination of capitalism and the general homogenization of nation state governance.

Bibliography

Akin, David

2004   "Ancestral Vigilance and the Corrective Conscience: Kastom as Culture in a Melanesian society", *Anthropological Theory*, 4(3): 299-324.

Appadurai, Arjun

1988   "Putting hierarchy in its place", *Cultural Anthropology*, 3(1): 36-49.

Babadzan, Alain

2009   *Le spectacle de la culture : Globalisation et traditionalismes en Océanie.* Paris: L'Harmattan, Connaissance des Hommes.

Dodds, Eric Robertson

1959   *The Greeks and the Irrational.* Berkeley : University of California Press.

Guiart, Jean

1951   "Forerunners of Melanesian nationalism", *Oceania*, 23(2):81-90.

Jebens, Holger

2004a   "Introduction: Cargo, cult and culture critique". In H. Jebens (ed.), *Cargo, Cult & Culture Critique*. Honolulu: Hawaii University Press, pp.1-13.

2004b   "Talking about Cargo Cults in Koimumu (West New Britain Province, Papua New Guinea)". In H. Jebens (ed.), *Cargo, Cult & Culture Critique*. Honolulu: Hawaii University Press, pp.157-169.

2007   *Kago und kastom : zum Verhältnis von kultureller Fremd- und Selbstwahrnehmung in West New Britain (Papua-Neuguinea)*. Stuttgart: Kohlhammer.

Kaplan, Martha

1995   *Neither Cargo nor Cult: Ritual, Politics and the Colonial Imagination in Fiji.* Durham N.C.: Duke University Press.

Kaplan, Martha
2004   "Neither Traditional nor Foreign: Dialogics of Power and Agency in Fijian History".
           In H. Jebens (ed.), *Cargo, Cult and Culture Critique*. Honolulu: Hawaii. University Press,
           pp.55-79.

Keesing, Roger
1989   "Creating the Past: Custom and Identity in the Contemporary Pacific".
           Contemporary Pacific, 1(1-2): 19-42.
Nd.   Papers, 1962-1993. MSS 427, Box 18, Folder 2. Mandeville Special Collections Library.
           Melanesian Archives. University of California San Diego.

Kilani, Mondher
1983   *Les cultes du Cargo mélanésiens: mythe et rationalité en anthropologie.*
           Lausanne: Éditions d'en bas

Lattas, Andrew
1998   *Cultures of secrecy: reinventing race in bush Kaliai cargo cults*. Madison: University of
           Wisconsin Press.

Lindstrom, Lamont
1986   *Kwamera Dictionary: Nikukua Sai Nagkiariien Nininife*. Canberra: Australian National
           University, Pacific Linguistics, Series C95.
1990   *Knowledge and Power in a South Pacific Society*. Washington/London, Smithsonian
           Institution Press.
1993a   *Cargo Cult: Strange Stories of Desire from Melanesia and Beyond*. Honolulu: University of
           Hawaii Press.
1993b   "Cargo Cult Culture: Toward a Genealogy of Melanesian Kastom".
           Anthropological Forum, 6(4): 495-513.

McDowell, Nancy
1988   "A Note on Cargo and Cultural Construction of Change". *Pacific Studies*, 11: 121-134.

Macintyre, Martha
2010   Debates, Remarks and Comments. ASAO Sessions 2009-2010: Kago, Kastom and Kalja.
           Old Theories and New Realities in the Study of Melanesian Movements. Unpublished
           documents.

Robbins, Joel
2004   "On the Critique in Cargo and the Cargo in Critique: Toward a Comparative Anthropology
           of Critical Practice". In H. Jebens (ed.), *Cargo, Cult & Culture Critique*. Honolulu: Hawaii
           University Press, pp.243-260.

Rohde, Erwin
1925   *Psyche: The Cult of Souls and Belief in Immortality among the Greeks*. London: Kegan Paul,
           Trench, Trubner.

Sahlins, Marshall
1992   "The Economics of Develop-Man in the Pacific". *Res Anthropology and Aesthetics*,
           21: 12-25.
1999   "Two or Three Things I know about Culture". *Journal of the Royal Anthropological
           Institute*, 5: 399-421

Scott, Michael W.

2010a   Debates, Remarks and Comments. ASAO Sessions 2009-2010: Kago, Kastom and Kalja. Old Theories and New Realities in the Study of Melanesian Movements. Unpublished documents.

2010b   "The Matter of Makira: Conquest, 'Cargo' Talk, and the Gendering of Peoples in Medieval Europe and Neo-colonial Melanesia". Paper delivrered to the 2009-2010 ASAO Meetings. Unpublished documents.

2012   "The Matter of Makira: Colonialism, Competition, and the Production of Gendered Peoples in Contemporary Solomon Islands and Medieval Britain", *History of Anthropology*, 23: 115-148.

Sullivan, Nancy

2005   "Cargo and Condescension". *Contemporary PNG Studies* 3: 1-13.

Tabani, Marc

2005   *Alors vint John Frum : une tragédie cultuelle des Mers du Sud.* Marseille: CREDO Production, video film, 75 minutes.

2007   "Cargo, Cult and Culture Critique, a Review of literature", *Oceania* 77(3): 371-373.

2008a   *Une pirogue pour le paradis: le culte de John Frum à Tanna.* Paris. Maison des Sciences de l'Homme.

2008b   "Political history of Nagriamel on Santo, Vanuatu", *Oceania* 78(3): 332-357.

2010   "The carnival of custom: Land dives, millenarian parades and other spectacular ritualizations in Vanuatu". *Oceania*, 80(3): 309-328.

Tonkinson, Robert

2004   "Encountering the Other: Millenarianism and the Permeability of Indigenous Domains in Melanesia and Australia". In H. Jebens (ed.), *Cargo, Cult & Culture Critique*. Honolulu: Hawaii University Press, pp.137-256.

Williams, Francis Edgard

1923   *The Vailala Madness and the Destruction of Native Ceremonies in the Gulf Division.* Port Moresby, Territory of Papua: Edward George Baker (Anthropology Report 4.)

Chapter 2

Between "Cargo" and "Cult"

Doug Dalton

Cargoist Returns

When I returned in 1999 to visit the village where I had resided fifteen years earlier, I had lost contact with the people with whom I had lived and the rumour was that I had died. The local provincial member whom I met in the capital Madang was able to radio ahead notice of my impending arrival a couple of days before I hiked up to the village from his house at the mission station along the road below the mountains. When I arrived I found my closest friend Borum casually cutting grass at the end of the path where it entered the otherwise empty village. I later learned that the village elders had thought someone might be trying to assume my identity for some potentially nefarious purpose. After embracing Borum I received an overwhelming welcome from the village residents and many old friends who came back to the village from their gardens and bush houses, and I was given space to sleep in the house of the son of an early native Lutheran missionary from outside the area who had married and spent his life there, no doubt because he was so familiar with and sympathetic towards Western ways. He was unusual among the villagers in being utterly sceptical of the many magical supernatural notions that exist in an uneasy syncretism with the Lutheranism which outwardly dominates the village.

The following day Borum took me to visit one of his relatives and another close associate of mine in his bush house but, as it turned out, he was away that morning and we instead sat with his first-born son. His son, I was told, was doing something utterly unheard of in the culture, that is, forgoing marriage. In my understanding and from what I know of his family, this could mean only one thing: he was undertaking the most profoundly disciplined practice of magic and sorcery possible. We visited him for a short while, sitting outside the house eating the sugar cane he brought out for us. Imbibing sugar cane requires, of course, spitting out the masticated rind after swallowing the sweet juice, which supplies the perfect material for the work of a sorcerer. Considering the context of my return visit it seems clear that he employed his magician's prowess to divine my identity and especially my intentions on behalf of the village elders, although I suspect that he did a great deal more than that.

While we were conversing he put a question to me which he said he had always wanted to ask a "whiteman", namely, "Is it true that whitemen get their money from the graveyard?" I recognized this as a contemporary "cargo cult" idea known elsewhere in New Guinea. Borum, a pretty good Lutheran, proceeded to make fun of the proposition, pointing out the illogicality of it: "if that were true, 'whitemen' would make their houses midway between the graveyard and the store and do nothing but travel the well-worn paths that connect them", he said. I professed my ignorance. We took our leave and Borum took me on an unusual route, bushwhacking through a swampy jungle area to the hamlet of another good friend of mine from long ago, the former village evangelist. One of his long-lost brothers had returned after a long exile working on the coast and set up a trade store there. The store was equipped with something I had not seen previously in the village environs: it had a refrigerator powered by a gas generator. In what seemed like an unusual conjunction of cultures, I was given a cold *Coca Cola* in a remote, mountainous Papua New Guinea jungle, some hours' walk from the nearest road, immediately following my encounter with the local sorcerer.

After that my visit proceeded without further incident of that kind. I hiked to a number of hamlets outside the village, went to church and explained myself to the congregation, played volleyball in front of my host's house, made gifts and contributed to a feast for the Lutheran confirmation ceremony which took place during my stay. While I was there, the missionary's son asked me to send him a pair of binoculars: he wanted to use them to disabuse the other village residents of the notion expressed by the Neo-Melanesian word *glassim* that, when "whitemen" use such technology to view the jungle, they are able to see the hidden "inside" (*newendemo*) of the outward appearances of the plants and soil and view the animating living forces which inhabit them. I haven't heard back from him regarding the success of his endeavour.

The ideas which the local sorcerer related to me and which the missionary's son hoped to dispel are what has been called "cargoism" or "cargo cult thinking" in the literature, something like Robbins' "everyday millennialism" except that it is not necessarily millennialist (Harding 1967; Lawrence 1966-67; Robbins 2004; Young 1971). These ideas were vaguely shared by another man I knew from my earlier fieldwork who came to observe me during my most recent visit. He and a handful of residents from nearby villages were sometimes known to try and continue practising versions of the widespread failed "cargo cult" movement which took place around 1980 wherein they attempt to make money magically multiply in a cult house. This man used to question me about the "secret" which "whitemen" were not sharing with them, often in very allusive and obscure language.

These amorphous "cargoism" ideas lead me to engage with the enormous literature on "cargo cult" in order to delineate the nature of the phenomenon in question, which I claim does not entail a kind of reductionist sociology yet does involve its own social theory, and to discuss the utility of the term "cargo cult" and to examine the immensity of writings on, and the endless recurrence of, the phenomena of "cargo cult". I argue that "cargo cult" is a phenomenon which exists in and through the interaction between different cultures and I compare and contrast the metaphysical assumptions of people like the Rawa speakers I came to know and the Western (American) culture I inhabit. This impels me to redistribute the predicates associated with "religion" and "science" in Western thinking and then to discuss the diversity of experiences and views within Rawa culture which such broad comparisons seem to overlook. Finally, I suggest that a way to comprehend an indigenous understanding of "cargo cult" might follow the model of encounter in Javanese *wayang* theatre and consider the question of whether or not the missionary's son is likely to succeed in his endeavour.

"Cargoism" and the Trouble with "Cargo Cult"

The first point to make in the context of these examples of "cargoism" is that, whatever it is, "cargo cult" does not necessarily have to take the form of a "social movement", although it certainly may do so (e.g. Scott 2012). In addition, these examples are extraordinarily difficult for a Western observer to understand and explain. Each of these instances of "cargoism" is much more a matter of thinking than of social doing, and makes no immediate sense within a Western metaphysic. I therefore find Biersack's (2009) exploration of Paiela cosmology in relation to the question of materiality more to the point than attempting to explain "cargo cult" as a peculiar kind of "social movement" and find great value in Bell's (2010) pursuit of aesthetic experience in relation to objects as a way into fathoming the ontology they embody. Scott (2012) likewise finds that "cargo talk" in the Solomons produces material which is a vehicle for aesthetic experience. I could produce a remarkably similar cosmology to that which Biersack provides for the Paiela which I learned from a group of Rawa elders, albeit without much of the fine detail that Biersack was able to obtain, but I find I have to put Rawa ideas in a much broader context to fathom the extent of the difference between them and Western ideas.

My understanding of "cargo cult" is consequently most at odds with that of Hermann (Ch. 6), who argues for abandoning the term "cargo cult" in favour of "social movement". Hermann constructs as strong an argument as one possibly can, supporting her contention with statements from members of the clan of Papua New Guinea's most famous "cargo cult" leader Yali, as well as numerous scholarly references, and is easily able to show, as others have, that "cargo cult" is a derogatory term. However, as Macintyre (Ch. 5) also points out, not all New Guinea natives view the term that way. Indeed, the outsiders blamed for fomenting "cargo cults" in their settlement by the villagers whom Hermann interviewed may well have been from among the Rawa-speaking people I knew, for they have long-standing trade relations with the villagers on the other side of the Finisterre Mountains inhabiting the north coast where Yali worked and resided. However the Rawa people I knew rarely used the term *kago kalt* in the early 1980s after participating in a large-scale movement that failed, something that they were understandably reluctant to discuss. Even the "cargo cultists" who continued some of the movement's practices referred to their activities in broader, less certain terms as "working" or "making" "something". But I also heard a group of men excitedly sharing the news of a *kago kalt* movement then taking place on New Britain, which they heard reported on the provincial radio, in tones which made it clear that they thought it might be real and effective. During my most recent visit I never once heard the term, even from the sorcerer who conveyed to me current "cargo cult thinking".

Macintyre (Ch. 5) and Tabani (Ch. 1) posit from their field experiences that the defining features of "cargo cults" include the possession of charismatic local leaders, ritual activities to effect transformations in power and status and millenarian ideas which, however, the "cargo cult thinking" I encountered does not substantiate. Biersack (Ch. 4) and Macintyre (Ch. 5) both propose that millennial expectations and hopes for imagined futures are the essential features of "cargo cult", although Macintyre finds desired access to wealth to be the perduring element of "movements" on Lihir while Biersack finds millennialism itself and not "cargo" to be definitive of these "movements". However the "cargoism" which I encountered was actually anything but hopeful or millennial. The "cargo cultists" I knew were in fact generally quite dour, particularly about the state of relations with "whitemen". So I cannot endorse the idea that the phenomenon in question is millenarian which, while a worthy subject of study, is not the same as "cargo cult" and is not a study to which "cargo cult" can be reduced. As Biersack (Ch. 4) shows, one can have millennialism without "cargo" concerns. However one cannot have millennialism without the "cult" or religious ontology which is widely found in Inner Oceania and this ontology continues independently of millennial movements and hopes after they wane. What, after all, happens to "cargo cult" "movements" after they fail to bring the millennium? For the Rawa "cargo cultists" I knew, it did not go away but instead continues to exist in a less sociological, more intellectual, and not very hopeful form (see also Jebens 2010; Scott 2012; cf. Festinger *et al.* 1964).

A critical problem with explaining "cargo cult" from within Western discourse is that it is "impervious to the kind of argument through dependency that our rationalistic outlook fosters" (Wagner 1979: 164). The Western apprehension of "cargo cult" generally reduces it to sociological "movements" which have a certain functional teleology, even if an illusory fantastic one. Most sympathetic accounts point out that they function as innovative collective political or economic activities which sometimes succeed in achieving their purposes; even where they fail to significantly change political or economic circumstances, they always succeed at organizing people socially, thus serving their own tautological self-fulfilment as "social movements". While accounting for the functional rationality of "cargo cult" "movements", explanations also typically account for and discount their apparent irrationality as due to psychological stress and the unpredictability of a Western economic system although one can always suppose, as Macintyre (Ch. 5) does, that their unrealistic aspects represent a pan-human proclivity to engage in wishful fantasy. Lindstrom's (1993, this volume Ch. 7) study of the Western fascination with an ever-increasing variety and extent of uses of "cargo cult" as refractions of modern desire lends support to this premise.

Biersack (Ch. 4) is, of course, correct in saying that, from an indigenous perspective, the apparent "irrationality" of "cargo cult" simply does not exist. But I believe that she greatly understates the problem of comprehending the perspective of people in other cultures. Anthropologists were once subject to the critique of "ethnocentrism" – of misunderstanding other cultures by imposing foreign concepts – but from the early 1980s they also became subject to criticism for "othering" or, worse, "orientalism", that is treating other cultures as different and thus excluding them from colonial history and desired development. Although the critique of "othering" makes sense in a post-independence era where government and villager concerns alike are for "development", "othering" and "ethnocentrism" are logical opposites: if there are significant cultural differences, taken together these create a double bind which makes doing anthropology impossible since if a culture is not described in indigenous terms one is "ethnocentric", but if it is described as very different one is "othering".

These two opposite critiques are nonetheless consistent with the first proposition of the American Anthropological Association Code of Ethics that researchers' primary ethical obligations are to the people whom they study (American Anthropological Association 1998). The rhetorical strategy to navigate politically between them would seem to be to describe other cultures in indigenous terms as not so different that they cannot engage in Western development and participate in the modern world. However, this strategy does nothing to move "cargo cult" discourse beyond the classical functionalist evolutionary arguments that these "movements" are incipient forms of nationalism or modern economic enterprise, which might even appear to be like the two "stage" process of Ipili purposive activity of first conceiving and then enacting (Biersack Ch. 4). The reason I do not employ this strategy is that, in my understanding, human history is not a linear phenomenon but, rather, complex and nonlinear and therefore, by its very nature, unpredictable. I also think that anyone who wants development should get it; if I could I would bring it myself. I would just warn them to be wary of the kinds of characters they will likely encounter in the modern world. However the Rawa people I know are already quite aware of such dangers.

The approaches which account for "cargo cult" as a kind of "social movement" do so by associating it, in a dependency relationship, with something that it is not, that is politics, economics, society, millennialism, fantasy, hope, and so forth. Furthermore, these are generally things which exist on the Western side of the cultural divide between Western Europeans and the peoples of Inner Oceania. This form of argument also often logically assumes an evolutionary teleology whereby Melanesians will inevitably become like Westerners, since these "movements" are frequently thought of as incipient forms of the essentially Western things which they are not or, at least, not quite yet. Part of the frustration of explaining "cargo cults" is that, despite all of their successes and failures, they have never gone away. If "cargo cults" are anything they are "total" phenomena, simultaneously economic, religious, historical, social, aesthetic, moral, political, et cetera, and not reducible to any one of them (Mauss 1967 [1925]). I will argue that "cargo cult" involves a particular mode of social relation, but it is not predicated on the Western sociological logic of a type of ritual "social movement." Rather it is assumed by the ontology implicit in the "cargoism" which certain villagers expressed to me.

I have elsewhere argued that the imperviousness to rationalistic argument of "cargo cults" accounts for the apparently endless Western treatment attempting to explain them in rational terms (Dalton 2000). I found Worsley's (1968) comprehensive account a particularly good example which well reflects the broader literature.

As with "cargo cult" discourse in general, Worsley's discussion adds explanation upon explanation, moving from one to another in a very uncertain and unsettled manner until he ends up with a tautological formulation like the functionally self-fulfilling "social movement": assuming "cargo cult" to be a form of political resistance, he "finds 'cargo' madness to be the simultaneous result of oppression, consumer desires, European vagaries, and native ignorance that inspire bizarre behaviours which [he] describes as simultaneously vain, unreal, irrational, 'fantastic' failures, on the one hand, and 'quite practical', 'not ineffective' and 'rational', on the other, finally explaining them as an 'emotional outlet' found in 'imaginary projection' – i.e. as ends in themselves whose own self-fulfilling purpose is to 'express social and moral solidarity' and 'ethical values'"(Dalton 2000: 355; Worsley 1968: 247-248).

A related problem which I have also addressed concerns what to call "cargo cult" (Dalton 2004). Originally coined in a colonial news magazine by an Australian expatriate planter residing in Papua New Guinea, the term "cargo cult" was intended to denote the chaotic irrationality of what would undoubtedly proliferate if the system of inequality which the planters enjoyed were diminished (Lindstrom 1993: 19). The irony is that his prediction was apparently correct and the more sympathetic observers who saw in "cargo cult" incipient nationalism were apparently wrong, for these activities have continued to occur since independence, if not actually increased (Scott 2012).

My argument was that we keep the troublesome term "cargo cult" because to do otherwise endeavours to substitute a normalizing, neutralizing supposedly objective term for what is an inherently troublesome phenomenon. The value of the term "cargo cult" is in the uneasy relationship between the two terms "cargo" and "cult". Born of colonial anxiety, "cargo cult" captures and preserves the peculiar clash of cultures that gives rise to a variety of remarkable ways of thinking and acting in relation to the "whitemen" long occurring in Inner Oceania. I argue that "cargo cult" is most fundamentally a liminoid, betwixt and between phenomenon which exists in the space between strikingly different cultures and, as such, resists the kinds of understandings and explanations which Westerners employ, from their side of the divide, to try to make sense of them (Turner 1967, 1982)[1]. Therefore "cargo cult" defies attempts to apprehend the phenomenon in question in an

---

1. Turner found that in modern Western industrial societies "liminal" states and persona were often not so much transitional moments or episodes in ritual processes but, rather, permanent yet extraordinary and uncommon statuses; he coined the term "liminoid" to identify them (Turner 1982). In using "liminoid" here I mean to indicate that the modern clash of cultures that "cargo cult" embodies is apparently a permanent state.

objective manner by finding the correct name for it – "millennialism", "social move-ment", "fantasy" or what have you – as the ancient Greeks presumed themselves to do with the *logos*.

The most basic problem with naming "cargo cult" may be that it fundamentally involves islanders interpreting Western culture as *kago* (Wagner 1981); establishing a supposedly objective neutral term for it has the effect of removing ourselves as interpreters from the picture. Besides being unable to settle on a single rational explanation, "cargo cult" discourse therefore expends a seemingly endless amount of intellectual energy maintaining its frame of reference, sustaining its exclusions, and managing the boundaries of its own discussion. If "cargo cult" is indeed us looking at others looking at us, being objective by keeping ourselves out of the picture is an interminable intellectual task, which accounts for why "cargo cult" never goes away and the discourse about it has such an unsettled, inconclusive quality. While Biersack (Ch. 4) dismisses the "postmodern" reflexivity which accom-panied the critique of "othering", assuming instead the perspective of a transcendental ego, I find that, although it runs the risk of becoming self-indulgent, it is necessary that I understand my position as a participant-observer in order to comprehend the "cargo cult" I encountered[2]. So I would suggest that, regardless of its capacity for derogatory use, the term "cargo cult" not be abandoned because it preserves the uneasy relation between Western culture and Inner Oceania islander cultures, prevents the objectification of native cultures and precludes us from removing ourselves as subjects from the phenomenon. However, as Hermann (Ch. 6) rightly suggests, we should also keep the term "under erasure" to obviate the pretence that it is an objective category. In addition, since "cargo cult" is a resolutely indi-genous interpretation of Western *kago*, Tabani (Ch. 1) is correct in advocating that the local term *kastom* be employed for the indigenous perspective it embodies in relation to "cargo cult" (see also Scott 2012; Abong Ch. 3). Indeed in order to comprehend the phenomenon in question, it is not sufficient to employ only one term: it is necessary to have several.

---

2. As Derrida (1968) pointed out, the attempt to critically remove oneself from a discursive process in which one is involved yields two possible "false exits". One is the attempt suddenly and dramatically to step outside of the discourse, as in adopting the supposedly neutral, objective perspective of a transcendental ego in relationship to the discourse. However this strategy ensconces one within the discourse one pretends to escape from more firmly than ever, for it fails to consider one's own position in relation to the system one supposedly thereby escapes. The other strategy is to critique the system from a position within its own discursive formation. This false exit is both strictly impossible and abso-lutely unavoidable; it has the virtue of acknowledging its position in a discursive formation and, para-doxically, yields more accurate results.

The Sociology of Knowledge and Knowledge of Sociology between "Cargo" and "Cult"

The most fundamental problem for Western explanations and interpretations of "cargo cult" is doubtless that Westerners simply do not and cannot believe local villagers when they suppose that, when "whitemen" *glassim* the earth, they are able to see the "inside", otherwise invisible, life energies and forms of consciousness that comprise it. The villagers, on the other hand, do not believe that the universe is <u>not</u> an animated, consciously aware one. They simply take it for granted. Villagers assume that anything which has a physical form, and perhaps many an entity without one, is likely to have some sort of living conscious awareness. The "outside" appearances of things in nature possess an unseen interior living subjectivity which is continuous with human intelligence. Rawa people I know participate in their environment and seek to align themselves with it by dreaming of, and befriending, the bush spirits which inhabit the jungle where they make gardens and go hunting, much as they do with one another when men and women practise certain kinds of love magic.

When Europeans view the landscape through binoculars, they see waves of light reflected off the surfaces of solid matter made up of atoms and molecules, themselves composed of matter and energy. When the villagers I knew looked though my optical distance finder or SLR camera they reportedly saw the incomprehensible fuzz of something many of them supposed they otherwise knew better through dreaming and other mystical techniques. Since people of Inner Oceania mystically participate in nature, it is not something from which they separate themselves but is instead something to which they relate socially and culturally, so when "cargo cults" become "social movements", they would more accurately be thought of as "nature movements" or "nature-culture movements" or, better, all three at once.

Westerners, on the other hand, have, to use the expression Weber (1946) adopted, "disenchanted the world". Over a very long period of time Europeans developed a thoroughly materialist view of the universe (Tarnas 1991, 2006). By the time of Newton they had placed themselves as knowing subjects outside an objective universe which was considered to be completely impersonal and unaware. Stunned by the mathematical discoveries of Newton and others, Europeans came to consider themselves, in relation to a transcendental, monotheistic God, as semi-divine beings endowed with the special capacity to reason and thus understand a purely material, unconscious "nature". The objective of man became to control, dominate and subdue an earth that itself lacked any intrinsic meaning and purpose, for her and his own divinely sanctioned and guided benefit. Because of this, Westerners place themselves outside and above "nature", understood as an object for them to have power over, for themselves. Their relation to a separate "nature" is consequently one of agonistic control: when it proves recalcitrant or to have an intention other than that of humans, Westerners experience a frustration of purpose and become ever more active and forceful in their attempts to subdue their environment.

People such as the islanders of Inner Oceania who assumed otherwise are thought by Europeans to be seriously intellectually challenged and deluded and they have viewed their task from their position in a divine social hierarchy between God and such native peoples as one of tutelage in relation to their larger objective, with themselves in the vanguard of history. With the idea that man is the animal endowed with reason, islanders appeared less rational and, by implication, less human and more like natural objects, subject to manipulation, control and paternalistic guardianship, if not exploitation. And when "cargo cultists" kept obstinately refusing to go along with the Western disenchantment of "nature", Europeans invented all sort of derogatory evolutionary notions such as "cargo cult" which insult and belittle them, and they redoubled their efforts to refashion islanders in their own image, if not deriding them then at least sympathetically explaining them in terms comprehensible to the Western mind.

When Rawa people interact with their environment in the assumption of a consciously aware universe, they endeavour to create symbiotic, synergistic relationships wherever they can and to protect themselves when they cannot. The relations they forge with the lands they inhabit and domesticate are more profound and serious than most Westerners can possibly fathom. When they travel outside their inhabited space, particularly into another group's domesticated landscape, villagers are vigilant about detecting dissonance with other forms of consciousness and potential sorcery threats. As inevitable as such conflicts may be, Rawa people also recognize that a symbiotic relationship is a far more useful and productive one. In the heyday of Rawa prehistoric culture, successful hamlets sought to ally themselves with one another through a series of feasting rituals which inevitably led to intermarriages. Though hardly free from hostilities, Rawa villagers had thus created a network of alliances across their collective territories along the southern slopes of the Finisterre Mountains and acts of aggression between hamlets, while often serious, were relatively easy to bring into balance if not resolve.

Villagers told me that if a completely unrecognizable stranger appeared from out of nowhere on someone's territory, the immediate impulse used to be to kill them, but when the missionaries arrived holding Bibles and crucifixes instead of bows and arrows, they were given more latitude and eventually embraced. Alternatively Rawa people also told stories of how, when encountering strangers on their territory who were assumed to be manifestations of bush spirits, they were especially careful to interact with them in a friendly manner. The early native missionaries whom the Rawa people I knew had invited to establish a village and preach the gospel married into, and thus joined, the community. However the colonial government and businessmen endeavoured to set up a tutelary exploitative hierarchy. The general reaction, explained to me in plain terms by the village headman, has therefore been to embrace Christianity and resist the colonial government and capitalist inequality and exploitation. It took them some time to sort this all out.

If Europeans are stymied by the epistemological ideas of native peoples, the "cargo cultists" I knew were baffled by the Westerners' sociology. The only thing these "cargo cultists" could not figure out is why "whitemen" would not share their secret – the knowledge they obviously must have but for some reason will not share. "Some of us don't believe that whitemen are telling us everything" is how they explained themselves to me. Like Yali, but unlike most other villagers I knew, they were sceptical of Western Christianity along with other European motives. In Rawa understanding and practice, since two peoples joining together are more powerful and successful than they are existing separately, to most Rawa villagers the missionaries seemed to be offering a mutually beneficial relationship, but the government and businessmen just ended up creating a hierarchy which failed to produce many benefits for the local people despite promises to the contrary. Sometimes Rawa people can get government help to build a school or road, but while I lived there in the early 1980s they staged a tax revolt and are generally quite wary of government and almost any business enterprise other than their own.

It was only after Yali learned that not all Europeans believe in Christianity but instead more commonly believe in social evolution that he returned to the north coast, refused to cooperate further with Europeans and orchestrated a revival of native *kastom* in opposition to Western ways (Lawrence 1964, Wagner 1981). At that point he was apparently able to fathom the duplicity of European tutelage and thus the sociology which accompanies a materialist, disenchanted "nature". When Yali asked Diamond (1997) why it was that "whitemen" got all the "cargo", it was therefore likely to have been a rhetorical question which, mistakenly, Diamond took literally: what Yali actually meant was something more like "if you whitemen are really as supernaturally gifted and superior as you think you are, why is it that you can't share your cargo knowledge with us?" What Diamond missed but Yali comprehended was the selfish, materialist pursuit of power, rather than technological mastery, which is actually at the root of much European privilege (see Errington and Gewertz 2004). After a series of run-ins with colonial authorities, Yali was never heard from again and his fate is uncertain. I think he probably died of a broken heart (cf. Lindstrom 1993).

While islanders are thwarted by the sociological presumptions of Europeans, Westerners are baffled by the epistemological presuppositions of native peoples. The encounter between Western civilization and cultures of Inner Oceania can be characterized as a meeting between "materialist" and "religious" views of reality. One only need go back to Tylor (1889 [1871]) to find this understanding of the conflict between Western and native cultures. But one must change his commonly held view of "religion" as essentially a belief in supernatural spirits. As Ruel (1982) has shown, the notion of "belief" has come to have extraordinary and unusual significance through European history. At first it implied a sense of trust and of belonging to a community, and then conformity to an authoritative orthodoxy, later it became an inner organizing experience, and finally the modern Western "belief in belief", that is a supposedly universal human religious quality of acknowledging something beyond oneself which different groups of people imagine in different ways. In the process "belief" was separated from its original meaning as something "trustworthy" and "reliable" and became a distinctly European Christian idea, now conceived as malleable and subject to doubt across communities, and therefore set apart from the knowledge and the authority of "science" (Pouillon 1982). For peoples without this history, "religion" is instead understood as local knowledge which they gain from experience and share within their communities.

The problem with this kind of knowledge for Europeans is that it falls within the realm of religious "belief" rather than "science". To Western social scientists, who operate in a multicultural world in relation to a single, unified, material "nature", such "beliefs" appear as symbolic "tropes" and "motifs" in "semantic fields". For the general scientific community, this sort of knowledge is simply not reliable: not everyone is capable of having the sorts of mystical experiences Rawa people rely upon for such knowledge. In addition, these experiences are largely random and unpredictable and generally not subject to human control: they often happen to the people who experience them rather than being things they have control over, although talented practising magicians are supposed to have more deliberate access to this knowledge and can often convey it to others. Of course in the Western world the general populace also has limited access to the empirical experiences and lack the mathematical aptitudes which scientists rely upon to build and verify their models of the world, and generally take it on faith that what the scientists say is true[3]. Yet even then the public often judges scientific knowledge against the social hierarchy which Western materialism implies and, if it threatens to undermine the status and control which they otherwise enjoy over "nature" and people supposedly more "natural" than themselves, it becomes the subject of protracted political scepticism and public debate[4].

In addition, modern physics is largely silent on the question of conscious awareness in "nature". Consciousness is generally assumed to be something to do with the human brain and a matter for psychology; physicists are limited to measuring things such as the chemical action potentials of brain transmitters acting across synapses. Yet what is considered to be "consciousness awareness" is largely a matter of definition involving an "awareness" of "self" and attributing it to physical or biological systems beyond our own brains has always been problematic. While researchers demonstrate some such mental capacities in chimpanzees and gorillas, the ability of humans to comprehend the awarenesses of other kinds of system much beyond themselves, if they exist, is necessarily strictly limited: it would seem impossible for humans to intuit a natural definition of the concept of "awareness" for systems on very different scales or of a makeup that is very different from their own. And, beyond that, any operational definition and its measurement would be arbitrary and tautological.

However, modern physics apparently substantiates the assumption of an invisible or unseen side of reality which vastly exceeds human comprehension: the best cosmological theories to date suppose that about ninety-five percent of reality is completely imperceptible to us, comprised of "dark matter", which physicists posited to explain the gravitational coherence of galaxies of stars, which cannot be accounted for with observable visible matter, and "dark energy", which they posit to explain the observed acceleration of the expansion of the universe (Seife 2003).

One need only stop thinking of "nature" as opposed to "man" in terms of merely matter and energy and instead think of the cosmos in terms of information in order to start constructing a workable theory of a consciously aware universe. Any system which overcomes entropy and maintains itself for any length of time must

---

3. A community of shamans would therefore be analogous to a community of scientists in the Western world, for they are both groups of specialists in the production of knowledge to which not everyone has direct access but upon whom their larger communities nevertheless rely.

4. This is apparently the situation with the current political controversy over global warming. It is interesting to consider the different trajectories of recent debates about climate change and somewhat older ones about the teaching of evolution. In the latter case the scientific view has apparently held sway whereas, in the former, that has hardly proven to be the case.

organize itself according to mathematical principles beyond mere material and energy and atoms and molecules. Such a system must be self-organizing and adaptive to maintain itself in some degree of equilibrium in relation to the other systems with which it interacts; such a system must be nonlinear and thus entail a variety of recursive negative and positive feedback processes in order to be adaptive and self-organizing. To maintain themselves and adjust to changes, complex adaptive systems must exchange not merely matter and energy with the systems around them but also what is essentially information: the pattern of organization beyond matter and energy is a kind of code for the matter it organizes, and complex systems generally consist of patterns within patterns at different scales of encoding. It is through these that self-organizing systems maintain themselves and interact with one another (Campbell 1982, Gell-Mann 1994, Taylor 2001, Waldrop 1992).

The clearest examples of information systems outside of human consciousness are probably DNA and the immune system. The natural biological world is full of such systems, yet complex environmental, geological and cosmological systems must also encode information about the chemical physical states of themselves and one another. Whether or not or at what point such systems acquire "conscious awareness" is impossible to say with any certainty, but it certainly does not make much sense to discount out of hand the working thesis that systems beyond the human brain and sensory apparatuses have this property unless, perhaps, one chooses to continue to enjoy the sociological implications of a materialist philosophy, and/or one is completely insensible to reality.

The Western materialist notion of "nature" is the figure which appears out of the ground of a sociology of dominance and dependency, tutelage and exploitation, while the Rawa sociology of creating synergy and symbiotic relations, that is of a complex adaptive cultural system, is the figure which appears out of the ground of an epistemology which assumes a consciously aware universe. These contrasting world views are much more than simply ways of viewing the world. They make up the fabric of neural patterns within the human brain and configure the somatic experiences and ways of sensing, knowing and interacting with the world of their bearers. They also comprise the outer universe and guide their behaviour in constructing and creating their world. A great many peoples of Inner Oceania simply do not want to inhabit the world which is fabricated by the "whiteman". This is the view of "cargo cult". But it is also the view of many non "cargo cultists" I knew who have embraced a more or less syncretic Christian religious perspective while being wary of government and business.

Diversity, Uncertainty and Culture

Macintyre (Ch. 5) is right to bring up the issue of the diversity of opinions and ideas and variations in confidence within the local cultures where "cargo cult" occurs, something which the broad comparison I have drawn apparently ignores and obfuscates. Such diversity has, of course, been familiar to ethnographers of "cargo cult" for many years. Harding (1967: 22), for example, writes "To maintain that cargoism is a pervasive system of thought and belief, however, is not to suggest that all natives hold to cargoist tenets with firm intellectual conviction". I have touched upon individual differences within Rawa culture and New Guinea in my descriptions and endeavoured to keep my broad comparison true to the local variety I encountered. Ethnographers face a real dilemma in attempting to describe a shared culture amidst what is often an overwhelming amount of diversity. Besides recounting life histories and telling stories about individuals, classic solutions to this dilemma include providing an appreciation of the polysemy of collective symbolic representations and ignoring or omitting from the culture, or cultural element they embody, the people who fail to participate in them.

There are problems, moreover, with limiting descriptions and interpretations to the local ethnographic context: besides the academic division of labour it implies, I would argue that it also limits the ability to interpret and fully understand the cultural phenomena being described. Of course any theoretical construction employed in an interpretation implies the broad cross-cultural comparisons employed to build it. But removing the local culture from its broad ethnographic context and separating description from comparison produces a kind of ethnographic present that, in particular, eliminates the broad prehistoric context which can be critical for understanding the phenomenon in question, even where history and contemporary change are central to the study. It is akin to trying to put together a puzzle without all of the pieces.

In addition, different cultural traditions include within them different realms of uncertainty which inform their own dynamic and produce much local diversity. In a somewhat removed context, Lévi-Strauss (1987) described the Polynesian notion *mana* in semiological terms as a "transcendental signified": there is an endless variety of ways of attempting to signify *mana* and make it present, none of which are entirely equal to the task. Many Polynesian people therefore try to obtain *mana* in a great many innovative ways as fortunes wax and wane. Rawa people, who have prehistoric ties with ancient Polynesian seafaring cultures, judge the magical activities in which many engage, as well as social relations they attempt to extend, in terms of the "root" (*tamoni*) and the "fruit" or "food" (*owardi*) it bears. The "root" is the secret magical knowledge of the hidden "inside" (*newendemo*) mystical forces which enable the result. People generally employ one kind a magic until it stops working and then set about looking for another. This is the uncertainty and scepticism which is part of the system of magical knowledge and makes for a variety of opinions and beliefs regarding many claims to knowledge or relationship.

Besides the enormous variation in magical knowledge, there is a great diversity of practitioners: virtually every Rawa villager participates in magic to some degree but the variety is enormous. Any headman has to have very powerful magic, including sorcery, to look after his community, most men seem to have magic to make gardens, pigs and children grow, and many young men and women have experimented with different sorts of love magic. Some men have magic to make it rain or stop raining. Others practise magic to make their musical performances affect their audience, to win at card games and other competitions, to win court cases and, perhaps, to make money multiply. Many have magic to cure different kinds of illness and to protect against illness and sorcery.

There are apparently as many kinds of magic as there are human purposes. Some kinds of magic are relatively easy to obtain and work while others require a great deal more ascetic discipline. More ambitious or motivated women and men endeavour to practise more demanding sorts of magic, while others seem satisfied to depend on others to accomplish the goals they have that might be amenable to magical manipulation. Very few seem entirely to doubt the efficacy of all kinds of magic, although the very strong version of Christianity has provided that possibility and some people evidently follow it. One practising magician who was also a Christian simply explained to me that "God created everything on earth and we just use it". Some church preachings claim that magic employs false gods which are akin to demons. This makes them credible and creates a space for the uneasy syncretism of magic and Christianity which generally exists in the village.

The doubt which is part of magic is based on an even more fundamental uncertainty regarding the knowledge, extent and nature of conscious awareness found in the jungle environment. A number of different Rawa people used to tell me stories of villagers who had been covered up by landslides as the result of vengeance by supposedly "wild" pigs which they had killed. The narratives all agree that all and only those who had eaten the pig they had hunted were killed by the landslides, and it was said that some people would not eat the pork because, regardless of how much it was cooked, the blood remained fresh. This blood was an indication of the nature of the conscious awareness of these "wild" pig-bush spirits which some people noticed and acknowledged while others did not, for without such awareness they are hard to distinguish from mere wild pigs.

Viveiros de Castro (2004) describes how, in the consciously aware universe of Amerindians, in contrast to the intellectual problem of materialism, the conundrum is how to differentiate inert material from conscious awareness rather than how to distinguish awareness out of a materialist "nature":

> "If in the [Western] naturalist view a subject is an insufficiently analyzed object, in the Amerindian animist cosmology the converse holds: *an object is an incompletely interpreted subject.* The object must either be 'expanded' to a full-fledged subject – a spirit; an animal in its human, reflexive form – or else understood as related to a subject (as existing, in Gell's terms, 'in the neighbourhood' of an agent). But an important qualification must now be made: Amerindian cosmologies do not as a rule attribute personhood (or the same degree of personhood) to each type of entity in the world. In the case of animals, for instance, the emphasis seems to be on those species that perform key symbolic and practical roles, such as the great predators and the principal species of prey for humans. Personhood and "perspectivity" – the capacity to occupy a point of view – is a question of degree and context rather than an absolute, diacritical property of particular species". (Viveiros de Castro 2004: 470, his emphasis)

Viveiros de Castro goes on to say that the key determinant of conscious awareness is position in a social network: entities which exist in apparent isolation appear as mere material objects, but everything else has a degree of conscious awareness. The complexity and nature of the material system does not decide if an entity is endowed with awareness. Rather the relation with other systems does: it is quite possible to be a complex system capable of awareness and still be socially isolated from humans and thus apparently merely material. So for Rawa people the status of a "wild" pig which has been hunted may be the issue of some discussion, disagreement, uncertainty and debate, yet nevertheless subject to experimental test: it might be a feral, domesticated or similar pig whose awareness is capable of being in a symbiotic relation with themselves, or perhaps a "wild" pig-bush spirit whose synergistic ties to the land make that impossible and instead render it essentially, for them, immortal.

The doubt and uncertainty which are inherent parts of magical practice and of a consciously aware universe exist within individuals as well as amidst the variety of opinions, experiences and views in the community. These are the arenas where the dramatic struggle between materialist and religious world views takes place. In the following section I offer a model of this struggle, from the perspective of a non-materialist view of reality, within and between Western cultures and the cultures of people such as my Rawa friends and other indigenous peoples of Inner Oceania.

Living, Killing and Dying in the Multi-verse

The great historical debates about indigenous peoples among Europeans were between the monogenists, who viewed indigenous peoples as human like themselves, having souls and conscious awareness, and the polygenists, who saw native peoples as mere animals or natural material beings lacking human attributes and available to have their labour and other resources exploited (Stocking 1968). These debates, in other terms, were between more sympathetic and callous views of indigenous peoples. With the general acceptance of indigenous peoples as human in the latter half of the nineteenth century, these two positions were redistributed between Europeans who viewed indigenous people and their resources as available for exploitation and those who saw them instead as deserving of their uplifting tutelage. Many if not most Europeans hold both views more or less simultaneously[5].

For animists the question was not how far to extend conscious human awareness beyond themselves, as it is for Europeans, but where to limit it (cf. Connolly and Anderson 1987; Schieffelin and Crittenden 1991). Therefore Biersack's question regarding the relevance of materiality in Paiela cosmology (2009) and Bell's exploration of the aesthetics of materiality in the Purari Delta somatic experience (2010) are highly pertinent. Viveiros de Castro's reinterpretation of Lévi-Strauss' illustration of supposedly universal ethnocentrism (1998) is a vivid example of the historic clash between European materialist and indigenous "religious" views of reality.

"In the Greater Antilles, some years after the discovery of America, whilst the Spanish were dispatching inquisitional commissions to investigate whether the natives had a soul or not, these very natives were busy drowning the white people they had captured in order to find out, after lengthy observation, whether or not the corpses were subject to putrefaction". (Viveiros de Castro 1998: 475, trans. Viveiros de Castro; Lévi-Strauss 1973: 384; 1976: 329)

Much as with "wild" pig-bush spirits in the Rawa jungle, the indigenous question was whether "whitemen" were beings with a conscious awareness able to engage in a

---

5. This duplicity – supposedly doing good while actually doing well economically – is the subject of Derrida's critique of Western bourgeois mentality: while it is always good to do good, it is pure hubris to suppose that history is going to go the way that we imagine or will it to go, or that the European Enlightenment project is either inevitable or was ever bound to be successful; it is all too easy to delude oneself in a self-justifying manner into the pretence of making better a situation we can neither fully comprehend nor control, and supposedly to do good for the world while actually doing well for oneself. Therefore Derrida thematizes Baudelaire's assertion that, while it is never good to do evil, there is some merit in knowing that one is doing so: the worse vice is to do evil out of stupidity (Derrida 1996).

synergistic, mutually beneficial exchange relationship with themselves, or were those with another form of consciousness beyond their comprehension – "insufficiently analyzed subjects" and, in this sense, more like material objects – giving "whitemen" a kind of immortality in relation to themselves and making them, quite possibly, extraordinarily dangerous. For the "cargo cultists" I knew and others whose aim was to assert *kastom* over and against the dominance of "whitemen", the answer to this question was clearly that "whitemen" are beings of the dangerous and immortal kind. But for larger numbers of Rawa people who have adopted a Christian religious perspective over that of materialist business and government, the answer is more qualified[6].

It is interesting, in this regard, to consider that the Enga and Ipili Cult of Ain and *mata kamo* movements which resulted from the European contact experience turned out to be more concerned with obtaining the immortality of "whitemen" than their "cargo" (Biersack Ch. 4). More recently Jebens finds that even Nakanai who reject the term "cargo cult" as derisive view it as fundamentally a relation to the dead and continue to assume it implicitly: "The expectation of goods sent by one's own ancestors is a central aspect of a '*kago kalt*' or 'cargo cult', and thus people reject it decisively along with the term itself: 'Money and cargo do not derive from the ancestors, money derives solely from sweat'. Yet some of my hosts and informants were still convinced that the dead were indeed able to help them in achieving economic success" (2010: 97). Among other interpreters of Inner Oceania "cargo cults", Lanternari is unusual in seeing them as intrinsic combinations of the traditional "cult of the dead" and the modern "cult of cargo". However he nonetheless views them in fairly standard terms as a "reaction to an alien culture, which appears among them in the form of religious evangelism and of hitherto unknown material goods" (1963: 185). I would add, along with Biersack, that it is not so much material goods as a materialist philosophy that cultists encounter.

For Rawa people the choice is not so much how sympathetic or callous to be within a materialist hierarchy but how much to hate, or align themselves with, an ambivalent, duplicitous, materialist hierarchy imposed from without within a consciously aware universe. "Cargo cultists" who assert *kastom* insist on a real synergy against a false or half-hearted one, while Christian villagers continue to build communities and forge bonds from which they may derive some benefit where they

---

6. Papua New Guineans who join the middle classes, very few of whom I ever got to know well at all, apparently accept the Western European hierarchy they join while nonetheless feeling the obligations they have to local kin communities (Gewertz and Errington 1999).

can and to be wary of the Western world where they cannot. Either way, while the vibrancy of their communities is very satisfying, the experience of a Western materialist world is not a happy one. I can only imagine the cataclysmic and emotionally devastating impact of living in a religiously alive universe that is overwhelmed by a dead materialist one, which, moreover, one is hardly able to influence.

If Western ambivalence lies along a sympathy-insensibility continuum in a materialist universe, then Rawa ambivalence would seem to move between hateful defiance of, and resigned accommodation to, an imposed materialist hierarchy, from within a religious perspective that is nevertheless satisfying. I suggest that a model of the struggle this ambivalence entails, understood from an indigenous perspective, can be found in the multiple times and ontologies of Javanese *wayang* theatre plots described by Becker (1979).

McDowell (1985, 1988) has pointed to a nonlinear, "episodic" view of time, change and history which is widespread in Inner Oceania: instead of viewing history as a linear evolutionary progression, the people of Bun see it as a series of disconnected episodes involving radical ontological breaks[7]. Therefore many "social movements" appear to take the form of millenarian transformations and "cargo cult" seems to make more sense. Instead of describing the indigenous world view as a "cosmos" or "universe", it would hence be more accurate to call it a "multiverse". Becker (1979) describes a similar temporality which produces the coherence of Javanese *wayang* plot structure: *wayang* theatre depends on coincidental encounters between opposed cosmic forces to motivate actions rather than a Western-style, logical linear progression of events which sequentially and causally build on one another. The acts in *wayang* plots always involve scenes in a court or hermitage, a journey away from there and a return, and a chance encounter during the journey entailing a battle between contrary beings and epistemologies. Each type of being dwells within a different epistemology and concept of time and all of them exist simultaneously. Any scene may be transposed or omitted except for the movement away from, and the return to, the court, and almost anything else can be left out or brought in. The coincidental clash of conceptual universes remains the centre of the performance and is what makes it coherent. Unlike Western linear narratives, in *wayang* theatre time has no constraint except that it must be multiple.

---

7. It should be noted, in this regard, that the "many worlds" theory of particle physics is a perfectly coherent and accepted physical theory, some versions of which suppose that different universes exist with different physical laws (Davies 1988).

Wayang theatre draws upon the mythology of the two great epics, the Ramayana and the Mahabharata, and the coincidental encounter takes place between the hero Arjuna or his counterpart and a demon in the forest. When they meet, two worlds collide: the demon is purely corporeal whereas Arjuna is a religious devotee whose awareness disturbs the demon's physical comfort. After the demon attacks and a struggle ensues, Arjuna kills the demon, which he recognizes as evil, out of religious duty, but the demon is never dead forever: the balance is merely restored, for the battle between gross materialism and religiosity is an eternal struggle[8]. In the most famous book of the Mahabharata, Arjuna finds himself on the field of battle facing an army of his cousins. His cousins are irreligious, materialistic people who are aching to usurp the kingdom of their religiously-minded adversaries. Being a pious and kind-hearted soul, Arjuna considers becoming a world renouncer or forest monk rather than fight his cousins, but the religious avatar Lord Krishna counsels him that this course of action would actually be utterly self-indulgent and that he must instead devote himself to a higher purpose, do his duty and risk himself in the endeavour to kill and defeat his cousins, which he successfully does.

There is a stock character in mythologies across South and East Asia, particularly well expressed in Chinese Buddhism (e.g. see Ahern 1973), which is used to personify the sort of demonic beings encountered by Arjuna in *wayang* theatre, namely the "hungry ghost". These beings are "ghosts" because they do not exist in the real living world. Instead, they are so caught up in their own self-delusions that, for them, the rest of the world appears to be lifeless: it exists only to be used for the enhancement of their own magnified selves. This is why, as one of Becker's translators explained to him, demons move in straight lines, for they are always engaged in the linear calculation of their own immediate gains. Because they are so disconnected from, and therefore unable to communicate meaningfully with, a living reality, suffering a kind of autism, these "ghosts" are profoundly unhappy, insatiably "hungry" and greedy, and willing to sacrifice almost anyone and anything – they imagine others to operate much like themselves – in order to gratify their senses and aggrandize their exaggerated egos[9]. Some Chinese routinely use this character to describe Westerners whom they encounter (e.g. Kingston 1989).

---

8. As Biersack (2009) describes for the Paiela, intelligence is considered to be superior but materiality is nevertheless irreducible, hence, one could suppose, the eternal struggle between these two principles.

9. From the viewpoint of information theory, "hungry ghosts" become trapped in a runaway positive feedback cycle with their own selves rather than being subject to the equilibrating negative feedback they would otherwise experience in relationship to other beings in their environment with which they could have a symbiotic relationship.

Jimmy Stevens, President of the Nagriamel movement on Santo, depicts the internal struggle between materialist and religious views in a universe full of hungry ghosts very well when he asserts that, rather than living the life of a consumer in quiet desperation, one must do one's duty and assume the risk of being a determined political actor in order to remake a sensible world against an overwhelmingly materialist one (Abong Ch. 3). The internal religious struggle, in other words, involves thinking, feeling and acting in a way that transcends one's own calculated, material self-interest and egoistic self-enhancement in a world full of hungry ghosts. This inner conflict is fundamentally with one's own ego. In the drama of "cargo cult" movements, like that of *wayang* theatre, the actors often risk everything to remake a living reality in the face of a dead and dying one. Most fundamentally, this struggle involves establishing a relationship with otherness and one's own death.

Europeans who live in a materialist universe, unless they think they are going to heaven (as Derrida (1992) would say, "economically"), generally suppose that when one dies one simply returns to the state of matter. For Rawa people I knew, at least in the old way of thinking, if they have been initiated in a traditional way to be leaders, or are extraordinarily successful and magnanimous, they believe that when they die they will become stars or souls in heaven, looking down on everyone and continuing to provide animating life energy. Otherwise it is generally assumed that someone who dies continues to exist as, or merges with, some form of conscious awareness belonging to the jungle landscape around the place where they are buried. Even though Christian missionaries endeavoured to separate the dead from the living by establishing a village graveyard some distance from village residences, people have continued to visit the graveyard, beseeching their deceased relatives for various purposes, and have recently started to bury and enshrine ancestors near their houses again.

From this perspective, it makes sense to suppose that "whitemen" get their money from the graveyard, for it is by interacting with what is to them an essentially dead universe that Western people are able to produce the wealth which they enjoy. Like most "cargo cultists", for the man who asked me this question, becoming a sorcerer involved an enormous sacrifice of, and risk to, self. And like Yali's questioning of Diamond, asking this of a "whiteman" was probably a rhetorical strategy: it is more like pointing out what sort of universe "whitemen" inhabit and indeed create, putting a thought in his head and thus, in a way, trying to harm him and thus awaken him from his dogmatic slumber. Many people who engage in "cargo cult" in Inner Oceania would rather die in an enchanted universe than live in a dead materialist one. This was the gist of the statement of Jean-Marie Tjibaou, the leader of the

Kanak Socialist National Liberation Front in New Caledonia, whom Abong (Ch. 3) quotes at the end of his paper: "Dying is not hard, it is more difficult to stay alive and to feel like a stranger in your own country, to feel that your country is dying and being powerless".

Seeing and Being in the Worlds of Rawa Culture

I have to wonder how successful my friend the missionary's son will be in using binoculars to disabuse his fellow villagers of the idea that "whitemen" *glassim* the hidden "inside" life forces which inhabit the jungle landscape. It is difficult to tell because he seems to be anticipating a trend which is already apparent in the village. When I was there in the early 1980s, the people I knew were not only unable to operate my SLR camera, but many of them had some unusual ideas about being photographed as well. Candid photographs or pictures of relaxed, smiling subjects were nearly impossible to get. Only a few relatively young men who had some education or had some familiarity with Western ways were able to interact with a camera in an informal way. Everyone else looked very serious and stiffened up to pose for photographs.

One young man I encountered at a funeral wake showed me a very small and worn photograph of his mother and earnestly told me that it was the reason that she had died. His photo illustrated an understanding which people generally assumed: a photograph has the capacity to entirely envelop the perspectival viewpoint of its subject. The image provides a kind of feedback to the self of its subject which has such psychic power that it can completely captivate it. In doing so, a photo can reformulate a subject so dramatically as to remove it from the cultural network of relations which define it, effectively "killing" it. This is why I had "died" when I had lost contact with the people I had known back in New Guinea. And this is what the sorcerer I met was attempting to counter in asking me, the "whiteman", about getting money from the graveyard[10].

When I visited in the late 1990s there were a large number of young men and women who had no trouble using my camera. In fact, some had cameras of their

---

10. Paradoxically, for Western Europeans, in "killing" a being as a consciously aware subject and thus rendering it a mere material object, the subject is, like truly "wild" Rawa pig-bush spirits, rendered immortal to those for whom he or she is psychically "dead": it is by sharing perspectives and thus participating in a common world that life energies can be exchanged and passed on and that people, or at least their physical persons, eventually die.

own. And they were very familiar with posing for photographs with smiling, friendly faces which simulated those they had seen in *National Geographic*. Indeed many young school children regularly brushed their teeth, wore nice clean clothes and cared for themselves in such a way as to render them quite photogenic, as though they were anticipating the opportunity. In one house I visited I also found that one of the residents had decorated a portion of wall with full-page, glossy colour photographs from a magazine of the white faces of fashion models. Typically the people I asked had little to say about the pictures except that one young member of the family liked them. One could adopt Fanon's thesis (1967) that such images invoke a sense of racial inferiority, as Lattas has done (1998), and they doubtless provide a measure of the self that most people are unable to equal, particularly people of colour in a globe dominated by white people. But being photographed also shifts the position of the subject in relation to the self in a manner which is consistent with the comfort young people now feel in relation to photography.

The village where I resided has acquired a two-room primary school from the government which teaches grades one through six. Families used to have to select a son to send to school on the coast or, later, in other areas somewhat closer to the village. Now a much larger number of students, both boys and girls, are able to attend primary school. The school is full of students who have a much greater familiarity with Western culture than their elders. They know about cameras and magazines. I never got to know any of them very well but I did get to know a few Rawa people who were permanent residents of urban areas and similarly conversant with Western ways. They used to try to help me understand traditional Rawa culture by explaining to me that "our elders used to say X, now we think Y". Although their own understanding of reality had changed dramatically, they never actually said that their elders had been wrong, only that they now know differently. Their elders, after all, had been quite successful in domesticating the landscape and growing their families. But they had lived in a different world and experienced a different reality.

Even when people were critical of an older generation for the fighting, vengeance raids and sorcery in which they had engaged, and about particular magical spirit beliefs, there was general agreement and recognition that the elders had accomplished monumental things. As is common elsewhere in New Guinea, the ancestors were sometimes said to be giant women and men who were capable of enormous feats surpassing the abilities of their descendants. People also shared with me the missionary narrative that the ancestors had lived in an evil time of darkness but now people had come to see the light. Some of these apparently competing narratives were told to me by the same people, usually at different times although I have also known people to consider them simultaneously, using the achievements of the ancestors to juxtapose and correct the idea that they were all just "crazy".

These kinds of stories are often analyzed as indicating a sense of inferiority in the modern world, both to the ancestors and to Westerners. It does not diminish the alienation and suffering experienced by indigenous islanders of Inner Oceania to observe that what these interpretations have in common is a linear view of time and, by implication, an evolutionary historical trajectory. Although opposing views of history appear to be involved here, these stories are all compatible with an episodic view of time. McDowell (1985) illustrates this understanding of time in Bun with the example of a woman who insisted that her grandmother had not been a cannibal because she is still, in essence, alive and, since cannibalism was a practice of the ancestors in a completely different time, she therefore could not have been one. With such a nonlinear notion of history, Rawa ancestors sometimes appear to be crazy, at other times extraordinary and divine, or both, but always dramatically different. This is because they are different kinds of subject in a consciously aware universe and therefore inhabit a different world.

Of course different types of subjects inhabiting different worlds also exist simultaneously, as with indigenous islanders and Westerners. In educating their children in Western ways of thinking and being, the villagers hazard losing them to the community or risk them, in a sense, "dying" in much the same way that I did. So what village residents have done is to embrace and nurture these children in extraordinary fashion. While I was there in 1999, for example, I was able to help with a Lutheran confirmation ceremony for these very same children in which forty young men and women were brought into the church fellowship with an overwhelming outpouring of community support. As is the tradition in these sorts of ceremonies these days, the children were "pulled" into the village by elders who sang and danced while wearing decorations in the manner of the ancestors. The confirmation candidates were then passed on to a modern singing group who led them into the church. The children were thus brought into a new world by their elders who simultaneously gave over their world to a younger generation and took credit for making that possible.

Rawa people have decades of experience with Western culture beginning with men who travelled to find work on German plantations in Rabaul a hundred or more years ago. They have a fairly good understanding of how different and separated is the world which many "whitemen" inhabit and have also lost many of their members to it, who, when they found employment, never or rarely returned home. What they have done with their young school children is remarkable: refashioning them as subjects while holding them tightly within their communities, keeping their affection and attention for themselves. If these children are to become more like ghosts, one might say, at least they won't go hungry.

In the larger picture, however, it is not clear that my friend's project to change villagers' understandings of *glassim* will be particularly successful. Not all children of school age attend the community school and there are many Rawa villages without one. A great many Rawa people continue to inhabit a world in which they dream of the bush spirits who dwell in their land and maintain other mystical connections with the living universe in which they participate. In addition, it is perhaps even more remarkable to find a very serious practising magician and sorcerer of the sort I met among the young men of the village. When I was there in the early 1980s, the villagers bragged about having successfully eliminated the practice of sorcery from their communities. They had sought to do so in an effort to bring to an end a period of great conflict and violence which followed upon the German colonization of the north coast. In a world full of hungry ghosts, however, having a dedicated sorcerer in the community now seems like a good idea: his statements were certainly disconcerting to me. He seems equal to the task of keeping alive a universe which is otherwise threatened with dying.

Between the missionary's son and the sorcerer, the young school children, their elders and the many villagers who spend most days in their bush houses near their gardens and pigs, between cargo and cult, the Rawa villagers I know seem well poised to negotiate their existence successfully in the living worlds they inhabit.

Acknowledgments

I gratefully acknowledge the monetary support which a National Science Foundation grant was able to afford me. I also very much appreciate the support which Roy Wagner gave to me and for pointing me in the direction of an anthropology of the subject. I am extraordinarily grateful for the opportunity they provided me. My sincere thanks go to the organizers of this collection, Marc Tabani and Marcellin Abong, for their direction and leadership, and to the other contributors for their many excellent papers and inspiration. I am especially thankful to my colleague Jim Jordan for his careful reading and comments and for suggesting and providing resources. I also thank Lamont Lindstrom for suggesting resources and for his editorial comments. I am most appreciative of the support and discussion of Dr Brian Bates and the members of the Delta of Virginia Chapter of Lambda Alpha, particularly Meghan Banton, Lauren Hilt, Alyssa Foley, Stephanie Neeley, Alexis Yorcsyk and Samantha Zerio. My undying gratitude goes to the many Rawa-speaking people I know for their generosity of spirit, honesty and strength, and for their insight into the human condition.

Bibliography

Ahern, Emily M.
1973   *The Cult of the Dead in a Chinese Village*. Stanford: Stanford University Press.

American Anthropological Association
1998   *Code of Ethics of the American Anthropological Association*. Approved June 1998. http://www.aaanet.org/committees/ethics/ethcode.htm.

Becker, Alton L.
1979   "Text-building, Epistemology, and Aesthetics in Javanese Shadow Theatre". In A.L. Becker and A. Yengoyan (eds), *The Imagination of Reality*. Norwood, NJ: Albex Publishing Corp., pp.211-243.

Bell, Joshua A.
2010   "Re-membering the Tom Kabu Movement. Histories of Material and Sensory Transformation". Paper delivered to the 2009-2010 ASAO Meetings.

Biersack, Aletta
2009   "How Matter Matters in Paiela Millenarianism, and What Light This Could Cast upon Melanesian Cargo Cults." Paper given on the panel "Ethnographies of Consciousness," organized by Josh Fisher, AAA annual meeting, Philadelphia, 12/6/09.

Campbell, Jeremy
1982   *Grammatical Man: Information, Entropy, Language, and Life*. New York: Simon & Schuster.

Connolly, Bob and Anderson, Robin
1987   *First Contact*. New York: Viking.

Dalton, Doug
2000   "Cargo Cults and Discursive Madness", *Oceania* 70(4): 345-361.
2004   "Cargo and Cult: The Mimetic Critique of Capitalist Culture". In H. Jebens (ed.), *Cargo, Cult & Culture Critique*. Honolulu: University of Hawaii Press, pp.187-208.

Davies, Paul
1988   *Other Worlds: Space, Superspace and the Quantum Universe*. New York: Penguin Books.

Derrida, Jacques
1982   "The Ends of Man". In *Margins of Philosophy*, Alan Bass (trans.). Chicago: The University of Chicago Press, pp.109-136.
1992   *Given Time: vol. I. Counterfeit money*. Peggy Kamuf (trans.). Chicago: The University of Chicago Press.

Diamond, Jared
1997   *Guns, Germs, and Steel: the Fates of Human Societies*. New York: W.W. Norton & Co.

Errington, Frederick and Gewertz, Deborah
2004   *Yali's Question: Sugar, Culture, and History*. Chicago: The University of Chicago Press.

Fanon, Frantz
1967   *Black Skin, White Masks*. Charles Lam Markmann (trans.). New York: Grove Press.

Festinger, Leon, Riecken, Henry W. and Schachter, Stanley
1964   *When Prophecy Fails; a Social and Psychological Study of a Modern Group That Predicted the Destruction of the World*. New York: Harper & Row.

Gell, Alfred
1998   *Art and Agency: An Anthropological Introduction*. Oxford: Clarendon.

Gell-Mann, Murray
1994   *The Quark and the Jaguar: Adventures in the Simple and the Complex*. New York: W. H. Freeman and Co.

Gewertz, Deborah and Errington, Frederick K.
1999   *Emerging Class in Papua New Guinea: the Telling of Difference*. Cambridge, U.K.: Cambridge University Press.

Harding, Thomas G.
1967   "A History of Cargoism in Sio, North-East New Guinea", *Oceania* 38(1): 1-23.

Jebens, Holger
2010   *After the Cult: Perceptions of Other and Self in West New Britain (Papua New Guinea)*. New York: Berghahn Books.

Kingston, Maxine Hong
1989   *The Woman Warrior: Memoirs of a Girlhood among Ghosts*. New York: Vintage Books.

Lattas, Andrew
1998   *Cultures of Secrecy: Reinventing Race in Bush Kaliai Cargo Cults*. Madison, WI: University of Wisconsin Press.

Lawrence, Peter
1964   *Road Belong Cargo: A Study of the Cargo Movement in the Southern Madang District, New Guinea*. Manchester: Manchester University Press.
1966-67 "Cargo Thinking as a Future Political Force in Papua and New Guinea", *Journal of the Papua and New Guinea Society* 9(1): 20-25.

Lanternari, Vittorio
1963   *The Religions of the Oppressed: A Study of Modern Messianic Cults*. Lisa Sergio (trans.). New York: Mentor Books.

Lévi-Strauss, Claude
1973 [1952]   "Race et histoire". In *Anthropologie Structurale Deux*. Paris: Plon, p. 377-422.
1976   "Race and History". In *Structural Anthropology Volume II*. Monique Layton (trans.). Chicago: The University of Chicago Press, pp.323-362.

1987   *Introduction to the Work of Marcel Mauss*. Trans. Felicity Baker. London:
        Routledge & Kegan Paul.

Lindstrom, Lamont
1993   *Cargo Cult: Strange Stories of Desire from Melanesia and Beyond*. Honolulu: University of
        Hawaii Press.

Mauss, Marcel
1967 [1925]   *The Gift: Forms and Function of Exchange in Archaic Societies*. Ian Cunnison
              (trans.). New York: W. W. Norton & Co. Inc.

McDowell, Nancy
1985   "Past and Future: The Nature of Episodic Time in Bun". In D. Gewertz and E. Schieffelin
        (eds), *History and Ethnohistory in Papua New Guinea*. Sydney: University of Sydney,
        pp.26-39.
1988   "A Note on Cargo Cults and Cultural Constructions of Change". *Pacific Studies* 11: 121-134.

Pouillon, Jean
1982   "Remarks on the Verb 'To Believe'". In M. Izard and P. Smith (eds), *Between Belief and
        Transgression: Structural Essays in Religion, History, and Myth*. John Leavitt (trans.).
        Chicago: University of Chicago Press, pp.1-8.

Robbins, Joel
2004   *Becoming Sinners: Christianity and Moral Torment in a Papua New Guinea Society*.
        Berkeley: University of California Press.

Ruel, Malcolm
1982   "Christians as Believers". In J. Davis (ed.), *Religious Organization and Religious Experience*,
        London: Academic Press, pp.9-31.

Schieffelin, Edward L. and Crittenden, Robert
1991   *Like People You See in a Dream: First Contact in Six Papuan Societies*. Stanford, CA:
        Stanford University Press.

Scott, Michael W.
2012   "The Matter of Makira: Colonisation, Competition, and the Production of Gendered
        Peoples in Contemporary Solomon Islands and Medieval Britain", *History and
        Anthropology*, 23(1): 115-148.

Seif, Charles
2003   *Alpha & Omega: The Search for the Beginning and End of the Universe*. New York: Penguin.

Stocking, George
1968   *Race, Culture, and Evolution: Essays in the History of Anthropology*.
        Chicago: The University of Chicago Press.

Tarnas, Richard
1991   *The Passion of the Western Mind: Understanding the Ideas That Have Shaped Our World
        View*. New York: Harmony Books.
2006   *Cosmos and Psyche: Intimations of a New World View*. New York: Viking.

Taylor, Mark C.
2001   *The Moment of Complexity: Emerging Network Culture*. Chicago: The University of Chicago Press.

Turner, Victor
1967   *The Forest of Symbols: Aspects of Ndembu Ritual*. Ithaca: Cornell University Press.
1982   *From Ritual to Theatre: The Human Seriousness of Play*. New York: Performing Arts Journal Publications.

Tylor, Edward B.
1889 [1871]   *Primitive Culture: Researches into the Development of Mythology, Philosophy, Religion, Language, Art, and Custom*. New York: Holt.

Viveiros de Castro, Eduardo
1998   "Cosmological Deixis and Amerindian Perspectivism", *Journal of the Royal Anthropological Institute* 4(3): 469-488.
2004   "Exchanging Perspectives: The Transformation of Objects into Subjects in Amerindian Ontologies", *Common Knowledge* 10(3): 463-484.

Wagner, Roy
1979   "The Talk of Koriki: A Daribi Contact Cult", *Social Research* 46(1): 141-165.
1981   *The Invention of Culture*. Chicago: The University of Chicago Press.

Waldrop, M. Mitchell
1992   *Complexity: The Emerging Science at the Edge of Order and Chaos*. New York: Simon & Schuster.

Weber, Max
1946   "Science as a Vocation". In H.H. Gerth and C. Wright Mills (eds and trans.), *Essays in Sociology*. New York: Oxford University Press, pp.129-156.

Worsley, Peter
1968 [1957]   *The Trumpet Shall Sound: A Study of Cargo Cults in Melanesia*. London: Schocken Books.

Young, Michael W.
1971   "Goodenough Island Cargo Cults", *Oceania* 42(1): 42-57.

Chapter 3

Metamorphoses of Nagriamel

Marcellin Abong

Introduction

Nagriamel or the New Union of Custom Chiefs (NUCC) is a customary movement that emerged in 1965 on the island of Santo in what was then the New Hebrides. Nagriamel was the initiative of chief Paul Tari Buluk, a traditional island leader, and of Jimmy Stevens, the son of a Tongan mother and Scottish father. Comparable in many ways to other sociopolitical movements in Vanuatu and elsewhere in Melanesia, such as the John Frum movement on the island of Tanna (Tabani 2008), it encouraged a return to "custom" (*kastom*) and the restoration of indigenous land rights, particularly land that Europeans had appropriated but not yet commercially developed. Nagriamel was the first political movement to command a national audience in the New Hebrides which became Vanuatu upon its independence in July 1980.

The name "Nagriamel" was derived from common north New Hebridian words for two plants, *ngaria* (Santo), a croton, and *mel* (Santo) or *mwele* (Ambae), a cycas palm, which were regarded as sacred and powerful ritual symbols. Croton represents the fruitful earth and cycas serves to cement traditional agreements, alliances, and transfer of property. There can be little doubt that the multiplicity of important and traditional meanings associated with its name has had much to do with the success of the movement. At its high-point in July 1980, when movement leaders attempted to establish the independent state of Vemarana rather than recognize an independent Vanuatu, supporters came from "15 islands" including Espiritu Santo, Malo, Aore, Tutuba, Mavea, Ambae, Maewo, Pentecost, Pele, Malekula, Banks, Torres, Ambrym, Paama/Epi and South Tanna.

Both the John Frum and Nagriamel movements challenged practices and social policies imposed by the Condominium as well as the values of Christianity. But, unlike the John Frum movement, Nagriamel ideology was less millenarian and less influenced by Christianity. Most of its members consider that its main message is to advocate an "authentic" return to tradition. It reacted against mission and colonial measures that sought to dishonour ancestral spirits and obliterate "dark" customs and ancestral practices including singing, dancing, drinking kava, wearing our feathers and other physical decorations, or to force us to hide our nudity by means of rags and to impose on women the wearing of austere mission dress. The aim of most missionaries was to abolish custom, to destroy the lifestyle we had inherited from our ancestors. On some islands like Tanna, Presbyterian missionaries established a strenuous church government known as *Tanna Law*. Their repression of *kastom* was assisted by certain local chiefs. They established church courts to punish our brothers who had remained "heathen".

The anti-custom politics of early mission Christianity were paradoxically eased by competition among denominations. Some converts left the Presbyterians, for example, to join the Seventh Day Adventist church which taught the Bible in English rather than in vernacular languages. Others followed often more tolerant Roman Catholic priests who were less opposed to kava drinking and ceremonial display. In the Northern Islands, the Church of Christ was the first to advocate indigenous autonomy within a mission. But it was the eventual emergence of diverse indigenous movements which forced the missionaries to change their attitude towards traditional values. In the first half of the twentieth century, movements hostile to stricter forms of Christianity multiplied in several Northern Islands. On Santo, for example, these included the prophetic movements of Rongofuro and Avu Avu, and the Naked Cult, the movement of Mol Valivu. On Malakula, other movements emerged such as the Malakula Native Company, the Tavala cult of Albert Reret, the Natakaro cults of Joseph, the Vuinamwangwe cult and the Saratangaulu cult. And Ambae was the home of the Tavala Prophetess.

Our islands fell under the guardianship of foreign powers between 1906 and 1980. This exercise of co-sovereignty between France and Great Britain was unique in the annals of colonization. The inefficiencies of a "Condominium" colonial government, with two languages, were often parodied as a "pandemonium". But even worse than its ineffectiveness was the Condominium's endorsement of the legal inferiority and submission of Melanesians who were relegated to the status of noncitizens. By 1940, the indigenous population of the New Hebrides was about 40,000, living alongside a few hundred European settlers. Some have estimated that the population was six times as numerous before the coming of the Whites. Most Melanesians continued to live off the fruits of their lands and seas, although much land had been alienated.

Colonial control began to weaken during the Second World War. The entry of the United States into the war against Japan and strategic wartime developments greatly changed a stagnant colonial situation. Hundreds of thousands of American servicemen landed in the New Hebrides between 1942 and 1946. Thousands of islanders were recruited by the US Army to build and fit out its bases on Efate and Santo. Where once there was only bush, within a few months the military built a multitude of roads, airstrips, ports, hospitals, barracks and other amenities to enhance the daily life of soldiers including restaurants, cinemas and playing fields. In hundreds of warehouses, enormous quantities of goods, military equipment and vehicles accumulated. This new vision of the world paralleled a concomitant decline of the French-British authority.

To the great surprise of our grandfathers, a significant number of the US soldiers who were based in the New Hebrides were African-American. This striking fact offered proof that potential equality between Whites and Blacks was possible; that we were not eternally condemned to being the simple boys of the *masta*. The road towards this ideal was very long and it is still far from being fully achieved. But a new collective consciousness had appeared. Whereas for millions of people around the world the war brought terrible slaughter, for us it marked the beginning of liberation. Wartime experience sparked indigenous movements that precipitated our fight to win back our lands or, at least, to prevent the additional alienation of our land. Well before the birth of the first modern political parties, the Nagriamel movement was the first to enunciate these claims and to demand dignity for all, regardless of skin colour.

Beginnings and Structure

The beginnings of Nagriamal was centred around Vanafo, along the Sarakata river, and the adjoining village of Moru, where associated gardens and plantations were located. Buluk had lived in Veliara, further inland, but Moru had been his ancestral land for generations, although his family had shifted due to hostilities with another group. He returned to Moru when the opposing faction had been killed, and the proximity of the river permitted him to get closer to the plantations. These combined areas subsequently became known as the 'headquarters' of the movement and simply as Vanafo (Hours, 1974). Prior to 1964 there were only limited numbers of people living at Vanafo, primarily man-Santo and Buluk's distant relatives, who had all been living here since the foundation of the Nagriamel. From 1965, however, this began to change and by the start of the 1970s there could be found a greatly increased number of people from many different islands: 40 huts belonging to people from Santo, 24 man-Aoba huts, 12 man-Paama huts, 14 man-Ambrym huts, 2 man-Pentecost huts, 3 man-Epi huts, and 1 hut each of man-Malo, Efate and Malekula. Many of the inhabitants from outside Santo tended to leave their families on their own islands, which promoted frequent travel to and from their home islands. The population at Vanafo, therefore, fluctuated greatly. During quieter periods there were some 300 individuals but during events such as the twice-annual meetings this increased to 800 people. Nagriamal's full membership throughout the archipelago was much greater with some 15000 people who had enrolled and paid for membership (Hours, 1974).

Due to the mixed origins of the people at Vanafo, the movement can to a certain extent, be seen to be a non-traditional movement, a new and different form of political development. It had its nominal 'capital', but the varied population at Vanafo tended to retain a certain autonomy, with the placement and grouping of huts organised around particular members' island of origin and religious beliefs, i.e. man-Aoba from Ndui Ndui and members of the Church of Christ all lived in the same area. Nevertheless, the movement's politico-economic organization reveals a specific character, being hierarchical and federalist. The seven most senior indigenous titles were:

1/ Chief President (Jimmy Stevens)
2/ Assistant Chief
3/ Land Owner (Buluk)
4/ Chief Committee
5/ Committee members
6/ Committee Secretary
7/ Union Secretary

These titles were followed by a list of a further 30 titles of decreasing importance, with *guard of school children* and *women's club* at the end. Each of these titles was represented by a badge that noted the initials of the grade, and it was worn on the left arm or on the chest. Everyone in Vanafo wore a badge. The same badges were also worn at Nagriamel's other centres on other islands (Hours, 1974). The committee was the deliberating body; it settled disputes and made sure that respect for law and order was upheld. The committee acted according to custom and had a highly traditional character. Important decisions were taken by the Chief President and discussed in the committee if necessary.

Both Custom and the Church played central roles in the socio-political structure of Nagriamal. Symbolic references to the Holy Bible and the Church were frequently used in tandem with or melded with customary practice, although generally perceived as of secondary importance. The bible was generally referred to less as a

Holy book than as a book providing a civil code. Numerous notices in the village with the chief's signature were preceded by the mention 'Witness' or 'by witness'. This attestation points to a charismatic element that clearly developed at Vanafo. The name Jimmy T.P.S. Moses stands for Jimmy Tubo Patuntun Stevens, with the addition of the messianic name 'Moses', after being baptized and entering the Church of Christ in 1967 in Vanafo. This political move was hugely successful as it brought a large important community from Ndui Ndui on Aoba to Vanafo. Many man-Santo converted to this religion at the same time, including Buluk and his men. They developed into the chief's most faithful supporters. The choice of the name Moses suggesting that he had great skills; he carried the law, he freed his people, and he was baptized at a certain age (Hours, 1974).

Why Ambae?

A significant number of Nagriamel supporters on Santo came from the neighbouring island of Ambae (Aoba). What was the reason for their support of the movement? Jimmy Stevens called upon the inhabitants of Ambae for several reasons. At the time they were the best educated population within the New Hebrides due to the success of Anglican schooling. Jimmy Stevens was a good strategist and he decided to have a church built in Vanafo in order to evangelize the *malmal* ("*malmal*" means "penis-holder") or *man bush*. Stevens wanted to expand access to education, then still controlled by the missions, and he wished to accelerate the process of emancipation by encouraging parents to send their children to school. At first he wanted to seek help from the Catholic mission, but he hesitated to do so since opting for Catholicism would imply his support for the French side. He also considered asking for the establishment of an Anglican school, but he had the same concerns in that this might privilege connections with the British administration. Instead he started negotiations with the more local Church of Christ which had become independent of foreign mission networks and any connection with France or Great Britain. The Church of Christ was by then exclusively run by native pastors. Stevens decided that he would invite this church to Vanafo to evangelize the *malmal* from all over Santo. Accordingly, he sent a letter of invitation to Pastor Abel Bani, church leader on Ambae. Even though Stevens had a previous connection with Ambae (his mother came from there), his request for pastors and teachers for Vanafo was at first declined.

Many Church of Christ pastors hesitated to ally themselves with a man who wanted to re-establish polygamy and who thought that custom was more important than the church's message, but eventually Pastor Abel Bani decided to set up a church in Vanafo. Bani sent one of his elders, Charley Ngole, with his son Wilson Viratamboel, to Santo. In 1967, they were the first to take charge of educating the *malmal* and of teaching them the word of God and the Bible. Shortly after their arrival, Charley Ngole and his son were joined by a group of people from Ambae who also moved into Vanafo. For four years, Ambae settlers continued to flock to Nagriamel's head-quarters. Daniel Ngole, a close relative of Charley Ngole, remembered:

> "When we first came to Vanafo, we slept under the trees, under the *nakatambol* (*Dracontomelon vitiense*) trees. We didn't bring anything with us, but we had faith in this movement, as we have faith in our Highest Lord. When it rained, we hid under trees to protect ourselves from the rain with banana or *laplap* leaves." (personal communication)

Charley Ngole died in 1974 after having done much for Vanafo's population and especially for the *malmal*; his body was buried there, according to his last wish. The elder James Garae Bakeo was also active during this period. Pastor Bani had assigned him responsibility for the communities of Vunamele, Malo and the small islands next to Santo. Later, the settlers from Ambae proposed that he be appointed the Republic of Vemarana's Minister of Foreign Affairs and Manager of Finances because of his natural abilities, his experience and his excellent contacts on Santo. Charley Ngole had to offer part of his land and his nieces to Jimmy Stevens in order to allow James Garae Bakeo to quit his post as elder of the Church of Christ. Bakeo came to Luganville to occupy an intermediate position between the Ambae church, directed by Abel Bani, and the Vanafo mission, managed by Charley Ngole. Jimmy Stevens himself was eventually baptized by Pastor Abel Bani. This baptism was symbolic because Stevens wanted to demonstrate that he, like his followers, was a supportive member of the church.

During his tours of the fifteen Northern Islands where his movement had influence, Jimmy Stevens preached his message and revolutionary *kastom* philosophy. He was most successful on Ambae. In 1968, people from the large village Nduindui on Ambae's west coast built a big *nakamal* (men's house) measuring 20 metres in honour of Nagriamel. They called this *Fonda Onebulubulu* which means "to come and add something". In front of this large structure, they piled up stones to symbolize the gathering of several clans and tribes into one organization. Jimmy Stevens was invited to its inauguration, but he did not attend. Instead he travelled to Longana on East Ambae for a meeting with Walter Lini, leader of the Vanuaaku Party, who would go on to become the first Prime Minister of Vanuatu. Stevens made it a priority to hear Lini's views on Nagriamel.

On his numerous tours around the islands, Stevens learned a great deal about indigenous societies as people told him their histories and the myths of their islands. On Ambae, people shared the story of *Anqa Tagaro*, a tradition of a civilization that existed in an earlier time. This was identified as "Bali Hai" in the novel *Tales of the South Pacific* by the American writer James Michener. These myths are connected to beliefs about the island's Manaro volcano. They tell the story of the kidnapping of the guardian of wisdom and knowledge, someone by the name of Moltare. Moltare was later said to be kidnapped by the Americans during World War II. He was taken to America and it was thanks to his knowledge that the United States succeeded in becoming the world's most powerful nation.

When Jimmy Stevens heard this story, he wanted to obtain this power and to make the Americans and Man Ambae his allies. The elder Albert Reret from the Ambae village of Tavala became his adviser. Reret considered himself to be a holder of traditional wisdom. He had a strong personality and had aroused the hostility of several missionaries. He was also a man of exceptional character; he emphatically refused any relationship with the Western world and its educational system. The only thing that mattered to him was the powers of *kastom*. But he interpreted *kastom* according to his own philosophy, one that Europeans generally described as a "Cargo Cult" (see Lindstrom, 1993). One of Reret's companions remembered: "He was the first one who wanted to obtain the goods from the store. But in order to buy them, he was not obliged to work. What he ate, he got from nature: sugar, biscuits, cans of food, etc."

Without ever going to Vanafo, Reret became Jimmy Stevens' long distance adviser, his spiritual guide, his ears and eyes. But in 1974, when he finally decided to visit Vanafo, he was beaten by Stevens' guards who had warned this diehard heathen not to prophesy in Vanafo. A year later he died from his wounds. Before he died he predicted Jimmy Stevens' and Nagriamel's ultimate failure.

Nagriamel and Vemarana on the International Scene

Nagriamel's actions motivated the awareness of indigenous ni-Vanuatu about land alienation. However, as former president of Vanuatu Georges Ati Sokomanu (or Kalkoa) observed in 2005: "Jimmy Stevens' real problem at this time was that he hadn't transformed his movement into a political party." When Nagriamel was founded, it was not an organized party but rather an indigenous land rights movement, one that also wanted to reform agriculture. Subsequently it took many forms including that of a secessionist state and later a political party, even though Stevens once denied this:

> "The Nagriamel is not a party. The Nagriamel is not politics. It is the heart of our men, it is their custom. But, in order to make it glow again [...] we have to use the right method [...] the Nagriamel existed before I did. But we have to reform it once more – to make it ours and to put its emblem on the flag we will hoist. That is my work. People ask me: we want the Nagriamel to become strong for our future generations. I tell them I will do the best I can [...]." (Stevens, quoted in Van Trease, 1987: 160)

Many things have been said about the Nagriamel movement and Jimmy Stevens' intentions have often been analyzed. His ideological orientation, meshing with that of chief Buluk and his partisans from the bush, ensured Stevens the role of indigenous hero. It is more difficult to see him as a partisan of nationalism. Rather, Stevens and his message at times took on the character of a cargo cult, although Stevens himself always refused this identification: "One day he was talking with disdain about the John Frum members – with whom he had no intention to associate – and about cargo cult members in general: I am not waiting for a big steamer to come along. I already have a black steamer. The earth is my steamer." (Stevens, quoted in Lindstrom, 1993: 163)

In fact, Nagriamel refused the sort of nationalist ideology that members of the opposing Vanuaaku Party were then cultivating. Stevens preferred a utopian vision of an ideal state in the hands of the custom people, a state like the one that had existed before the arrival of the colonists:

> "I noticed (considering the political evolution of the New Hebrides before Independence) that many political parties emerged, each of them with a different point of view. I was worried that this might affect the Nagriamel's state in Vanafo, and suggested that we establish a separate group in Luganville [...] This bureau's [the Vemarana's] objective would be to take charge of the political questions and to ensure that these questions did not reach the rest of the movement. I was the leader of the Nagriamel and the President of the Vemarana at the same time." (Stevens, 1995: 237)

> "The Nagriamel is part of a federation, of a state that we call Natakaro. In the Nagriamel's constitution, Natakaro represents all the islands of the New Hebrides. Unfortunately, when the White people arrived here, they have replaced the name Natakaro by 'New Hebrides'. Before the White people arrived, there was a law, that certain people called Natamata or Namangi, which prohibited any other law from governing the country." (Stevens, quoted in Bernard, 1983: 73)

Nagriamel did make alliances with certain foreigners in the hope that these would benefit its followers and lead to the raising of their political awareness and emancipation. Stevens claimed: "Nagriamel existed before I did. But we have to reform it once more – give it its coherence, its flag, the colours we hoist. That is my work. [...] The Nagriamel will be for you, my black children" (quoted in Van Trease, 1987: 160). But as it turned out the hopes of the Nagriamel leaders Jimmy Stevens, Paul Tamlumlum, John Bule and Jimmy Kaku were in fact being realized by the Vanuaaku Party which would mobilize the islands of the archipelago to obtain independence in 1980. Vanuaaku leaders like Donald Kalpokas, Walter Lini, George Sokomanu, Kalkot Matas Kelekele, Sethy Regenvanu, Barak Sope and Onen Tahi were the men who led the country to independence. Like Nagriamel, in order to guarantee the protection of indigenous land national leaders adopted the Constitution of the Republic of Vanuatu which stipulated that "All the land of the Republic of Vanuatu belongs to the indigenous custom owners and their descendants" and that "Only indigenous citizens have the right of perpetual ownership of the land."

Nagriamel's Foreign Relations

At the end of the 1960s Jimmy Stevens' personal power had increased, thanks to the help of several American entrepreneurs. In 1967 Stevens was approached by Eugene Peacock, an American land speculator who wanted to invest in the New Hebrides. For Nagriamel's *man bush* this alliance was wonderful, but it proved to be pernicious. To further his cause of land recovery, Stevens came to rely on the help of foreign speculators and land sharks. Peacock's enterprise, with a registered office in Hawaii, made an agreement with Stevens to buy immense areas of land on Santo. He proposed subdividing these areas into small parcels to sell to American veterans of the Vietnam War (Beasant, 1984: 45).

Peacock's activities were closely followed by the colonial administration which thought he was a disturbing element. France, especially, was at that time trying to ingratiate itself with Stevens and Nagriamel by accelerating the distribution of material assistance to the movement. The Condominium blocked Peacock's land speculation with new laws on land subdivision and an increase in taxation on the commercial exploitation of unoccupied parcels of land. These legislative manoeuvres corrected earlier Condominium law that, in 1971, had given the New Hebrides the status of a "fiscal paradise". This status had attracted doubtful speculators like Peacock to the New Hebrides and more specifically to Santo.

Peacock attempted a diversion in his battle with the Condominium and with those political parties suspicious of his actions. His French associate Jean-Jacques Hénin cemented economic cooperation with Nagriamel by founding SODEPAC, a company for land-clearing and cattle-raising that hired Stevens' men exclusively. John Beasant reported, although this has yet to be proved, that considerable sums of money were transferred to Nagriamel so that Hénin would be appointed the movement's Development Adviser and subsequently its Financial Head (Beasant, 1984: 48-49). The page of Nagriamel's doubtful alliances and foreign sponsors was far from being turned. It would later rebound with the Leconte[1] and the Phoenix Foundation affairs.

France wanted to save Stevens' dignity and restore Nagriamel's reputation and, while it was also concerned with its own interests in the New Hebrides, it continued to interfere with local politics on Santo. To contest the powerful investors coming to Santo, France sent the billionaire Monsieur Leconte to the island. Leconte had been involved with nickel mines in New Caledonia and already owned land on Santo. Nagriamel came to an agreement with the French government: one hectare of land would go to Leconte for every hour that Vanafo settlers used mechanical tools he lent them in order to prepare Nagriamel's own fields. In return, Leconte had to build roads, import equipment and bring running water and electricity to Vanafo. These promises were partly fulfilled. Thanks to Leconte, there is today a road that links Vanafo to Matantas.

France succeeded in securing Nagriamel's support in order to defend its own interests. The alliance between Leconte and Nagriamel was also a test for the French administration in its strategy of redistributing land. By developing infrastructure, France wanted to raise the self-esteem of indigenous people yet protect its own interests. The French colonial administration admitted: "If the agreement between

---

1. During a meeting in Vanafo in August 1977 between Stevens and the two delegates of the Condominium, Monsieur Gauger, the French delegate, explained the alliance between custom and the progress that France would bring: "Monsieur Gauger spoke about the importance of custom and the local sense of identity. At the same time, he said, custom could adapt to modernization as, for example, in the supply of electricity". Jimmy Stevens replied: "I, as the Chief of the islands of Santo and the village of Vanafo, am happy to tell you about a feast that lasted for 3 days. First, we celebrated rice and the French cattle, our cattle in Vanafo. The money for the cattle came from the French government and all of us indigenous people were OK, we have worked on the project. The rice comes from the indigenous people's land and was cultivated thanks to Paul Buluk and financed by Monsieur Leconte. Yesterday, we celebrated the roads paid by the governments, especially the road that leads from Vanafo to Matantas [...]. And today we celebrate our community clinic and our *nakamal* [...] I want everybody in our village to understand the importance of our *nakamal* and the community clinic [...] I think that the women of this village are all happy that we have our community clinic, because their children are healthy. This proves that a community clinic, a road, running water and other things have given us healthy children". (Extracts from a speech collected and translated by Peter Crowe, 1987: 151-159).

Stevens and Leconte succeeds, it will be easier to find a solution for the problems with the ownership of land. If it fails, Stevens will not be able to keep the promises he has made to his partisans, and they will drop him" (quoted in Beasant, 1984: 23). However, in spite of cooperation between France and Nagriamel, the agreement ultimately was not successful. Leconte ended up throwing in the towel, progressively abandoning his investment projects in the New Hebrides because he was sceptical about political game-playing and dissatisfied with the amount of potential profits.

Many Nagriamel supporters were hostile towards foreign investors and it became impossible to hide the fact that Jimmy Stevens had made agreements with them. Stevens argued: "I want my people to be free of all the rules of the Condominium, not an independence to chase away the Whites, but the Blacks shouldn't be controlled by them any longer" (Stevens, quoted in Van Trease, 1987: 163). French and other foreign influence in Vanafo were becoming evident: there was a Francophone school, the community clinic was French and Nagriamel headquarters now boasted concrete buildings and well-equipped offices as well as tractors and cars. These signs of financial prosperity obliged Stevens to explain the situation and in a 1977 speech he reaffirmed his five priorities and Nagriamel's fundamental principles:

> "1. To work to develop a flourishing economy in the future;
> 2. The earth is the basis, the essence of all things. Most of our lands belong to the New Hebrides by custom and the Europeans have no rights to them. But, Nagriamel does not claim all the land that the foreigners use. Jimmy Stevens wishes to see all the people living together in peace and mutual respect. This is why Nagriamel's logo depicts a black hand shaking a white hand;
> 3. To work together in harmony so that White landowners can stay after independence and maintain their businesses as long as they respect legitimate indigenous rights;
> 4. Political independence and economical autonomy will remain priorities for the inhabitants of the New Hebrides;
> 5. The re-establishment of custom." (Stevens, quoted in Abong, 2009)

From 1975 Jimmy Stevens and Nagriamel also started receiving a significant amount of help from Michael Oliver, the president of the mysterious Phoenix Foundation, established in Carson City, Nevada. Oliver's real name was Moses Olitsky (Van Trease, 1987: 149). He was a Lithuanian Jew who had escaped from Nazi concentration camps to make a fortune in the United States as a real estate broker. He promoted a radical libertarian ideology. He was convinced that United States fiscal policies would lead to the weakening of the dollar and to economic and political instability culminating in a dictatorship.

Ludwig Von Mises, an Austrian economist, was the Phoenix Foundation's mentor. Von Mises had argued that market laws were a total process that influenced all human activity. Economic ultra-liberalism was seen as the guarantee of universal liberty. Oliver decided to create the Phoenix Foundation in 1975 to carry out Von Mises' teaching alongside John Hospers' ideology. Hospers was a philosophy professor at the University of South California and a former libertarian candidate in the 1972 US presidential elections. He preached minimal state control, a system of voluntary taxes, and the total deregularization of the capitalist economy.

During the 1970s, Oliver judged that the United States had become a "fascist-socialist" state and he investigated other countries in the world where he could apply his program. In 1972, he tried to construct a small village on piles over the submerged island of Minerva, a reef between Fiji and Tonga. This venture failed when the Tongan King Tupou IV sailed to the island in his yacht and tore up the Phoenix Foundation flag that had been planted there. A further attempt saw Oliver going to Abaco, an island in the Bahamas. He hoped to provoke the secession of Abaco from the rest of the Bahamas by creating the "Abaco Independence Movement". But his actions, declared illegal by the Bahama's legitimate government, failed.

Oliver next set his sights on Santo. The Phoenix Foundation tried to manipulate and control Jimmy Stevens and the Nagriamel movement in various different ways. Oliver became Stevens' employer and influenced Nagriamel for several years. He paid for Jimmy Stevens' trips abroad, to the United States in particular. He became the Nagriamel's silent partner. With the help of Oliver's advisers Thomas Eck and Robert J. Doorn, a philosopher and jurist, the Phoenix Foundation wrote a constitution for the Republic of Vemarana. Little by little Jimmy Stevens embraced the goal of Nagriamel's transformation into an independent state, named Vemarana, which would secede from the New Hebrides.

The control that the Phoenix Foundation had obtained over Nagriamel went hand in hand with Jimmy Stevens' growing delusions of grandeur. On 10 August, he declared himself Chief President Moses and declared the day a Nagriamel holiday. This kind of attempt on the part of multinational capitalists to penetrate a country by corrupting its political parties and leaders, who in turn become indebted, is a classic stratagem. However, Stevens' suspect collaboration did not greatly diminish his local prestige. He continued to rule the hearts of many followers with his charismatic speeches. Although he may have held their support, his doubtful alliances ultimately led to the failure of his movement. He had presented himself as a champion of indigenous *kastom* and land rights, but his compromises with foreign investors in the end made Nagriamel less independent.

Stevens tried to compensate for his loss of autonomy by reinventing custom in a host of ways but he tended to view *kastom* through the distorted lens of his own desires and fantasies. This tendency is illustrated in a speech he gave shortly before his death:

> "I think the Nagriamel will continue to move forward. In the meantime, to make sure that we will continue the way that was shown by Moli Stevens, I have killed one hundred pigs and ten more so the name Stevens will become royal. In Bislama, *natamata* means royal. After my death, my *natamata* descendants will be treated in a royal way by all the coming generations […]. This plan is very closely related to my family […]. Before my arrest, I had 25 wives, but the Mobile Force made a lot of fuss about them, so I have decided to take a new group of wives. I have many children, 15 of them are boys. I am very attached to the number 15. I was born on 15 June. On 15 January, the chiefs of Vanafo laid their hands on me. For the Whites, the number 10 has special significance. For the Israelites it is the number 12. For me it is the number 15. I organize my work and my life by increments of 15. And of course, there are 15 Nagriamel islands. It is my wish that one day every district will be ruled by one of my sons and his family." (Stevens, 1995: 243, trans. Marcellin Abong)

The Road Towards Independence and the Drama of Rebellion

In 1971 a petition from Nagriamel was sent to the United Nations to assert the archipelago's independence. This demand was presented by an Indo-Fijian lawyer named Dr Ramrakha who had been hired by Stevens around 1965 during negotiations with France for the restitution of Société Française des Nouvelles-Hébrides (SFNH) lands to indigenous owners. The "Republic of Vemarana" file was entrusted to Ramrakha and a Vemarana flag was hidden in a bamboo stick and taken to New York to be displayed during his speech at the United Nations.

This attempt was a failure as only Japan supported the independence claim. This initial failure, however, did not slow Stevens' secessionist plans. On 27 September 1975, he unilaterally proclaimed the independence of the Nagriamel Federation in Vanafo. This declaration was signed by Stevens "with the authority of the Upper Council of the Nagriamel Federation":

> "We, the people of the various New Hebrides islands, do hereby declare, in accordance with United Nations Resolution Number 1514, of 14 December 1975, our independence from any foreign country. Our islands were never under the sovereignty of any other nation, and we were never a colony of any nation. The authority for our action comes not only from United Nations Resolution Number 1514 but, also, from the demand by our people for independence. We can provide the genuine results of a poll taken recently, which we offer to any neutral nation for their inspection and verification. Our new nation is a federation of settlements and the government is elected in accordance with fair democratic principles. We are dedicated to the rights and dignity of all individuals, regardless of race, creed or religion. All rights and individual belongings shall be fully protected and defended. Our boundaries are as follows:

1. All of the villages of Santo, except Luganville, until it wishes to join us.
2. All of the islands surrounding Santo, including Aore, Aoba, Malo, Maewo and Sako.
3. All of the islands in the Banks and Torres Groups of the New Hebrides.
4. Any other settlements in the New Hebrides wishing to join us and to enjoy these rights as free and independent people.

We are firm in our belief that the races of the world should cooperate and that all people should live in peace and harmony. And, for this reason, our motto includes not only our traditional Na-Griamel sign, but also a handshake between people of all races. This motto is now shown on our flag and shall be included on all of our official documents. Our new nation shall be known as the NA-GRIAMEL FEDERATION, and our independence is effective immediately. We extend greetings to all countries of the world." (quoted in Bernard, 1983: 52, trans. Marcellin Abong)

The ethnologist Pascal Bernard who was living in Vanafo at the end of the 1970s noted:

"The constitution is presented in a short document of seven pages. The cover shows the movement's emblem: the handshake of a white and a black hand, and above it a bouquet of *namele* and *nangaria* leaves. The title is: 'Constitution of the Federation of Natakaro (Formerly New Hebrides Islands)'. The constitution is made up of nine articles, handwritten by Jimmy Stevens himself, with the stamp of the 'Nagriamel Chief President Union Council'.

The text states that each group (a geographic and social unit) has control over its own territory and authority over its own laws, custom and traditions. The role of the government of the Federation is reduced to the essential activities of the protection and defence of the life and rights of each person. The electoral procedure consists of groups appointing the members of the Upper House, that is a kind of traditionalist Senate, and the Lower House or the Nasara (the name that is given to 'the house of the initiated men' in the Northern Islands). The executive power is assured by the Chief President of the Nagriamel Federation. The military organization is subordinate to civil power. The declaration of rights insists on the defence of life and all freedoms (of conscience, religious choice, speech and press, assembly and claims to land)." (summarized in Bernard, 1983: 52, trans. Marcellin Abong)

The system of proposed Vemarana government was illustrated by a diagram. If we look at this organizational diagram, in light of information I have gathered in Vanafo, we are far from the principles of the minimalist state that the Phoenix Foundation had wished to create.

Government System of the Republic of Vemarana
(Collected by Marcellin Abong)

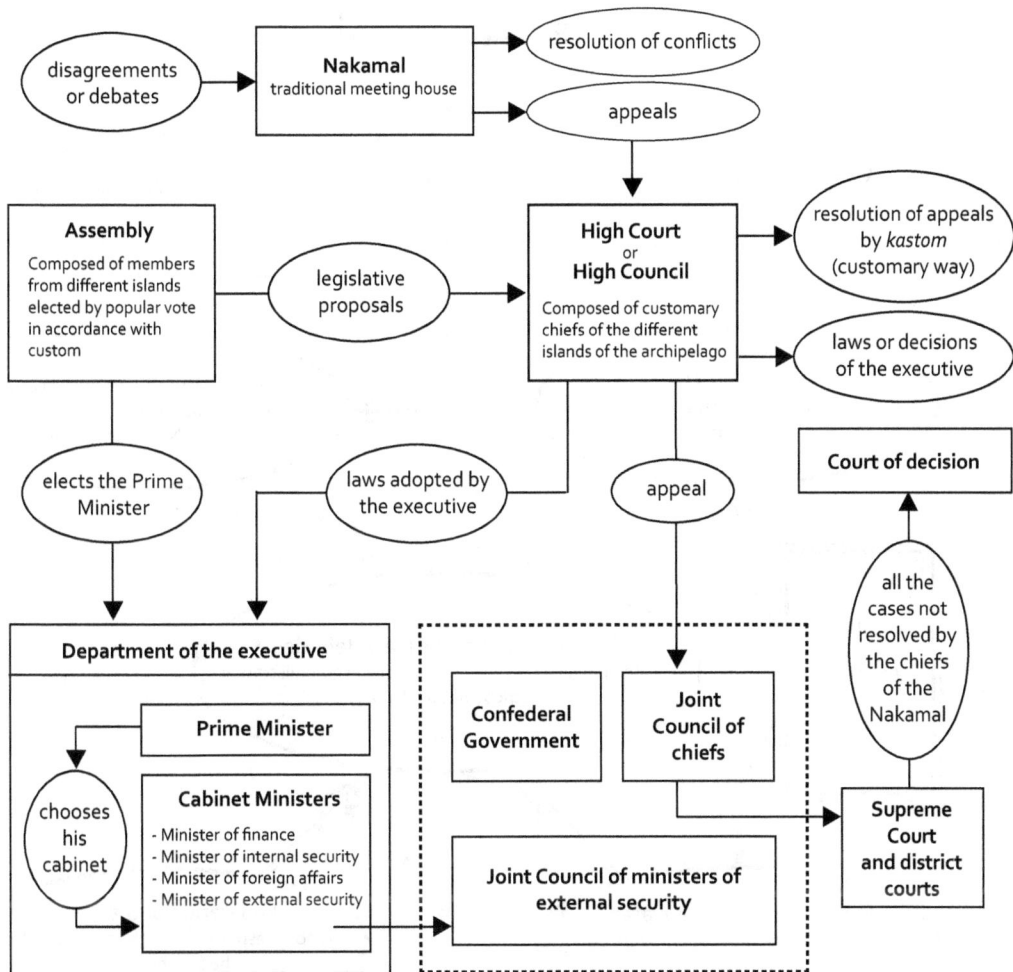

disagreements or debates

Nakamal
traditional meeting house

resolution of conflicts

appeals

Assembly
Composed of members from different islands elected by popular vote in accordance with custom

legislative proposals

High Court
or
High Council
Composed of customary chiefs of the different islands of the archipelago

resolution of appeals by *kastom* (customary way)

laws or decisions of the executive

elects the Prime Minister

laws adopted by the executive

appeal

Court of decision

all the cases not resolved by the chiefs of the Nakamal

Department of the executive

Prime Minister

chooses his cabinet

Cabinet Ministers
- Minister of finance
- Minister of internal security
- Minister of foreign affairs
- Minister of external security

Confederal Government

Joint Council of chiefs

Joint Council of ministers of external security

Supreme Court and district courts

Federal organization proposed by the Nagriamel
for the Republic of Vemarana (published in *Jeune Mélanésie*, 13 May 1980).

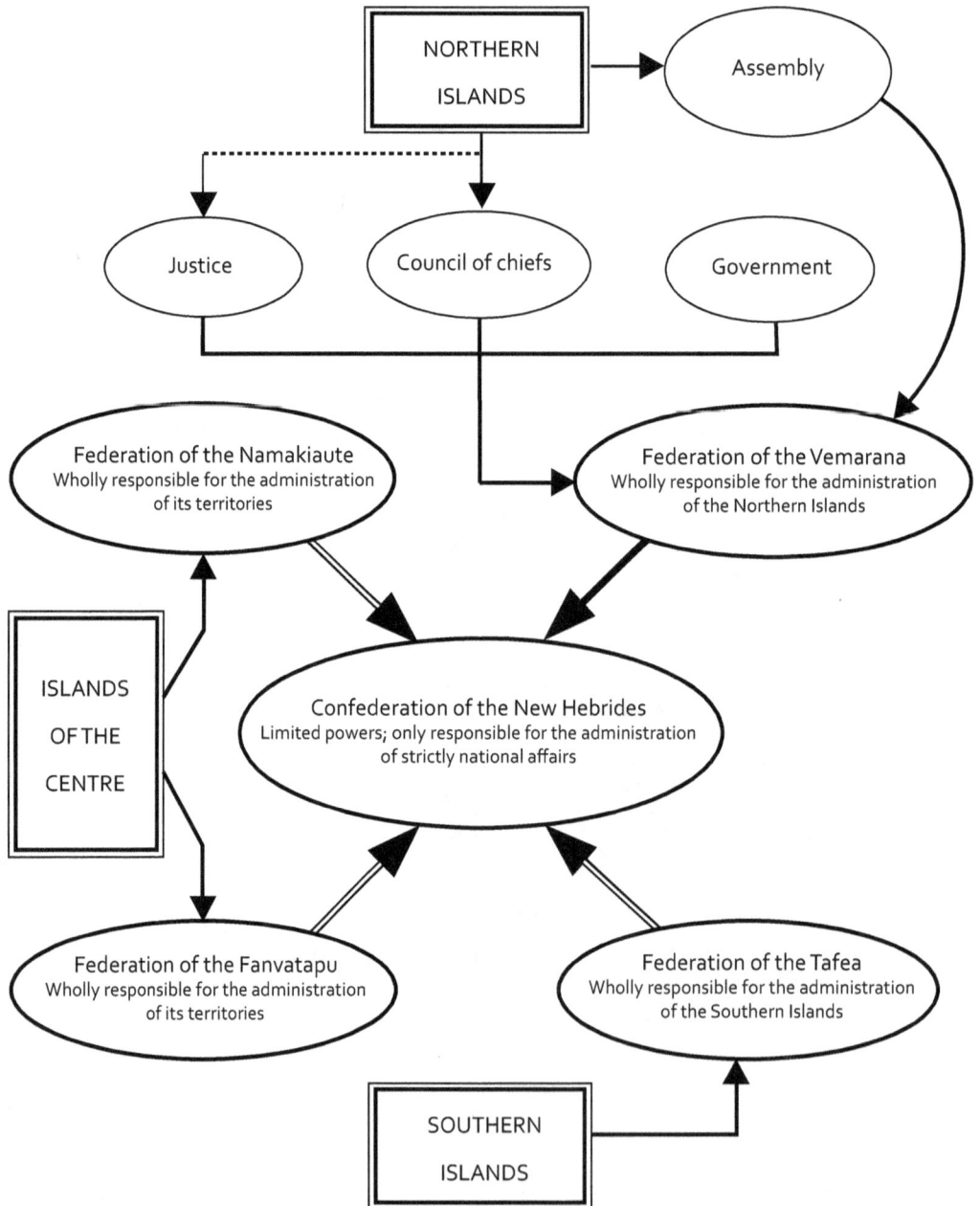

Nagriamel had accepted the adoption of a national constitution signed in October 1978, under the aegis of a government of national union. But the movement's failure at the election of 16 November 1979 represented a turning point in its history. Nagriamel and its political allies were faced with an incoming independent government led by their rivals in the Vanuaaku Party. And from this time, too, the French authorities played a double game. France publicly accepted the imminent independence of a new state led by the Vanuaaku Party, but did not exclude other possible outcomes.

Francophones in particular feared that the Vanuaaku Party's electoral victory might allow it to change the national constitution as originally drafted. This provoked a genuine shock in the Francophone camp and the political situation rapidly deteriorated. Jimmy Stevens announced on Radio Vanafo (provided by Oliver) that the elections had been rigged and he threatened Vanuaaku Party members living on Santo, which led to their exodus from the island. In January 1980 Jimmy Stevens had declared the separate independence of Santo and Tanna and he gave British officials seven days to leave. When the British suggested sending troops to Santo, French General Inspector Jean-Jacques Robert refused in spite of British protests. This situation lasted for six months, until the day before Vanuatu's independence in July 1980. Every attempt at reconciliation failed although discussions went on for weeks.

In May the Vanuaaku Party-led administration declared that the New Hebrides, renamed Vanuatu, would become independent on 30 July 1980. In reply, Nagriamel's members took possession of the municipality of Luganville. After a night of riots, Stevens delivered a dawn speech on Radio Vanafo, which had been renamed Radio Vemarana:

> "This is the road that leads towards deliverance and freedom, protected and defended by the Independent Federation of the Nagriamel, Santo, and New Hebrides. This is the service of radio diffusion at 25° south latitude and 168° west longitude of planet Earth or Urianta, under the rays of the Milky Way. Today, the Vemarana was born. The people of Santo named it this way and the people of Santo work for its administration. Come and join the Vemarana, it doesn't matter of which race you are, so we can help the Vemarana's government to part from the country of Vanuatu. The Nagriamel has been independent since 1976, so if we understand things well, the independence of the Vanuatu government will only start from July 1980. Be careful, because the independence of Vanuatu is not the same as the independence of Vemarana." (Stevens, quoted in Beasant, 1984: 94)

During the days that followed, the new government of Vanuatu ordered a total blockade of the island of Santo, but this had little effect. But then, on 15 June 1980, 200 British Marines arrived on Santo. The French had previously sent 55 policemen to Santo to ensure the defence of its representatives. These manoeuvres reinforced the oppressive atmosphere. There had also been trouble on the island of Tanna, and the day of 11 June 1980 was marked by the assassination of Alex Yolou, leader of the Francophone camp there. On Santo, Vemarana had enjoyed two months of effective independence. But, as independence day came closer, the Vanuaaku Party supported by Andrew Stuart, the British Commissioner, demanded that the nation's independence be respected.

On 17 June 1980, the incoming Prime Minister Walter Lini signed an agreement with Papua New Guinea to supply troops to intervene on Santo and quash the secession. The Kumul Force, composed of 300 men, two patrol ships and four aeroplanes (Bernard, 1983: 117), arrived and took up positions on Santo on 18 August 1980. The first day of the intervention, the Papuan Commander Colonel Toy Huai's restoration of state power went smoothly as his troops had occupied Luganville's strategic positions. Inspections and arrests began. On 30 August 1980, Papuan troops killed Stevens' eldest son during shooting aimed at the vehicle in which he was driving in the company of two others.

The next day Papuan troops occupied Vanafo and Port-Olry, the other bastion of Nagriamel resistance. They found Jimmy Stevens seated on a chair under the village's big banyan tree and supported by a group of several hundred followers, men, women and children. Among them there were also a few Europeans who had taken shelter in Vanafo. Several hundreds of Vemaranists were arrested during these operations. In spite of Jimmy Stevens' arrest, along with those of his followers, fighting continued in north Santo for several days. From September to November the Papua New Guinea army, the Vanuatu Mobile Force (mainly composed of members of the Vanuaaku Party) and aeroplanes of the Royal Australian Air Force which transported prisoners to Port-Vila continued to patrol Santo. Numerous brutalities were recorded and there were many violent arrests. The official number of arrests given by the Vanuatu government is 2,774. Rebels were sentenced to five to seven years' imprisonment. Several hundred French settlers escaped legal pursuit by fleeing to New Caledonia, and 127 foreigners ultimately were expelled from the country, 110 of them French citizens (Beasant, 1983: 143).

"Jimmy Stevens was charged with 11 crimes on 21 November 1980. These included:

1. Military action involving the use of arms;
2. at his direction sending men to cause damage to the British Paddock [the colonial official residence area];
3. arbitrary detention of delegates and policemen;
4. possession of stolen objects: dynamite, munitions;

5. organization of an illegal movement;
6. incitement to break the law;
7. illegal production of passports;
8. distributing copies of the illegal [Vemarana] constitution;
9. financing of an illegal association;
10. prejudicial conduct against public order;
11. broadcasting by an illegal radio station." (Paitel, 1985: 262-263, trans. Marcellin Abong)

Stevens would plead guilty to all charges and he took complete responsibility for the rebellion. He was sentenced to fourteen and a half years in prison and fined 220,000 vatu. In his defence, he declared:

"I am one of the big custom chiefs of the Nagriamel and I would like the President of the Court to treat me like a custom chief. People have asked me to do things, and I accepted. I didn't think about all the consequences. Today, I can see all the damage that has been done and I realize that I made a mistake when I accepted the role of Prime Minister of the Vemarana. I listened to too many people, the French representatives had promised they would never let me down, General Inspector Robert had promised me... They all promised me... I have been in charge of the Nagriamel for 20 years, nobody was killed because I made a mistake, but Vanuatu has killed three of my men: Alexis Buluk, Alexis Yolou on the island of Tanna, and recently, one of my sons. This is all I have to say." (extracts from Jimmy Stevens' defence at his trial, quoted in Bernard, 1983: 125-126, trans. Marcellin Abong)

Nagriamel Today and Tomorrow

The number of Nagriamel followers has continued to increase although many outside the movement may not be aware of this. In Vanuatu's last general election of 2008 for example, Nagriamel supporters from Malo elected Vanuatu's only Nagriamel Member of Parliament, the honorable Avo Molisale who represents the Malo/Santo constituency. A Nagriamel candidate for the SANMA (Santo, Malo, and Aore) Provincial Council also received the highest number of votes among those running. On Ambae, where Nagriamel support remains strong, the movement's candidate for Parliament Mr Edmond Oke received over 400 votes. And in a recent by-election on Epi, Nagriamel supporters helped elect Yoan Simon, a considerable accomplishment considering that Epi has been a stronghold of the Vanuaaku Pati.

Malo, comparatively, has the greatest number of Nagriamel supporters towards other political parties. On Santo, Nagriamel members compose a third of the Provincial Council and another Nagriamel leader serves on the PENAMA (Pentecost, Ambae, Maewo) Provincial Council. Some Nagriamel followers continue to support other political parties including the UMP (Union of Moderate Parties), the Vanuatu Republiken Pati (VRP), the Peoples Action Pati (PAP) and even the Vanuaaku Pati. Many Nagriamel leaders assert that Nagriamel is a belief system rather than a political party and even though a person might affiliate with another political party he still supports Nagriamel's founding principles.

Today, Nagriamel stands at the crossroads. Some claim that Nagriamel does not have enough popular support to elect more than one or two Members of Parliament, but my analysis suggests it should be able to elect at least five. Currently, however, the movement faces some internal division and dispute over ownership of the name Nagriamel itself. The executive of the movement's political arm claims that it controls the right to decide electoral strategy and choose candidates. Members of this executive, originally supporters of the former Tabwemasana Pati on Santo, claim to be founders of the national Nagriamel movement. An opposing group, which calls itself Nagriamel James Garae Bakeo Grup, believes that the Santo-based group has cached a large sum of money somewhere that elder James Garae Bakeo helped obtain. Bakeo, now deceased, was the former Minister of Foreign Affairs, External Trade, and Economy in the short-lived Vemarana Republic and a close collaborator of Jimmy Stevens. He was reputedly involved in dealings between Nagriamel and investors from the United States and New Caledonia. The Nagriamel James Garae Bakeo Grup is led today by Alic Garae Bakeo, James Bakeo's son. Jif Frankie Stevens leads a third faction, the so-called Original Nagriamel, which is still located at Fanafo, Jimmy Stevens' headquarters on Santo. Finally, there is a fourth faction, the Hanga Takaro Nagriamel on Ambae, which also claims to be the backbone of the Nagriamel Movement today.

Given these disputes over leadership of the movement, and claims to the Nagriamel name itself, the wider movement has found it difficult to unite. Rumours of the agreement that James Garae Bakeo may have signed with American investors in the name of the "Republic of Vemarana Development Corporation" (supposedly registered in Panama) have also sparked outside interest and interference, particularly associated with Alic Garae Bakeo's faction. A locally powerful ni-Vanuatu businesswoman of Asian origin, Thi Tam Goiset, has become involved with Bakeo. This woman, a member of a large family whose wealth grew during Vanuatu's colonial era, has large investments throughout Vanuatu and has become involved in a number of schemes, humanitarian and otherwise, with village communities. On Tanna, she has been implicated with various John Frum movement factions, receiving a title from one of these. She has also received the chiefly title Lenavao Moli from one Nagriamel faction. She now claims the right to speak for both the John Frum and Nagriamel movements, but many supporters dispute her right to do so. The businesswoman claims that traditional exchanges of gifts are the basis for her customary right to speak today on behalf of Nagriamel and John Frum, although many remain confused about this.

The remaining significant issue, therefore, concerns who is to serve as Nagriamel's spokesperson. When Jimmy Stevens was released from prison he announced: "I now turn over the work to my Black children." This statement recalls Charles de Gaulle's proclamation in Algeria when he said "I have understood you" (*Je vous ai compris*) in that Jif Moli Stevens meant that his generation of John Frum and Nagriamel leaders had altogether failed in achieving their goals. His speech only alluded to the work that the children of Nagriamel were by then beginning to take up. Today, as we witness the steady increase in Vanuatu's customary lands being put up for sale, Nagriamel's original struggle to preserve land has withered on the vine and now needs a new and active campaign to bring it back to life. However, the policies of Nagriamel's newly elected leaders, as expressed in political posters and platforms during the 2008 elections, did not significantly focus on the promotion of tradition and culture. This, too, leads to questions about Nagriamel's vision for the future preservation and development of Vanuatu's traditional cultures.

Conclusion

I have attempted to clarify several misunderstandings about the Nagriamel movement and its leader, Jimmy Stevens. These include the assertion that Stevens excluded *kastom* from his struggle, or that he used *kastom* only to serve his own interests. They also include the associated argument that Stevens used his name and titles in order to ensnare and mislead his followers. Kolig's psychological analysis of Stevens' character (see Kolig, 1981 and 1987) argues that he used his name as an emblem, which suggests that he was someone with a split personality, almost a borderline case of schizophrenia.

I believe that this portrait of Stevens is pointless and almost offensive, considering his significant influence on the history of our country. He deserves more respect even if he did make mistakes. The ultimate source of these mistakes was the original establishment of the Anglo-French Condominium. Political rivalries, an economic war, and social struggles were added to tribal conflict. Colonialism may have brought economic transformation but this was the sort of progress depicted in the following image: A man standing on the border of an abyss who says: "I have taken a big step forward!"

I prefer an anthropological and biographical approach to Stevens' life history which places his struggle in its cultural and historical context. It is important that we try to understand the original orientations of Nagriamel's philosophy and its associated positive actions. An anthropological approach to Stevens' names and titles could be parsed as follows. By struggling to revive *kastom* and by recreating it in so doing, Stevens from the start established himself as a protector of *kastom*, as its guardian. However, in associating his body and soul with *kastom* he also resorted to non-customary parameters. "Jimmy" was his *man olbaot* (common) name, but one day he woke up after he had "had a dream", to use Martin Luther King's words. "Stevens" sounded American, and this supported his persona as liberator. For him, America was not a mythical country where cargo comes from, but rather represented the awakening of a political conscience spurred by the presence of the US military in the New Hebrides during World War II. America had become the imagined source of equality and fraternity.

Similarly, Stevens' revival of *kastom* served to contest colonial oppression. His assumed title "Tupu" underlined his claim to aristocratic status. He opposed his vision of a Black King to the "White Shadows" who previously had been the colonial rulers of the black islands; an enlightened monarch descended from the heart of darkness. His other titles "Patuntun" and "Moli" reminded followers of his vocation as a guide, the custom guide of Santo and the supreme beacon of *kastom* for all the Northern Islands.

In short, Jimmy was a charismatic man. His destiny was exceptional, his journey extraordinary. But without Nagriamel supporters, its *nalnal*, its "nudists" from the Dark Bush only wearing their courage and integrity, Jimmy Stevens would never have become Pantuntun, or Moli. We cannot analyze Stevens merely as an individual. His empathy with Nagriamel supporters gave rise to his status as a cult leader: the person who established custom rules of the Northern Islands. His canonization as a cult character is not merely secular, it bears supernatural significance. Beyond becoming Pantuntun and Moli, Stevens also claimed the titles of Jif (Chief), President and Prophet: Jif President Moli Tupu Pantuntun Moses. Each of these titles magnifies the previous one. But even if he was a neo-customary monarch, Stevens never became a despot. Several of his followers' testimonials state that their Jif was not a soft person but that he had a safeguard that prevented him from going astray. He knew very well that he was nothing without Nagriamel supporters, and that is why he could claim a Biblical-like status as the movement's patriarch.

Jimmy Stevens was not always an enlightened man, but he was thoughtful. He could recognize his mistakes. It is true that he ordered James Garae Bakeo, at the time the interim Vemarana Minister of Economic Affairs and Foreign Exchange, to sign over to foreign private investors a lease of more than 40,000 hectares of land in Matantas on the island of Santo and in Loanatom on Tanna. But before he died while imprisoned in hospital, he admitted that he never should have associated with foreign speculators, especially not with Michael Oliver and his American investors. Stevens had been blinded by the manoeuvres and manipulations of these American investors and the dollars they showered on him. But who could blame a person who had never encountered the merciless forces of neo-liberal capitalism? Walter Lini's Melanesian socialism, too, has subsequently led Vanuatu to accept help from Australia, New Zealand, France, China and Japan. Which leader of the Vanuaaku Party has ever explained to us that "communalism" and the redistribution of land to custom owners would one day lead to the construction of concrete buildings all over Efate's coast? That it would lead to our people selling their land for a Toyota? That new Christian sects would come to tell us that Jesus prefers rich people and that only their pastors' miracles will save us from the disasters caused by our ancestral principles? If we forget our Dark Bush (our traditional indigenous) political economy will this not result in our being drawn inexorably into the new world order advocated by George Bush and others?

Militants of the past and the present may object to my interpretation, but they must admit that the memory of Jimmy Stevens is not exclusively theirs to control. He has become a historical and political character for everyone in Vanuatu. In 2004, after he died, one follower claimed that she saw Stevens shine like a sun. She predicted that his body will be sent to Mount Tabwemasana and his ashes scattered from the top of the hill in the direction of the USA. Many of Stevens' followers similarly have come to honour his spirit.

With globalization, our cultures have now become integrated into the global village. It is unfair to accuse our youngsters, who as a result have been plunged into confusion, of not respecting custom: *kastom* has an obscure connotation for many of them. We don't know how to explain it, we don't know how to put it into practice, and sometimes we don't even regret its disappearance. If we want our children to share our culture, elders must acknowledge cultural change. New traditions are emerging. Different generations must inevitably share this contemporary global culture with our Pacific neighbours and with friends all over the world. There is no doubt that Jimmy Stevens had understood this back in the 1960s. But his presentiment was hard to share with his followers.

The future can no longer be directed solely by custom. But if we get our people involved we can offer them new way of seeing things, an acceptable life that goes beyond mere survival. In order to move forward, we have to celebrate what we have in common, our shared memory of custom as this developed within a context of colonial oppression. For Stevens custom was *natangwata*, the work of the first-born. Stevens was a precursor in his celebration of *kastom* as a foundational symbol but his actions transcended all past cultural expressions – whether in the context of the clans, the tribes, the islands or other traditional forms of collective identification. The Nagriamel movement speaks to all of us. *Natangwata* is the oldest son of all the clans, the oldest of all our brothers, the bearer of a shared spirit, the basket that contains the complete set of our original words. For Jimmy the foundation of any indigenous claims was culture. But there is no culture without institutional and therefore political frameworks. Let us remember the sad end of Alexis Yolou on the island of Tanna. He was not killed because he had a full bank account but because he asserted ideas for the indigenous cause, seen from his own perspective on *kastom*.

This concern for indigenous rights pushed Nagriamel to assert island rights and the legitimacy of *kastom*. Today, Vanuatu's land is being alienated all over again by land speculators, harming indigenous people who often no longer have the strength to contest such "investors", – a new kind of settler who comes to plant dollars instead of coconut trees, with the approval of state authorities. We must remember the lessons from the past. The younger generation needs to remember Nagriamel's demands in support of indigenous rights. Its actions caused rich men who bought up indigenous lands to feel insecure; it also discomfited members of the Vanuaaku Party and British and Australian agents – everyone who wanted to claim power in favour of his own exclusive interests.

Our elders, our man bush, had once understood this message and they supported Jimmy Stevens and his law of the Dark Bush. Stevens said that in order to maintain one's dignity one should not become a simple consumer which would lead to a life of despair. One should instead become a determined agent within the national economy and claim the power to decide one's own existence. This explains why Stevens encouraged Ambae people to come to Santo. He sought their help in order to create a new form of cultural diversity at the heart of the future Republic of Vemarana. He believed that people should work their land productively but not just to feed themselves alone, that they should uphold their ideals and not merely follow the law of the strongest.

This paper seeks to rehabilitate Nagriamel, a political movement of which our elders should no longer feel ashamed and from which our youngsters should draw inspiration. Let us remember, with great respect, our ancestors' travels along the sad path of humiliation. Let us not forget the blows they suffered, the kicks, the whipping

– insults and injury for which our former "masters" have never apologized. Our grandfathers' claims were systematically refused by the colonial administration and its repressive system. Their mistake was being Melanesian, being black – and claiming their rights. Our grandfathers taught us that we, too, should be willing to die for these basic rights. Our children should know that they will die with us if we do not protect our freedoms. Let us remember what Jean-Marie Tjibaou, leader of New Caledonia's Kanak Socialist National Liberation Front, said only a few days before his assassination: "Dying is not hard, it is more difficult to stay alive and to feel like a stranger in your own country, to feel that your country is dying and being powerless." After suffering oppression and humiliation we, too, must remember Nagriamel and our ancestors who struggled with so-called "progress and civilization": we must dare to fight in order that one day we shall win.

Bibliography

Abong, Marcellin
2009   *La pirogue du Dark Bush : aperçus critiques sur l'histoire du Nagriamel.*
        Port-Vila : VKS Publications.

Beasant, John
1984   *The Santo Rebellion, an Imperial Reckoning.* Honolulu: Hawaii University Press.

Bernard, Pascal
1983   *Le Nagriamel : tradition et nationalisme au Vanuatu.* PhD Thesis.
        Université Paris-X-Nanterre.

Hours, Bernard
1974   "Un mouvement politico-religieux néo-hébridais : le Nagriamel",
        Cahiers ORSTOM 11(3-4): 227-242.

Kolig, Erich
1981   "The Paradox of Santo, Vanuatu", *Pacific Perspective* 10(1): 57-61.
1987   "Kastom, Cargo and the Construction of Utopia on Santo, Vanuatu: The Nagriamel
        Movement", *Journal de la Société des Océanistes* 85(2): 181-204.

Lindstrom, Lamont
1993   *Cargo Cult. Strange Stories of Desire from Melanesia and Beyond.* Honolulu: University of
        Hawaii Press.

Paitel, Patrick
1985   *L'enjeu Kanak.* Paris: Editions France-empire.

Raff, E.
1928   Extract from a Letter from Rev. E. Raff, Vila New Hebrides, 10th January 1924.
        In F.E. Williams, *Orokaiva Magic.* London: Clarendon Press, pp. 100-101.

Stevens, Jimmy

1995   "Le mouvement Nagriamel". In H. Van Trease (ed.), *La politique mélanésienne : stael blong Vanuatu*. Christchurch/Suva: Macmillan Brown Centre for Pacific Studies and Institute of Pacific Studies, University of the South Pacific, pp. 237-244.

Tabani, Marc

2001   "Histoire politique du Nagriamel à Santo (Vanuatu)". *Journal de la Société des Océanistes* 113(2): 151-176.

2002   *Les pouvoirs de la coutume à Vanuatu : traditionalisme et édification nationale*. Paris: l'Harmattan.

2008   *Une pirogue pour le Paradis : le culte de John Frum à Tanna*. Paris: Editions de la Maison des Sciences de l'Homme.

Van Trease, Howard

1981   "Arrière-plan historique du problème de l'aliénation des terres à Vanuatu". *Rapport de la conférence régionale sur la gestion des terres*. Port-Vila: Institute for Pacific Studies, University of the South Pacific, pp. 27-44.

1987   *The Politics of Land in Vanuatu: from Colony to Independence*. Suva: Institute of Pacific Studies, University of the South Pacific.

Van Trease, Howard (ed.).

1995   *La politique mélanésienne : stael blong Vanuatu*. Christchurch/Suva: Macmillan Brown Centre for Pacific Studies and Institute of Pacific Studies, University of the South Pacific.

Chapter 4

Beyond "Cargo Cult": Interpreting *Mata Kamo*

Aletta Biersack

> "New Guinea equals the Stone Age in the popular imagination;
> for better or worse, it is in dialogue with various versions
> of this myth that every scholar of the region must write."
> (Rutherford 2005: 136)

In *Writing Culture* and what is widely regarded as its companion text, *Anthropology as Cultural Critique*, Clifford, Marcus, and Fischer reoriented anthropology away from "the field" and exotic others and towards a critique of anthropology as an exoticizing, orientalizing discourse. Instead of the naïve, tacit assumption that anthropological accounts offered scientific, objective portrayals of their subjects, these authors subversively proposed that anthropological writings were akin to literature: "always caught up in the invention, not the representation, of cultures" (Clifford 1986: 2). The task that befell anthropology, then, was to critique the discursive constructions of anthropology, exposing the rhetoric and presuppositions that informed these constructions, as well as the historical circumstances and politics of anthropological inscription.

The spirit of this postmodern initiative is alive and well in Lamont Lindstrom's book *Cargo Cult: Strange Stories of Desire from Melanesia and Beyond*, which critiques the category "cargo cult" as a "discourse" that Lindstrom dubs "cargoism" (1993: 13; see also Lindstrom Ch. 7 and Clark 1992). "Cargoism" was originally coined by Thomas Harding to characterize Melanesian perceptions: "Cargoism is nothing less than the Melanesian world view applied to the task of providing meaningful interpretation of European culture" (1967: 21, quoted in Lindstrom 1993: 62). In this usage, "cargoism" signifies an ethnographic reality: the Melanesian mentality in its struggle to understand European culture. Lindstrom's usage of the term anchors "cargoism" not in the exotic terrain of the thought processes of anthropological others but in the domestic terrain of our own representations. "Cargo cults are Melanesian, but cargo cult accounts belong to us" (Lindstrom 2004: 17). By this he means that our narratives (including those of anthropologists) about so-called cargo cults reflect our own "insatiable wanting" (*ibid.*) for material goods. Lindstrom makes several powerful points. First and foremost, the birth of the "cargo cult" construction cannot be extricated from colonialism and the tendency of colonial officers, missionaries, and colonial anthropologists such as F. E. Williams to envision Melanesians as primitives (see also Lattas 1992; McDowell 2000; Dalton Ch. 2, Hermann Ch. 6). Hence the language of early writings on "cargo cult" events – "madness", "disturbance", "trouble", "hysteria", "frenzy" – and the underlying notion that cargo cult activities were "either 'irrational' behaviors of primitive peoples or [...] signs of mental instability or cultural collapse" (Leavitt 2004: 170; see also Hermann 1992 and Ch. 6; Otto 2004: 210). Secondly, early writers simplified, reduced and then generalized certain aspects of putative cargo cults to all of Melanesia, "nativizing" them in the sense of locating them in the pre-European or pre-colonial past, so that everything about Melanesian culture – indeed, about Melanesians themselves – is really about cargo (Lindstrom 1993: 63-64). The effect of this nativization is to identify Melanesia as radically other. Ironically, though, to move to Lindstrom's third point, the obsession with cargo is ours and not theirs, for it is we, not Melanesians, who are the materialists. Lindstrom powerfully concludes that "cargo cult does not exist per se; rather, it appears in the dirty mirror of the European self – a cultic other as a reflection of the imperial self" (*ibid.*: 7).

The value of Lindstrom's poststructuralist or postmodernist effort – in this case, to deconstruct the notions of cargo and cargo cult in reflexive ways by discrediting the Western imperial lens – lies in the way it sensitizes us to possible distortions in the anthropological record. Yet I share Michael Harkin's concern in *Reassessing Revitalization Movements* that such efforts "tend to dissolve the object of study into the ether of postmodern reflexivity" by reading "markers of difference" as part of a problematic "discourse of exoticism and essentialism" (2004: xvi), thus calling into question the persisting anthropological effort to penetrate *other* discourses and *other* discursive constructions by understanding *other* cultures and to do so *in their own terms* (cf. Lattas 2007 for a parallel point)[1]. How to do this without ethnocentric distortion remains the challenge for Melanesian anthropology.

Bearing in mind the postmodernist critique, this chapter resumes the interpretive task, asking whether "cargo cult" is an apt epithet for a ritual movement that occurred

---

1. Indeed, Marcus and Fischer, in their introduction to the second edition of *Anthropology as Cultural Critique*, distance themselves from *Writing Culture*. "For us, the decline of a certain construction of ethnographic authority never augured the end of anthropology but rather the opportunity to reorient its core practices" (1999: xxviii). Such reorientation requires acknowledgment that anthropological writing always exists within "a stream of already existing representations produced by journalists, prior anthropologists, historians, creative writers and of course the subjects of study themselves. And, therefore, a primary framing task of any ethnography is to juxtapose these pre-existing representations, attempting to understand their diverse conditions of production, and to incorporate the resulting analysis fully into the strategies which define any contemporary field project" (*ibid.*: xx).

in the mid-1940s in what is now called Enga Province, Papua New Guinea. In developing my hermeneutic strategy, I find Nancy McDowell's "A Note on Cargo Cults and Cultural Constructions of Change" (1988) helpful. Like Lindstrom, McDowell questions the existence of cargo cults. The problem, according to her, is that we have extracted "a few features" from a "semantic field" (*ibid.*: 122) (a term McDowell borrows from Lévi-Strauss's *Totemism Today* [1963: 18; see McDowell 1988: 121]) and conjured these extracts as a discrete institution – the so-called cargo cult of anthropological writings. To move beyond the reification and institutionalization of what is essentially a piece of a wider network of tropes and meanings, McDowell proposes restoring the original semantic field and reading the "few features" (*ibid.*) labelled "cargo cult" in the context of that field. Understanding so-called cargo cults through the prism of indigenous semantic fields could reveal undergirding sophistications that give the lie to the caricature of so-called cargo cultists as irrational, even "mad," and, of course, "primitive" (see Dalton 2000a, 2000b; Kamma 1972). By the same token, it might expose similarities between these and Westerners (McDowell 2000), challenging the us/them binarism at play in Lindstrom's "cargoism" and the pejorative, condescending Western constructions of Melanesia it bespeaks.

Ipili speakers occupy adjacent valleys: the Paiela valley to the west ("western Ipilis") and the Porgera valley to the east ("eastern Ipilis"). In the mid-1940s[2], a cult began at Lyeimi (aka Lyeime, Lyemi, Ljaima, Lyalyame, Lyalyalaim, Yeimi and Yeim), a location north of the Lagaip River where Tayato (aka Taro) Enga lived (see Wiessner and Tumu 1998: 14, map 2)[3], and swiftly moved throughout Enga- and Ipili-speaking territory. Mervyn J. Meggitt, who first described the cult in a blockbuster article that remains the indispensable reference for those interested in it (1973, 1974), referred to it as the "Cult of Ain" or "Ain's Cult". Ipili speakers called it *mata kamo* (aka *mara kamo*) or "shaking magic" because participants who were most inspired and transported by the proceedings shook. The chapter begins with an introduction to the cult, emphasizing its manifestations among various Enga groups (Feil 1983; Golub

2. Sharp dates what he refers to as the "Lyeimi Movement" from 1944 to 1945 (1990: 112). Wiessner and Tumu say the cult lasted from 1943 to 1945 (2001: 301). Reithofer states that the cult originated "around 1944" (2006: 190). Patrol Officer Dwyer indicates that the cult swept "through the Wabag sub district in 1945" (Wabag Patrol Report 8, 1952-1953; T. Dwyer, PO, January 31 to February 29, 1953), and Patrol Officer Graham Hardy writes that the cult "swept through parts of the WABAG Sub-District soon after the last WAR", that is, World War II (Laiagam Patrol Report 3, 1956-1957).

3. Lyeimi was a borderland where "mostly Taro [aka Tayato] Enga or mixed communities in which Ipili-Pogera or Tokowaeme Nete have intermarried with Taro Enga clans and live in the manner of the Taro Enga" (Sharp 1990: 112). Patrol Officer Graham Hardy indicates that the influence of Hewa (aka Ewa, Kewa) was "noticeable" (Laiagam Patrol Report 3, 1956-1957: 7).

2001: 173-178; Jacka 2002: 202-206; Meggitt 1974; Wiessner and Tumu 1998: 383 and 2001). But the ethnographic heart of the article concerns Ipili versions of the cult (see Biersack 2011a and 2011b, which also covers Enga, Somaip and Huli versions of the cult). *Mata kamo* varied from one location to the next. In some locations the ostensible effort was to obtain wealth; in the Paiela valley, however, wealth acquisition was not a goal. What was common to all performances of *mata kamo* was a ritual reorientation away from the ancestors and towards the sky and beings associated with it, a reorientation that fulfilled the explicit directives of the cult leaders. In keeping with McDowell's article, I offer an interpretation of *mata kamo* in light of the "semantic field" that undergirds all Ipili variants, regardless of whether acquiring wealth is a motive: Ipili cosmology, which discursively constructed the world in anti-Copernican, anthropocentric terms. I shall argue that *mata kamo* constituted a concerted, often exuberant, effort to escape the human condition as Ipili speakers defined it by instantiating a millennium of "supernatural bliss" (Worsley 1968: 12), one that Ipili cosmology prefigured in its notions of the sky and skyward life. In some places, acquiring abundant and/or superior wealth, including at times artifacts of white material culture, served as a sign of that millennium and must be understood with respect to Ipili millenarian discourse and as a dimension or aspect of a millenarian cult or movement. To interpret *mata kamo* in cargoistic terms, as evidence of indigenous materialism, is to miss the point of *mata kamo*, which was to transcend the material conditions of terrestrial life by celestializing human life.

Introduction to the Cult of Ain

The Cult of Ain or Ain's Cult began in the middle 1940s and moved quickly from its point of initiation in Lyeimi southward to other Tayato Enga places (Wailya [aka Waiya, Walia] [Jacka 2002: 204], Tumundan (aka Tumandan, Tumandane, Tumundane) [Meggitt 1956: 117 and 1974: 23-25; Wabag Patrol Report no. 2, 1952-1953: 12-13; Wiessner and Tumu 2001: 315]), and from there eastward, southward, and northward to other Enga locations (see *ibid*.: 305, map 2), attracting participation from Yandapo (aka Yandapu) (Meggitt 1974: 42), Maramuni (*ibid*.: 42-43), Mae (aka Mai) (*ibid*.: 43-45), Waka (ibid: 32-37) and Tombema (Feil 1983) Engas[4].

---

4. The cult was also proselytized to the Karinj-speaking Somaip (Reithofer 2006: 187-212), the Huli (Frankel 1986: 28-29; Glasse 1995: 73; Meggitt 1974: 32), Konema (west of the Paiela valley), and the Porgera (Biersack 1998: 55-60; Gibbs 1977: 12-21; Jacka 2002: 205-207; Meggitt 1974: 27-32) and Paiela (Biersack 1991: 268-272; 2005: 141-152) valleys.

There are several stories of how the cult began (Biersack 2005: 146, Jacka 2002: 208-209, Meggitt 1974: 21, Sharp 1990: 114-115, and Wiessner and Tumu 2001: 311). The best known is Meggitt's: the cult began when the ghost of Ain, a Tayato Enga member of the Kamani patriclan, visited one or more of his sons in a dream or dreams and told them that existing rituals were to be abandoned and that a new ritual was to be put in their place, one that offered sacrifices not to ancestral figures or traditional mythological beings, as existing rituals did, but to the ur-ancestors, as it were, the ancestors of all ancestors – the sun and the moon – "the father and the mother of us all" (1974: 21). In accounting for this ritual innovation, Meggitt argued that the area had suffered recently from a decade of calamities. Frosts had destroyed sweet potato crops, many had died from outbreaks of influenza and dysentery, and pig herds had been decimated by anthrax (*ibid.*: 18-19). During these disasters the existing ritual repertoire had proved ineffectual, making people receptive to ritual innovation.

This was also the time when Australian adventurers and explorers first entered the area (*ibid.*: 15-16), exposing local people to white people for the first time – to "their very appearance, their puzzling activities in mapping the terrain, sending radio messages and the like, their multitudinous possessions, their weapons, their use of aircraft" (*ibid.*: 16) – and leaving a "deep impression" (*ibid.*). A permanent patrol post was opened up at Wabag, the capital of today's Enga Province, in 1942 or 1943 (*ibid.*: 17), and interest in white material culture was sparked by the miniscule but high-impact presence of those white men who manned the post or who passed through it.

The signature event of the cult was the massive sacrifice of pigs to the sun. A tall house and/or high platform was built, pigs were hoisted up on it, and each pig's snout was held up towards the sun as the sun was summoned to receive the gift. The pig was then killed and baked and feasted upon by participants. Such prestations opened up an exchange with the sun that would hopefully result in a quid pro quo of improved health, the acquisition of wealth and/or an ascent to the sky. In the sky, cult participants would live with the sun and the immortal "sky beings" (*yalyakali* in Engan) (Brennan 1977: 16; Wiessner and Tumu 2001: 304), who had been made by the sun and moon and who had borne the ancestors (Brennan 1977: 15-17; Meggitt 1965: 107; Wiessner and Tumu 1998: 181).

There were several other core features of the cult among Enga speakers (see Meggitt 1974: 39-41).

1. Cult leaders stared at the sun along the shafts of spears and shook. In some places, cult leaders exposed themselves to fire to prove the power and veracity of their teachings. Participants "followed suit and became 'shaking men'" (*ibid.*: 39), even holding embers in emulation of the cult leaders (*ibid.*: 25).

2. The Cult of Ain strove to supplant past ritual with its own innovations. Thus, each clan was told to abandon ancestral rituals involving stones (the *kepele* ritual [Gibbs 1978, Wiessner and Tumu 1998: 192-194] being the most important of these) and bachelor purification rituals called *sangai* or *sanggai* among Engas (Meggitt 1964, 1974: 39; Wiessner and Tumu 1998: 216-237, 2001: 313). Ritual paraphernalia were burned or discarded, as were all weapons.

3. A belief that participants would enter the sky world was widespread.

4. Participants also expected to receive an abundance of valuables, traditional and/or white.

5. Male and female participants bathed in local streams, violating the strict segregation of the sexes that the prevailing conventions at the time imposed.

6. New food taboos were promulgated and warfare was banned.

7. The cult leaders were paid handsomely as the imparters of new knowledge.

Engan versions of the cult speakers contained an unmistakable cargoic aspect. A recurring inspiration in this regard was a cow's tail that had shown up in Wabag and that signified to local people the kind of gigantic pig that everyone would soon possess. "News of this phenomenon rapidly spread through the western Enga group, together with the assurance […] that somewhere, perhaps in the sky world of Enga cosmology, people had whole herds of these desirable beasts" (Meggitt 1974: 25). Although Meggitt believed that participants in the original version of the cult at Lyeimi did not expect to receive wealth, Peter Sharp tells a different story. Sharp worked as a medical officer with the Department of Health in Papua New Guinea from 1975 to 1980, "the greater part of that time being spent in Enga Province" (1990: 112), and he had ample opportunity to collect stories about the Cult of Ain at Lyeimi in this period. In his article "The Searching Sun", Sharp wrote that the Lyeimi cult leader[5] "predicted the coming of new men, crops, new technology and new domestic animals. He took the Kamani [Ain's patriclan] early one morning and showed them strange animal tracks in the mud" (*ibid.*: 114). The cult leader also "had the tail of one of these new beasts which men later recognized as a bullock's tail" (*ibid.*), and he showed this tail to cult participants (*ibid.*).

A common method for receiving the wealth the cult promised was to create artificial pools. Such pools made their first appearance at Lyeimi, where the cult leader

5. The spelling of the names of the four sons of Ain varies considerably from text to text. I have chosen to avoid using specific names, simply referring to "the cult leaders" or the "Enga cult leaders". I do mention one of these by name, Wambilipi, using Meggitt's (1974) spelling. As the cult moved out from its point of origin, the original leaders picked up disciples, who joined them as cult leaders or who took over the leadership of the cult, especially at points furthest from Lyeimi.

or leaders told followers to dig holes that would fill miraculously with water and that could be used for unspecified ritual purposes (*ibid.*: 112). At Tumundan pits were again dug, this time around the dance ground, a flat plaza that was (and still is) used throughout the highlands for dancing, giving and distributing gifts, and speech making. The Tumundan pits were filled with magically prepared water, and participants were told that pearlshells would eventually materialize in them (Meggitt 1974: 25). It was also predicted that "pigs would appear in the women's houses and new crops [...] would sprout in the gardens" (*ibid.*). Meggitt attributes these expectations to "the garbled stories reaching the Taro [aka Tayato] of the fabulous quantities of shell valuables and exotic foodstuffs [...] possessed by the Europeans at Wabag" (*ibid.*), directly east of Tumundan.

The Engan cult leaders would go on to convert the Waka Enga living along the upper Wage River. There, holes were again dug around the dance ground and water poured into them, with the expectation that "new wealth from the sky" would eventually appear in the pits (*ibid.*: 34). A period of darkness was predicted, but once the darkness had dissipated, those who had shaken were instructed to visit the pits "to remove the pigs, pearlshells and steel axes placed there by the sky-people" (*ibid.*: 35).

The emphasis upon wealth acquisition only intensified as the cult moved down the Wage River. At the southern extremity of Waka Enga territory, the cult leaders promised participants that the sun would send "new bigger pigs and other valuables" (*ibid.*: 36) and that these would appear in the pits the shakers dug around the dance ground and filled with water. A cult house was built and a ring of cordyline was planted opposite its door. Within this ring, a wreath of spears was erected, and followers were told to cook all meat on top of these spears "as gifts to the sun" (*ibid.*), until such time as the "new wealth" appeared in the pits.

There were variations on this theme among the Yandapo, Mae (aka Mai) (Meggitt 1965: 105; Wiessner and Tumu 1998: 54), and Tombema (Feil 1983) Engas. Pits were dug, water was poured in and participants waited for pearlshells, huge pigs and steel axes to appear in the pools. The strategy was to appeal to the sun to send this wealth. Among the Mae, for example, participants killed their pigs to demonstrate to the sun their fidelity to the new ritual regime. Those who sacrificed would receive "dozens of pigs" (Meggitt 1974: 43) that would materialize mysteriously in women's houses and emerge from pools (*ibid.*). Also – and this seems unique to the Mae – many cowrie shells, pearlshells and steel axes would be found lying around (*ibid.*). The usual washing rite was part and parcel of the effort to attract abundant wealth to each participant. According to Meggitt, the cult leaders put all the pearlshells they had received in payment for their services into the water so that the essence of the pearlshells "would float down and enter the bodies of the bathers to ensure that they would receive the promised valuables from the sun" (*ibid.*: 45).

In tandem with this motif of wealth acquisition was another: the theme of ascending to the sky. Meggitt believed that this promise was not made until the cult arrived in Tipinini at the eastern edge of Ipili-speaking territory. Yet a patrol report written in 1952 makes it clear that cult participants at Tumundan expected to ascend to the sky. The people of Tumundan were exhorted to slaughter pigs on a high platform to appease the sun and, if they did, "everyone who died went to live on the sun" (Wabag Patrol Report no. 2, 1952-1953: 12-13). Indeed, Meggitt's first account of the cult at Tumundan described the same quid pro quo: those who foreswore the old rituals and who obeyed certain prohibitions would ascend into the sky to live with "sky beings" forever (1956: 117). This pledge was coupled with the companion pledge that participants would "receive great wealth in pigs and goods" (*ibid.*). The theme of an ascent to the sky may in fact have been present from the very beginning. In fall 1993, I had a chance to talk to a man named Kaiya, who was living at Tipinini at the eastern edge of the Porgera valley at the time. Kaiya had attended the cult at Lyeimi, and he told me that participants there were promised that they would go to the sky, the "good ground" (*yu epene*). "Good ground" is a common Ipili epithet for the sky in *mata kamo* times.

Ascending to the sky was clearly something Enga speakers could imagine at that time. In 1938, about six years before the onset of the Cult of Ain, another cult broke out at Wailya. According to Jacka, the cult was in reaction to rumors of the presence of white men in the area (2002: 200-201) and, no doubt in light of the violence that sometimes did happen in first-contact encounters, Kaiyamba's followers prepared to ward off the white menace. Kaiyamba died at the hands of the white men, and his band of followers was routed (*ibid.*: 201). If Kaiyamba's cult was clearly about resistance, it was not just about that. Kaiyamba identified himself as the son of the sun (*ibid.*: 200), and he also told participants to prepare to go up into the sky (*ibid.*: 201). While Jacka suggests that Kaiyamba was the source of the notion of an ascent to the sky, I would suggest instead that Kaiyamba and his followers were inspired by the semantic field (to use McDowell's and Lévi-Strauss's term) they shared with other Engas. If I may generalize from Paul Brennan's account of Engan religion (1977): Engas acknowledged a supreme being, Aitawe, personified by the sun, who together with the moon, a female, created the sky beings (*yalyakali*). These in turn bore the ancestors of the various Enga phratries, which populated the earth rather than the sky. The *yalyakali* had access to the water of life and were thus immortal. The human descendants of the sky beings would have been immortal but for the fact that human mothers rejected the water of life in favor of the milk they breast-fed their offspring, and "thereafter all the burdenless accoutrements of the sky world were, of necessity, exchanged for the care and toil known to the earthlings" (*ibid.*: 16; see also Meggitt 1965: 107-109; Wiessner and Tumu 1998: 181)[6]. In announcing himself to be the son of the sun and in promising an ascent to the sky, Kaiyamba, I would suggest, spoke the language of Engan millenarian discourse.

The Cult in the Porgera Valley

I have just summarized the principal themes in the Enga variants of the Cult of Ain. From these materials, it would appear that a case could be made for calling the Cult of Ain a cargo cult. But did the cult seek first and foremost to acquire wealth, especially white wealth (including white manufactured items), satisfying local appetites for material possessions? Is the category "cargo cult" an apt representation of the cult's core project?

In searching for the answers to these questions, I turn to the cult among Ipili speakers. Moving southward out of Lyeimi, the cult arrived at Tipinini, on the eastern edge of the Porgera valley[7]. Then it moved westward, arriving at Anawe and Mungalep, both of which are near the present Porgera mine on the western side of the Porgera valley. From there, it moved further northward, to Pitika and Politika, and then westward into the northeastern side of the Paiela valley. I begin this section with a generic account of the cult in the Porgera valley, as described by Meggitt (1974: 27-31) and Gibbs (1977: 12-18). I then describe the cult at Tipinini, the easternmost point where Ipili is spoken within the Porgera valley[8]. With respect to the cult at Tipinini, I draw upon Jacka's (2002: 206-207), Gibbs' (1977: 18-21), and Meggitt's (1974: 31-32) accounts, supplementing these with my own research in the fall of 1993.

---

6. Meggitt, too, characterizes human life in negative terms: "[...] it is the lot of the Mae to be gardeners and warriors. Men must toil to wrest a meagre livelihood from a harsh environment in which violent death is [...] an everyday occurrence" (1965: 108). He attributes this state to "the behaviour of the sky beings in the past" (*ibid.*), a behaviour he does not describe.

7. Jacka and Meggitt differ as to how the cult came to the Porgera valley and to Tipinini at its eastern edge. Meggitt indicates that the cult moved from Tumundan and to the Porgera valley/Tipinini (1974: 26). Jacka argues that the cult went to Wailya, a Tayato Enga location southwest of Lyeimi. Then it branched out, some of the brothers going to Tipinini while others went to Tumundan (2002: 200, figure 2).

8. Tipinini is at the easternmost edge of the Porgera valley. Many living there are functionally bilingual in Ipili and Engan. Jacka claims that Huli is also spoken there (2003: 10), albeit to a lesser extent than Engan or Ipili. Wiessner and Tumu place Tipinini within the Tayato Engan ethnic area (1998: 15, map 2).

Many of the details of the cult in the Porgera valley are already familiar. The brothers urged the abandonment of traditional ritual practices and a turning to the sun ("our father") for help (*ibid.*: 27). Pigs were clubbed to death with a "small steel tomahawk" (*ibid.*: 28) on a high platform and offered to the sun, the cult leaders stared at the sun along the shafts of spears and "shook violently" (*ibid.*), and they held embers to demonstrate the validity of their teachings (*ibid.*: 27). Participants were commanded to bathe under a waterfall that the cult leaders created using a sluice-like arrangement "to cleanse and prepare their bodies for the ascent into the sky-world" (*ibid.*: 29). The wives of the cult leaders used a stone to scrape a pearlshell, the dust thus generated falling into the water and entering the vaginas of the bathing women so that they would not contaminate their husbands during intercourse (*ibid.*: 30). For greater purity, copulation was suspended for a month (*ibid.*: 29).

In addition to feasting upon the carcasses of the slaughtered pigs, the pigs' kidneys were magically prepared and eaten with particular leaves. As had happened in the upper Wage River (*ibid.*: 36), a sow's innards were buried in the middle of a circle of stones that had been placed on the dance ground and a cordyline shrub was planted on this partial grave. This then marked the site of a large house built for the occasion, the main post of which was driven within the circle of stones ringing the partial grave. The house would shelter people when, within a few months, "massive discharges of lightning would signal the coming of a great darkness that would cover the land for days or weeks" (*ibid.*: 28)[9]. Those inside the house would say magic to "invoke the help of the sun to disperse the cloud of darkness" (*ibid.*). "Then enormous *moropae* pythons would hang suspended from the sky, and all the people and their pigs would make their way into the sky world along the 'paths' formed by the bodies of the snakes" (*ibid.*). "[…] once they were established in the sky-world, the progeny of their pigs would attain great size, becoming as large as that much discussed beast whose tail had been displayed at Wabag" (*ibid.*: 27). If participants abandoned fighting, observed the newly promulgated food taboos and maximized their purity by bathing and by abstaining from intercourse, there would "be no more sickness or death among you and hence no more ghosts or any need for rituals to propitiate them" (*ibid.*: 30).

9. Terms meaning "time of darkness" have been reported throughout the region with which this chapter is concerned. Scholars link the "time of darkness" to a volcanic eruption on Long Island in the Bismark Sea off the north coast of New Guinea in the 1600s that darkened the sky with tephra ashfall. In several locations, preparing for a time of darkness, which the sun would then disperse as a preliminary to participants ascending to the sky, was a striking dimension of *mata kamo* activities. See, for example, Jacka 2002: 205, Reithofer 2006: 204, and Wiessner and Tumu 2001: 316.

Gibbs' account corroborates this intermixing of themes: wealth acquisition but also attaining immortality. A spirit that dwelled at the boundary of sky and earth predicted the end of the world, indicating that cult participants, as long as they observed certain prohibitions and performed certain rituals, "would not die but be received into the sky" (1977: 12). Offerings to ancestral spirits were abandoned, pigs were ritually sacrificed to the sun, sweet potatoes were specially prepared and consumed and several food taboos were put in place. The day following the massive slaughter of pigs, the kidneys were barbecued, holes were poked in them using the wing bones of a fruit bat, and then they were eaten. Gibbs claims that the procedure of poking the kidneys with bat wing bones echoed existing magic to promote health (*ibid.*). Participants bathed, singing the songs the cult leader taught them. The sample song Gibbs supplies urged participants to "[f]orget your beliefs and take on good ways" (*ibid.*). Everyone went inside the large house that had been built for the occasion and that was called *ongi* ("time ends, or darkness" [*ibid.*]) and "waited for the imminent end of the world which was to be heralded by a time of darkness" (*ibid.*: 12). Presumably (and as at other locations) the end of the time of darkness also heralded the promised ascent to the sky, where participants were to find wealth (*ibid.*: 14). "The visitors […] showed the Ipili a piece of woven material, a steel axe and wood cut with the axe. In *tawetoko* [literally the "sky bridge," but which may also be translated as sky] the Ipili would have axes like this, along with pearl shells and other valuable things. There was also reference to a horse's tail, […] an indication of the size of the pigs in *tawetoko*" (*ibid.*: 13). As proof of the validity of his teachings, the cult leader "handled hot coals and touched people with a short spear he was carrying. This made many people go into fits of shaking (men today describe them as being 'drunk')" (*ibid.*).

Meggitt alludes to (but fails to name) six or seven locations within the Porgera valley where Cult of Ain rituals were performed (1974: 27). Tipinini, where the theme of wealth acquisition was pronounced, was no doubt among these. According to Jacka, the cult leaders created small pools of water there, and, when Tipininians gazed into these, they saw metal houses, goats, cars, sheep and planes (2002: 205). As participants washed, cult leaders sat above the bathers and scraped pearlshells so that pearlshell dust would powder the bathers' bodies, making them shiny, healthy and likely to attract wealth (*ibid.*). A large round house was built to accommodate Tipininians as they waited for a "time of darkness" to pass (*ibid.*), after which they would ascend to the sky (*ibid.*).

Those with whom I discussed the cult emphasized the promised ascent to the sky. As I shall show, the notion of ground's end was fundamental to the Ipili worldview, and a cult leader claimed that the sun had warned him about the imminence of ground's end. In that context: pigs were sacrificed to the sun in Cult of Ain/*mata kamo* fashion and people feasted upon their carcasses. The shaking state was induced both by looking at the sun along the shaft of a spear and by consuming the pigs' kidneys. Shakers were *ke*, I was told. To be *ke* is to "be confused; not know; not be in one's right mind, be crazy; be in a trance" (Ingemann n.d.: n.p.). Ipili speakers translate *ke* into *longlong* ("crazy" or "mad") as well as *spak* or "drunk" in Tok Pisin (aka Neo-Melanesian). Hence, Gibbs' informants claimed that Porgeran shakers were "drunk".

Once the Enga cult leaders were gone, a young, unmarried woman named Ipiyama (aka Ipayeme, Ipiama) enticed her followers with promises that they would receive white manufactured goods. A man named Wambe chanced upon her one morning and she showed him a piece of black wood. "Wambe looked at the wood and then had a vision of […] axes, knives, houses with iron roofs and cars" (Gibbs 1977: 19). Ipiyama showed this same piece of wood to her followers the night before she led them to a pool on Mount Tongapipi (aka Tongopipi) (*ibid.*). According to Meggitt, Ipiyama told her followers they would find "a great number of new pigs and pearlshells" (1974: 31) at the bottom of the pool. As people looked into the water, they saw "houses, cars, airplanes, cattle, all the things of the white man" (Jacka 2002: 206). Despite the fact that Ipili speakers fear water and do not swim, they entered the water and ultimately drowned (Gibbs 1977: 19-20; Jacka 2002: 207; Meggitt 1974: 31-32).

The motive of wealth acquisition was prominent in the accounts of Ipiyama's spin-off cult I collected in the fall of 1993, when Pimbisu and Kainu, two old women, Muyu, an old man, and Yakop, a middle-aged man, shared their stories with me. Pimbisu told me that Ipiyama had invited everyone to a pool high up in the forests of Mount Tongapipi. En route, everyone had indiscriminate sex (see also Gibbs 1977: 19), even intercourse with siblings in violation of the incest taboo, the cornerstone of Ipili society. The next morning everyone got up early and assembled around the water. Timbapu, Ipiyama's hand-picked assistant, either held a mirror in his hand or put one on the surface of the lake. (Bush mirrors [*ipa lema lema*] were made by filling a small gourd with water and blackening the water with charcoal to create a reflecting surface for what was in essence a mini-pool.) Kainu, who claimed to be Timbapu's sister-in-law, described the water as being like a mirror (*ipa lema lema*). In this mirror, everyone saw stores and cars, cows and sheep, tin-roofed houses – it was like Australia, Pimbisu said. Why did participants want to enter the pond? "Thinking that in that good land [the sky] they would eat while resting [that is, without labouring, eating freely], they went into the water" (*Yu epene okona oto no pitimakale nembo talu ipa okona peainipia*), Pimbisu responded.

Meggitt's account of the cult in the Porgera valley stresses what he takes to be a "doctrinal shift towards an emphasis on a kind of bodily assumption [into the sky]", a shift he attributes to "the belief prevailing throughout the area [here he includes Enga-speaking territory] in the existence of a celestial world inhabited by the immortal offspring of the sun and the moon, a realm from which came [...], in the opinion of many, also the powerful, wealthy and seemingly indestructible Europeans" (1974: 27). Bill Gammage's wonderful book *The Sky Travellers*, concerning the patrol by Jim Taylor and John Black between March 1938 and June 1939, which brought the explorers into the Porgera and Paiela valleys, makes it clear that Engas and also Ipili speakers classified these white explorers as "sky people". "[...] most commonly the travellers' wealth, planes, wireless, guns and sometimes white or red skin [sky beings were said to be red-skinned] suggested that they were sky people, perhaps refugees from a sky battle, wandering the earth below, landless and womanless, seeking a place to settle" (1998: 1). Gammage describes two encounters between the patrol and Paielas in which white men were classified as sky men (*ibid.*: 132, 188), and Meggitt indicates that "many Enga regarded the Europeans [...] as being sky-people sojourning on earth, or at any rate as being in some way connected with the sky" (1974: 51). If nothing else, the white man's planes associated him with the sky (*ibid.*). But planes also associated the white man with the abundant and superior wealth they flew into the area in their effort to provision expatriate patrols (*ibid.*).

Whereas Meggitt saw events as taking a millenarian turn (*ibid.*: 27) among the Ipili speakers of the Porgera valley, the connections drawn in the local imagination among cargo, the sky and immortality were apparent in an earlier version of the cult among Enga speakers. At Tumundan, magically prepared water was put in pits dug around the perimeter of a dance ground with the expectation that pearlshells would eventually be found in them; "pigs would appear in the women's houses and new crops would sprout in the gardens" (*ibid.*: 25). But this was not all. Those who sacrificed pigs to appease the sun were assured that "everyone who died went to live on the sun and [...] then the dead would be brought back to earth to live on their former land" (Wabag Patrol Report 2, 1952-1953: 12). What characterized this cult, it seems, was a perceived concatenation of desiderata: cargo, an ascent to the sky and the achievement of immortality. Meggitt, in his 1956 description of the cult at Tumundan, certainly makes it sound that way. In "The Valleys of the Upper Wage and Lai Rivers...", he wrote, "all those who killed their pigs in a certain manner, eschewed the old rituals and obeyed certain prohibitions would supernaturally receive great wealth in pigs and goods. They would take these with them when they ascended into the sky to live forever with *Jaljakali* [*Yalyakali* or "sky man"], the sky being" (*ibid.*:

117). I return to this point below, but first I explore narratives of cult participation from the Paiela valley, which differ from those already examined in not emphasizing wealth acquisition.

The Cult in the Paiela Valley

From Pitika and Politika in the northwestern corner of the Porgera valley, the Engan cult leaders moved westward into the Paiela valley: to Piawe and Bealo in the northeastern corner of the Paiela valley and then onto Takopa and Asiaputenga in the central eastern side of that valley. In the Paiela valley, cargo acquisition ceases to be a goal and ascent to the sky for the purpose of achieving a better life and ideally immortality becomes the primary motivation for cult participation. In this section I substantiate this claim with an analysis of two stories of cult participation in the Paiela valley. Lewambo (with whom I discussed the cult in February 1995 and October 2000) participated in the cult at Asiaputenga. His account gives us a sense of how festive and licentious the cult was. After Asiaputenga, cult leaders moved to Tombena, a location just outside Kolombi, the site of the only airstrip in the Paiela valley, then crossed the Pakupale River and moved to Taninga in the northwestern corner of the Paiela valley. Kau (aka Kauwambo), with whom I discussed the cult in the fall of 1993, November 1995 and October 2000, participated in the cult at Taninga.

Lewambo's Story

Lewambo was a young boy living at Kolombi and just beginning to attend the *omatisia* ritual, a *sangai-* or *sanggai*-like ritual designed to grow bachelors and ready them for marriage, when three of the original Engan cult leaders, together with a sister named Lauwe, entered the Paiela valley. Three others came as well: Taiyako, Kome and Aleka. Kome and Aleka would bring the cult to the western shores of the Pakupale River. Lewambo (like other Paielas) referred to all the cult leaders as "spell owners" (*kamo anduane*).

At Asiaputenga, the cult leaders built a tall building and hoisted the pigs up onto the roof using a ladder and rope. The pigs' noses were pointed upward towards the sky as the cult leaders summoned the sun and moon to receive the gift – "*Alu Nai o, o yia peyo geyo*" ("*Alu* sun o, o I am killing and giving you pig") and "*Alu nai maiyawana gula, alu nai yia geyo*" ("*Alu* sun and moon, I am giving you pig"). The name of the owner of each sacrificed pig was uttered as the pig was offered up. "We killed and dropped the pigs repeatedly so that we would go to the sky." So many pigs were killed that they could not all be eaten, and the surplus was left on the ground to rot.

The pigs' kidneys were barbecued and placed on a bed of certain leaves, and a bone from the wing of a bat was used to jab the kidneys as a spell was said to promote the desired ascent to the sky. Similarly, sweet potatoes were scraped with pearlshell and bespelled and then (like the kidneys) cooked in the fire to promote an ascent to the sky. The consumption of the kidneys in particular made participants "crazy" or *ke*. In Paiela versions of *mata kamo*, sugar cane was also eaten. The accounts of this aspect of the ritual are sketchy. Participants brought in sugar cane and fought over it; then the stalks were broken up so that everyone could get a piece. As participants ate the sugar cane and sweet potatoes, they walked around "crazily" looking up at the sky and saying, "Let's go to the sky" (*Tawe pimakale* [literally, "Let's make sky"]). Then the pigs were taken out of the oven and feasted upon.

The day after the feast, everyone went to the Ipa Pukuma, a stream in the vicinity of Asiaputenga, which Lauwe, the sister of some of the cult leaders, straddled and defiled. Even so, the purpose of washing in the stream was to cleanse participants' bodies in preparation for ascending to the sky. Pearlshells were placed across the river (a detail, like the details about Lauwe, that is unique to Lewambo's narrative), and the spellmen stood upstream saying magic as bathers stood downstream. At the time cross-gender contact was strictly regulated, intercourse being the only context in which males and females were proximate. But in *mata kamo*, men and women bathed together and in ways that were maximally transgressive, establishing intimacy in a setting where *ceteris paribus* it should have been prohibited. Exposing the genitals in public was (and is) not done, but participants were so "crazy" that they allowed their aprons and grass skirts to be in disarray, revealing what these items of clothing were meant to conceal. Male and female bathers looked at each other's private parts, an act that was normally reserved for intercourse because of its erotic impact. Some garbed themselves in tree leaves when their clothing became totally dysfunctional. Menstruators and women who had just given birth ordinarily sequestered themselves to insulate pure people from their impurities (Biersack 1987), but Lewambo indicated that women who were menstruating or who had just given birth bathed with men and that men looked at these defiled women, contaminating themselves as they did so.

After participants washed, they danced, to the same effect. The spellmen wore wigs festooned with the feathers of the *paitauwa* bird (the Raggiana bird of paradise [Ingerman n.d.: n.p.]), carried spears on their shoulders and danced. Lauwe held a bow and jumped around with it. "We danced virtually naked, with our genitals exposed, and we did not worry about that. We were delighted because we would go to the sky, so we danced," Lewambo said. One woman was so "crazy" that she hurled stones at the men; a woman who was nursing her child was also *ke* and dropped the child and ran away.

The cult leaders encouraged everyone to abandon their weapons and their ancestors and ancestral rituals and to sacrifice only to the sun. In the pre-colonial period Paielas fed pork to the skulls of deceased parents to promote their own health. To take better care of these skulls, offspring built small shelters at the base of trees, creating a canopy over the structure to shield it from the rain. In *mata kamo*, the skulls of parents were taken out of their houses and "discarded" in the river to rid the world of what, from the *mata kamo* perspective, was the wrong kind of spirit: a dead terrestrial, rather than an immortal celestial, spirit. The *kepele* cult – as described by Gibbs, a "clan ritual" (1978: 436) designed to change the luck of a line that had experienced serious misfortunes (*ibid.*; see Gibbs 1978 on the Ipili version of *kepele* and Wiessner and Tumu 1998: 107-109, 192-194, 198-212 on the Enga version of *kepele*) – was a particular target of the cult (Meggitt 1974: 24, Wiessner and Tumu 2001: 311). Lewambo told me that the paraphernalia for the *kepele* ritual – especially the *kepele nu* ("*kepele* netbag" or "*kepele* womb"), a wicker figurine in the shape of a man with a large penis (Gibbs 1978: n.p., photograph b [see also Raich 1967]), as well as the *kepele kulini* ("*kepele* bones"), the special stones that were deployed in the *kepele* ritual – were burned.

Kau's Story

Kau was a boy living with his widowed mother and maternal uncle at Tatonga on the western bank of the Pakupale River when word came that people had already gone to the sky at Taninga in the northwestern corner of the Paiela valley. All three travelled northward to participate in *mata kamo* under the leadership of Taiyako, along with Kome and Aleka, all of whom seem to have been disciples of the original Engan cult leaders.

The cult leaders promised that participants would ascend to the sky if they performed the rituals they were taught. A house was built, and pigs were carried up to the roof using a huge ladder, an operation Kau likened to carrying the pigs up to the sky. On the roof, the snout of each pig was held up to the sun as the sun and the moon – the sun's wife, some say – were summoned to receive the gift. Then the pig was killed and dropped to the ground. People came from other locations on the western bank of the Pakupale River to kill pigs at Taninga. The slaughter of pigs was massive.

As the pork was being cooked, participants washed in the Bolo River. Paiela participants tend to dwell on this aspect of the ritual, as the violations of customary male-female relations were truly egregious. Kau's account paralleled Lewambo's: men and women removed their clothes and bathed naked in the water as the cult leaders said magic. At this point, Kau, a small boy, became frightened and ran off, but others followed and brought him back, and one of his kinsmen hoisted him onto his shoulders and walked into the water with him, committing him to ritual participation.

After the washing, the baked pigs were taken out of the oven and eaten. Participants also ate the pigs' kidneys, which were roasted over the fire, cut into pieces, laid on a bed of certain shredded leaves, poked with the bone of a bat as a spell was said, and then eaten.

In the morning sweet potatoes were scraped with a pearlshell and cooked in the fire. Participants also imbibed "sky water" (*tawe ipa*). This was poured down the shaft of a spear by one of the cult leaders as participants stationed themselves at the tip end and drank it. Some participants became *ke* or "crazy" from drinking this water and sang the songs the cult leaders had taught them in the way that intoxicated people sing today.

Kau was adamant that the purpose of the ritual was not to acquire wealth. Participants wanted to ascend to the sky, a goal all aspects of the ritual were designed to advance. The expectation was that the earth would be "lost" (*latako*) and that a rope would drop from the sky so that participants could climb above the clouds. "We were told that those who had participated in *mata kamo* would soon be going to the sky, and that we newcomers would follow them once we had performed the ritual," Kau said. Participants were thrilled to leave the ground and "go above," he said.

The cult leaders referred to the participants as "sky men" (*tawe akali*) or "sky people" (*tawe wanda akali*). As sky people, participants possessed a degree of ritual purity that nonparticipants lacked, and participants were told to avoid contact with ("to keep a distance from" [*wa tika pi*]) nonparticipants. *Mata kamo* created a caste-like difference between the pure and the impure, the enlightened and the ignorant, something Kau's story makes crystal clear. Kau's maternal grandmother and one other woman were too old to travel to Taninga and they were left at Taninga with a supply of firewood, water and sweet potatoes sufficient to last until Kau, his mother and his uncle returned. The two old women were still there, entertaining each other with *tindi* or folktales/myths and very much in need of assistance from more able-bodied people, when Kau's party came back. Fresh from cult participation, they bragged that they were now "sky people" and that the old women should "keep a distance", the time-honoured Paiela strategy for safeguarding purity in the presence of contaminants.

Kau's uncle took pity on the two women and killed a pig for them, but they were still prohibited from touching their purer "sky" kin.

Kau's story can be augmented with the information that Mata, Kau's mother, gave me in an interview in December 1976. Mata elaborated on the abandonment of intersexual taboos. Ordinarily fathers and their small children and males and females "kept a distance," she said, but the rule in *mata kamo* was "*not* to keep a distance" (*wa tika pulene*). Fathers played with their young children and they danced touching the elbows of their daughters; husbands and wives sat looking straight at each other; and, the greatest transgression of all, siblings married. Mata said that the cult leaders encouraged sibling liaisons. Mata also explained that, during the washing ritual, women lay down under the cascading water and spread their legs so that the water could enter and purify their vaginas, their intention being to protect their husbands from coital contamination.

The Case for Millenarianism

Among Ipili speakers, *mata kamo* cuts a broad swathe, from Tipinini in the Ipili far east to the western bank of the Pakupale River in the Ipili far west, and covering two valleys from their northern to their southern extremities. Across this terrain, the emphasis of *mata kamo* shifted. The most obvious goal of Ipiyama's spin-off cult at Tipinini – the Ipili location nearest to Wabag, the regional portal on the white world at that time – was wealth acquisition. Paielas had relatively little exposure to white material culture, and wealth acquisition was not a goal of Paiela versions of *mata kamo*. Instead Paielas zealously, "crazily", sought entrance into the sky world, there to achieve immortality. Thus, Lapu, a man who probably went to Taninga with Kau and his mother, and who in any case would have participated in *mata kamo* on the western side of the Paiela valley, told me in December 1976 that the cult leaders had promised that all who consumed the pigs' kidneys and who washed themselves in ritually prescribed ways would go to the sky and not die. Lewambo, speaking to me in October 2000, said that his father and mother had lived and died on earth and that he wanted to go to the sky to escape their fate. The sky was a "good ground"; it was where immortal *tawe akali* or "sky men" lived, he said. Similarly for Kau, who told me, also in October 2000, that participants thought they would go to the sky (the "good ground") and not die.

If acquiring wealth was not a goal in all versions of *mata kamo*, then the *mata kamo* project could not have been fundamentally "cargoistic"; it must have been something else. The constant across all versions of *mata kamo* was not a craving for riches but the desire to enter the sky. This section elaborates upon that point, concluding that *mata kamo* was at base a millenarian cult or movement and must be understood as such.

Wealth and the Sky Motif

While the cargoic aspects of *mata kamo* are striking, the sky motif was not only present but featured through the stylistics of the sacrifice in all versions of *mata kamo*. Pigs were hoisted up on high platforms or roofs, their noses were held upward in prestation to the sun as the sun was summoned to receive the gift, and then they were killed. Before *mata kamo* demonic spirits called *yama* (who attacked living human beings, sickening or killing them) were placated by slaughtering a pig and shoving its snout into a hole in the ground, the hole serving as the "road" along which the attacking *yama* could "come" and receive its gift and then withdraw, effecting a cure. This was called *kolo* (Jacka 2001) (also *ingape*). In the *mata kamo* sacrifice, the sky rather than the earth was used as a medium of communication with spirits, and these spirits were sky rather than earth beings. That *mata kamo* sacrifice was an inversion of *kolo* was an obvious aspect of the proceedings to all those whose *mata kamo* stories I collected. They also understood why this was so: the old rituals were to be replaced by new rituals oriented to the sky, for the principal message of the cult leaders was that ancestral rituals – all of which concerned terrestrial life and its travails – should be abandoned as participants turned to the sun for assistance (Meggitt 1974: 21).

To say as much is to suggest that those versions of *mata kamo* that appear to have been exclusively focused on wealth acquisition were as invested in engagement with the sky as those versions (Paiela versions, most notably) that focused on an ascent to the sky alone. Even in Ipiyama's spin-off cult, the Ipili version of *mata kamo* that seems the most blatantly cargo-oriented in its quest for material gains, ascending to the sky was the indispensable step, for it was in the sky that participants would receive the desired goods.

> "Ipayema began to talk about going up the sky bridge [the sky] so that [her followers] could go live in the sky world and receive all of the goods that Wambilipa and his brothers said would come. One day she climbed on the roof of the house while people were gathered inside and started urinating on them. She told them that she was giving them 'sky water' (*tawe ipa*) which would allow them to travel up the sky bridge if they drank it." (Jacka 2002: 206) [10]

---

10. The term *tawe toko* is typically translated as "skybridge". The word *toko* refers to a "level raised surface; floor, chair, table; on top of; bridge, fallen log on which people walk" (Ingemann n.d.: n.p.). The image of levelness is odd because *tawe toko* suggests some apparatus facilitating an ascent to the sky. I tend to translate it simply as "sky", to avoid the image.

Ipiyama's cult was not unique in this regard. If we cast our eyes back over the various cult accounts reported here, it is clear that the sky and its inhabitants were key to receiving the hoped-for wealth. A few examples from stories already told will suffice to make the point. Among the Waka Enga, pits were dug around the dance ground to receive "new wealth from the sky" (Meggitt 1974: 34), and pigs, pearlshells and steel axes were expected to be gifted by the sky people (*ibid.*). The Mae Enga hoped to receive "valuables from the sun" (*ibid.*: 45). In the Porgera valley, it was predicted that there would be a time of darkness that the sun would disperse. Then people would ascend to the sky along the "'path' formed by the bodies of the snakes" (*ibid.*: 28). The offspring of the pigs that those who ascended to the sky brought with them would be as big as the animal whose tail had found its way to Wabag and made such a sensation (*ibid.*: 27).

Mata kamo sacrifice opened up an exchange with the sun, an exchange that, in some locations, was expected to culminate in a countergift of wealth. The wealth would be gifted by the sun, or by his "sky being" offspring; and/or it would be received in the sky; and/or it would be received in what I have come to think of as sky spaces: those pools or pits of water that reflected (like the mini-pool indigenous mirror) the sky and its wealth – or so participants fantasized.

The Meaning of the Sky

But acquiring wealth was not the sole benefit. Participants would also become immortal, a promise that can be documented for all versions of the cult narrated here, including Tumundan (through Dwyer's account [Wabag Patrol Report no. 2, 1952-1953: 12-13] and Meggitt's initial reporting of the cult at Tumundan [1956: 117]) and Lyeimi (through Kaiya's account, according to which participants were told they would ascend to the sky, implying their eventual immortalization). What, then, were the connections between wealth and the sky, the sky and immortalization, and wealth and immortalization? To explore these connections, I return to Mc-Dowell's article "A Note on Cargo Cults and Cultural Constructions of Change", which urges us to approach cargoic activity through the "semantic field" (1988: 122) informing this activity. Given the ritual specifics of *mata kamo*, this semantic field is necessarily cosmological: a matter of sky and earth. Long before missionaries entered the area, and long before *mata kamo*, Ipili cosmology turned on a sky/earth axis, a dichotomy that bore on the nature of the human condition as Ipilis understood it to be. I begin making this argument with a discussion of *yu*, the Ipili construction of the earth, a construction I have distilled from diverse materials: magical spells, rituals and, most importantly, the very language Ipili speakers use to speak of the earth and human life on it.

In the precontact cosmos, the earth was the locus of all material, biological life. Terrestrial life (plants, animals and humans) was corporeal life: a matter of skin and bone (metaphorically the bark and pith of a tree, respectively, for example). All terrestrial life had a life cycle: entities were born, grew (their "skin" became "big"), declined (their "skin" became small and wizened), and ultimately died. Somewhere in the middle of this cycle reproduction occurred. Earth itself, the host of all life forms, had a body: a surface or "outer" skin ("ground skin" or *yu umbuaini*) and a subsurface, "inner" bone ("ground bone" or *yu kulini*), the living residing on the "skin", the visible surface of the earth, and the dead residing in the invisible interior of the earth or "earth bone" (*yu kulini*). Like all life forms, earth had a life cycle. Each earth came into existence, lasted 14 generations, and "ended", but only to begin again (Biersack 1991: 290-291, n. 15; 1995a: 20-23, 1996: 95-97; 1999: 75-76; 2001: 40; 2005: 139).

Examining a plethora of beliefs and practices in light of conversations I have had with Ipili speakers, Porgerans and Paielas alike, I have concluded that the fundamental principle of corporeal, terrestrial existence was what I call a "sacrificial principle": that life must be spent (or sacrificed) in the course of sustaining and reproducing itself, that life and death were thus two sides of the same zero-sum coin (Biersack 1995a: 22; 1995b: 257-261; 1996: 92-95; 1998: 52-55; 1999: 75; 2004: 111-112; 2005: 140-141; see also Biersack 2001: 85-89; Buchbinder and Rappaport 1976; Golub 2006: 271-272; Reithofer 2006: 180-182; Stewart and A. Strathern 2004: 184; cf. Bloch and Parry, eds. 1982). This principle applied to "work" (*peape*), a wide category that encompassed all purposeful activity, from gardening to sexual reproduction to marriage. Horticulture – clearing the forest, fencing and mounding the garden, weeding and harvesting it – was necessary for the maintenance of human life, but physical labor wore the body down (cf. Otto 2004: 215), contributing to its decline and hastening its death. Similarly, all purposeful activities related to reproduction – from coitus to parturition to nursing – were thought to promote aging and death, for both male *and* female reproductive partners. The exotic practices and related fears (pertaining to menstruation, coitus and other intersexual contact) reported for the area affected by the Cult of Ain (Biersack 1987 and 2004: 109-111; Kyakas and Wiessner 1992: chapters 5 and 6; Meggitt 1964; Wiessner and Tumu 1998: 217-218) are only intelligible when placed within a wider cluster of beliefs and practices envisioning regeneration as a source or cause of aging and death.

The importance of the body and its materiality in this worldview cannot be overstated. In the Ipili understanding, the body made human beings creatures of need; it was the primal instrument used to meet these needs; it anchored human existence in a spatiotemporal order, the earth, the resources of which enabled the body to meet its material needs; and it was to the body specifically, to the physical side of human life, that the sacrificial principle pertained.

In all particulars, terrestrial life contrasted with sky life. At the close of some myths, sky men and women (*tawe wanda akali*) ascend to *tawe toko* or "the sky bridge" (Gibbs 1977: 9), where they live forever in workless bliss, free of horticulture and reproduction, fertility and regeneration, and thus death. But it was the sun (*nai, aluni, ni, nitawe, ewa, onewa*) rather than sky people who dominated the sky, and it is through the solar symbol that the significance of the sky is revealed. Whereas humans had mortal bodies that both required and enabled the manipulation of things – *peape* or work – and that suffered and died as a result, the sun had no body, performed no manipulations and existed forever as a transcendent being. Ascending to the sky was tantamount, then, to escaping the human condition of earth-boundedness and, with it, work and mortality, rendering human life "blissful" (Worsley 1968: 11).

This, the millenarian goal of *mata kamo*, was most evident in those aspects of *mata kamo* that embraced an ascent to the sky, with immortality as the attendant benefit. But this millenarian goal was also subtly encapsulated in the economics of those versions of the ritual that were wealth-seeking. The sacrificial principle is reciprocity or equivalence in its cruellest guise: a life for a life, the *bekim* ("to give in return", "to reciprocate") principle that explicitly informs eye-for-an-eye revenge killings and that implicitly defined the human condition as a mortal condition. The ritual instantiated, at least in participants' fantasies, a far more benign transactional regime. Participants would receive more and better or bigger than they gave – more and better or bigger pigs (the cow's tail again!) and superior white manufactured items (the steel axe, for example, houses with tin roofs, cars, etc.) – and they would do so without damaging or forfeiting their life. The wealth participants sought had two defining characteristics: the one already mentioned, that it was more and/or better and/or bigger, but also that little or no "work" was required to obtain it (cf. Bashkow 2006: 107-110). This shift – from balanced to generalized reciprocity (Sahlins 1972), as it were, humans becoming the beneficiaries of the sun's largesse – itself constituted a release from the harshness of the terrestrial condition to which human beings had been consigned. The requirement that human beings had to "work" and suffer the consequences of a dilapidated, increasingly immobile and ultimately dead body had in effect been rescinded. *Whether receiving windfall wealth or achieving immortality, the project was essentially the same: to liberate human beings from their abject terrestrial condition, governed as it was by the sacrificial principle.*

Those with whom I discussed the cult were aware of the transformational implications of its economics. Pimbisu, for example, put the prospects of participating in a new workless order this way in explaining why Tipininians were willing to enter a forest pool despite their fear of drowning: "Thinking that in that good land [the common epithet for the sky in the *mata kamo* context] they would eat while resting [that is, without labouring, eating freely] they went into the water" (*Yu epene okona oto no pitimakale nembo talu ipa okona peainipia*). Nane Pasia, an articulate Paiela who participated in *mata kamo* at Masiapulika and Politika [11] in the southwestern corner of the Paiela valley, added the further benefit of life everlasting in explaining to me in our October 2000 conversation why participants wanted to go to the sky. The ground was "bad", he said. It was where people worked very hard, suffered and died. But life was not harsh in the sky. There, "we would not work, garden, and build houses; we would only be happy. We would not be buried in the ground; we would live forever".

Whether through wealth acquisition and/or an ascent to the sky, cult participants sought a total transformation. The human condition as Ipili speakers defined it would give way to the cosmically privileged, "blissful" condition beyond work, suffering and death of the sun and the sky beings. Indeed, participants acted as if (in the words of Kau) they had already gone to the sky. The notion that there was no life without death, no renewal of life without the loss of life, was implicit in Ipili fears of intimacy with one's spouse (cf. Meggitt 1964 on parallel Enga fears). But in Paiela versions of the cult in particular, spouses fearlessly bathed naked together as if there were now no penalty for such intimacy. Here and there (at Taninga, on the western shore of the Pakupale River, for example), relatives coupled in violation of the local incest taboo, which precluded marriage between all kinspeople. While considerations of space prevent me from developing this point at length, suffice it to say that the organization of social networks through marriage ("the exchange of women" [*wanda lawa lawa pi*]) and sexual reproduction, all of which depended upon the incest taboo, was the most important and pervasive category of "work" that Ipili speakers undertook (Biersack 1995b: 233-247). To overthrow the incest taboo was to relinquish the most important tool Ipili speakers wielded, effectively voiding a vast domain of effort, from precontact rituals to prepare male youth for marriage, to fattening, assembling

---

11. There are two Politikas of which I am aware. One lies in the southwestern corner of the Paiela valley. The other lies in the northwestern corner of the Porgera valley. *Mata kamo* ritual was performed at Politika in the Porgera valley. Cult leaders then moved westward into the northeastern corner of the Paiela valley. The ritual was also either performed at Politika in the Paiela valley or it drew participants from that location.

and distributing bridewealth, to maintaining and repairing networks through further exchange, to bearing and rearing children.

Madness's Reason

This interpretation has explained some aspects and dimensions of the ritual – why pigs were sacrificed to the sun, the association of the sky with wealth and immortality, and how wealth acquisition and the achievement of immortality were at root millenarian in their implications – but it has not accounted for the shaking (cf. Schwartz 1962: *passim* on *guria* in the Paliau Movement) and the *ke* ("crazy" or "mad") state with which *mata kamo* or "shaking magic" was associated. Lattas (1992) has convincingly argued that the emphasis upon "madness" in the early ethnographies or ethnohistories of "cargo cults" – most notably in F. E. Williams' "The Vailala Madness" – must be understood in terms of colonialism, which, inherently racist and Orientalist, required an inferior, possibly wild and uncivilized, subjugated other (see Kaplan 1995, who makes a similar point for "cargo cult" per se). Were *mata kamo* participants "crazy" (and thus irrational and inferior), or is there some other way of understanding the state Ipili speakers call *ke*?

To understand the state of *ke* and its significance, it is necessary to consider Ipili constructions of the immaterial side of human existence. Porgeras and Paielas recognize a single faculty, *nembo*, which may then be translated as will, soul, spirit and heart and which I choose to translate as "mind" to reflect the *nembo*'s association with thinking, knowledge, wisdom and decision-making. The *nembo* is located in the *yamapane*, a complex of heart and lungs (linking *nembo* or mind with action and speech), and it "carries" *mana*, in this case a Papuan rather than an Austronesian word meaning knowledge (cf. Goldman 1983: 44-45). The root of all purposeful action or "work" (*peape*) is said to be the *nembo* and its *mana*. The expression "First the mind, then the body" or "First we think, then we act" (*nembo ini, angini matili*) encapsulates in singsong fashion the two-sidedness of action: mind, which bears knowledge and which makes decisions, but also bodily movement or effort, which implements that knowledge (cf. Otto 2004: 216). The sun, as the source of light, was also viewed as the source of *mana*. He was the source of ancestral knowledge (*yumbanena mana*), and he was the source of the new knowledge that governed *mata kamo* and directed participants away from ancestral knowledge and towards a new dispensation. To break with ancestral custom – the specific charge given to all cult participants – required adhering to a new *mana*, of which the sun – through his intermediaries, the cult leaders – was the only possible source.

As already indicated, *ke* means to "be confused; not know; not be in one's right mind, be crazy; be in trance" (Ingemann n.d.: n.p.). It translates into Neo-Melanesian *longlong* or "crazy" and *spak* or "drunk". In my understanding of the term, the state of *ke* is symptomatic of a voiding of mind. A person who is *ke* is expected to act wildly or randomly (*ambe pua*), as if there were no mind governing the act. A "crazy" person is a person who "has no *nembo*" (*nembo na yene*). A new material world had been glimpsed (that of white people and their material culture), and/or a blissful state – free of hard work, suffering and death – was now sought. *Ke* could be interpreted as that liminal state in which the old learning was negated, making way for new knowledge, knowledge that would reform or revolutionize human existence.

Or *ke* could be interpreted as a state of trance in which participants communicated with the sun. Sharp's observations of the cult at Lyeimi, where the Cult of Ain started, are suggestive in this regard. He writes of the cult leader ("L.") there: "when offering cooked meat of sacrificed pigs while standing on a high platform L. stared at the sun and his body shook violently [...]. Observers felt at this time that he was communicating directly with the sun deity, because cultural expectation is that shaking means communication with spirits" (1990: 114). A patrol officer named Graham Hardy talked to the last surviving Enga cult leader in April 1957 and reported that he had claimed "to have had inspirations from God, personified by the Sun, who appointed him a headman" (Laiagam Patrol Report 3, 1956/57: 11; see also Jacka 2002: 204).

Those with whom I have discussed *mata kamo* corroborated this understanding of the shaking and the "crazy" state associated with it. Ipili speakers imagined the sun as a single eye (*nai lene*), and to look at the sun along the shaft of a spear (which many did) was to "exchange glances" (*anda lawa lawa*) with the sun, the *sine qua non* of all actual communication, which Ipili speakers define in interactional, intercorporeal terms. And so, in "looking up" (*anda iyu pi*), Lapu told me in our conversation of December 1976, participants entered into communication (*nembo lawa lawa pi*, "to exchange minds") with the sun. Only a few did this, he said, all of them *mata akali* or "shaking men," as he called them. These shakers (Meggitt 1974: 25; Reithofer 2006: 195-196; Sharp 1990: 113) spoke strange words (*pi waka waka* [lit. "language other other"; "gibberish"]) which were understood to be the words of the sun, words that conveyed the sun's *mana* or knowledge. Mata, Lapu's relative and Kau's mother, also claimed in December 1976 that the cult leaders were transmitting the sun's thoughts directly to participants. Similarly, during my Tipinini research in fall 1993, Muyu told me that one of the Enga cult leaders had told him that what he divulged to participants originated with the sun.

In *mata kamo*, Ipili speakers established contact with the sun – either directly, by shaking and becoming *ke*, or indirectly through cult leaders serving as intermediaries – for the purpose of learning new *mana* or knowledge: how to sacrifice and to whom, what foods to avoid, what spells to say, what songs to sing, how to purify the body, whether to "keep a distance" and with respect to whom, and whom to marry. Armed with this new *mana* or knowledge, they hoped to revolutionize their existence, in ways that the sky and its beings symbolized. The millenarian project of *mata kamo*, to perfect human existence, was thus utterly dependent upon "madness": that state in which the old mind or knowledge was voided and communication with the source of the new, true knowledge was established.

Conclusions

Taking my cue from McDowell, I have approached *mata kamo* through the semantic field to which it so patently belonged: Ipili cosmology, centred as it was on the radical difference between immortal sky beings and mortal earth beings. I have argued that the cargoic features of *mata kamo* are to be understood with respect to *mata kamo*'s millenarian goal: the effort to achieve immortality by ascending to the sky. To obtain superior and abundant wealth without having to work for it signified the same amelioration of the human condition that an ascent to the sky signified: a shift from a life blighted by labor, suffering and death to a life emancipated from those travails. That participants cavorted in the water with their spouses suggests that they believed themselves to have already been liberated. They were, after all, no longer earthlings but "sky people".

I conclude that *mata kamo* is best understood as a millenarian cult or movement. The goal of *mata kamo* was to transform the human condition by rendering human beings (in the poetics of the ritual) sky beings: free from hard work and other suffering, free ultimately from death. Acquiring abundant, superior wealth in return for paltry, inferior wealth (the exchange of pig-scale pigs for cow-scale pigs, for example) advanced but did not attain this goal. In most (possibly all) cases, such acquisition was mediated by the sky and its beings, symbolically associating wealth acquisition with the ritual's true purpose: to set human life on another footing by celestializing it (cf. Biersack 1996: 104-109, 2005: 141-146; Golub 2001: 178).

Mata kamo is not the only case where wealth acquisition is associated with the restoration or achievement of a state of perfection *sans* suffering, labor and mortality. The well-known John Frum movement of Vanuatu, for example, rested on certain predictions that sickness and work would end (Sillitoe 2000: 186). Similarly, so-called cargo movements among the Western Dani of what is now West Papua were concerned less with inducing a windfall of cargo (although they were interested in that as well) than in recovering the state of immortality they believed themselves to have lost (Giay and Godschalk 1993). Schwartz's fascinating account of the Paliau Movement (1962) contains many instances in which the ambitions of a leader or follower far outstripped the mere acquisition of cargo, in ways that paralleled the aspirations of *mata kamo* leaders and followers. How "cargoistic" would so-called cargo cults look if they were examined from the perspective of those ritual goals that had nothing to do with acquiring wealth?

Following McDowell, I have here approached *mata kamo* semantically rather than intellectually, through the criterion of rationality, as Orientalist inscriptions of cargo cult have done. My concern throughout has been to understand *mata kamo* as a millenarian movement devoted to perfecting or idealizing the world and, along with it, human existence. There is no doubt that some versions of Meggitt's Cult of Ain focused to a degree on obtaining white wealth (see discussion in Biersack 2011b), as did the Tipinini variant of the Cult of Ain. In all cases, though, obtaining wealth was inextricable from the goal of ascending to the sky, where the conditions of human life would be ameliorated. As among Ipili speakers, so too among Enga speakers: the constant across all known variants of the Cult of Ain, whether or not cargo was sought, was the celestialization of human existence (*ibid.*).

I am not alone, of course, in associating cargo cults with millenarianism. In his powerful introduction to "Alienating Mirrors: Christianity, Cargo Cults and Colonialism in Melanesia", Lattas reminds us that "millenarian movements express the power of the human imagination to idealise and posit a better world which is without pain, suffering and work" (1992: 2), and he goes on to describe the idealizations inherent in Melanesian cargo cults (*ibid.*: 2-3). Robbins leaves no doubt that he sees "cargo cultism" as millenarian insofar as it rests upon a critique of the present and strives to achieve a utopian, or at least, superior future (2004). Worsley, too, wrote of cargo cults as millenarian movements. "I use the term 'millenarian' to describe those move-ments in which there is an expectation of, and preparation for, the coming of a period of supernatural bliss" (1968: 12). The return of the ancestors, or "God, or some other liberating power" (*ibid.*: 11) would usher in the "reign of eternal bliss" (*ibid.*) that Worsley associated with millenarian movements. Similarly, Kenelm Burridge said of "cargo activities" that they envisaged "both new spiritual values (a new heaven) and a renewed sociomoral, economic, and political order (a new earth)" (1993: 276) and that they could therefore "be called millenarian type" (*ibid.*; see also Burridge 1969; Kamma 1972).

Worsley points out that millenarian movements are not restricted to Melanesia but "have occurred throughout the world" (*ibid.*; see also Stewart and Strathern 2002: 71), and it is in exploring so-called cargo cults as millenarian movements that the possibility of de-exoticizing them and of rendering them not only intelligible but *familiar* lies. This account of *mata kamo* has opened a window on the similarities as opposed to the differences between Melanesians and Westerners (see McDowell 2000). Any culturally competent Westerner would understand the thematics of *mata kamo*. They are even expressed in what to Westerners would be quite familiar tropes of sky and earth, life and death, mortality and immortality, a point that Burridge was careful to make as well (1969, 1993: 276). Since *mata kamo* and other variants of the Cult of Ain occurred in the mid-1940s, before the arrival of the missionaries in the area, and since many who have described the Cult of Ain have commented on the relevance of indigenous cosmology to its principal features, we can be certain that these tropes are *indigenous*. There are, then, substantial discursive similarities between Ipili speakers and Westerners, similarities that give the lie to the us/them binarism underlying Orientalist representations in general and Lindstrom's (1993) "cargoism" in particular. Aspects of *mata kamo* and the broader cult environment in which it arose do concern wealth acquisition, but these aspects must be understood with respect to the "semantic field" (McDowell 1988: 122) that gave them their meaning. This meaning, moreover, was millenarian: a matter of achieving a radical transformation in the human condition. The implication is clear: the way beyond Lindstrom's "cargoism" (1993) – which reads "a few features" (McDowell 1988: 121) as irrational, materialist and primitive – lies in interpreting so-called cargo cults as aspects of millenarian movements (cf. Otto 2009). Only then will it be possible to come to know their informing philosophies and their true aspirations – and to understand those caught up in them in their own terms. This, in turn, will return us to the ethnographic enterprise of opening "ourselves to the understanding of other cultures" (Robbins 2004: 257) and those who live and operate with respect to their parameters.

Coda

Sharp's article on the Cult of Ain provides us with further details on Wambilipi, the longest-living of the four brothers who inaugurated the cult. Wambilipi ("W." in Sharp's account) refused baptism in the late 1960s, when others of his clan had converted, because he considered himself to be a prophet of the same stature as John the Baptist and, in any case, he considered himself to have "introduced the ritual [baptism] [...]. There were none equal to him who could baptise him. When the others were baptised by the Lutheran pastor W. baptised himself. In the 1960s W. went to Laiagama [aka Laiagam] patrol post and approved of the Apostolic church there. He did not join the church there but said it was they who were joining him. The parishioners of this church opposed many traditions of this area. They smashed painted skulls [...]. They threw *kepele* stones [special ritual stones] into the river. Their services included speaking in tongues and they also conducted mass baptisms in rivers." (1990: 116)

Sharp goes on to note that Wambilipi "was reported as saying he was responsible for bringing the church and health services to the people. Because he was not being given his due he would take them away again" (*ibid.*). As a medical officer working with the Department of Health in Papua New Guinea, Sharp displayed in his article a tendency (uncomfortable to me) to medicalize the persons and phenomena he came across. To him, Wambilipi "had grandiose ideas, a nihilistic view of the world" (*ibid.*: 117), and clearly suffered from delusions of grandeur.

But was he delusional – or "mad", for that matter? Those who knew Wambilipi did not think so. Sharp asked them whether Wambilipi was *longlong* or "crazy", and he could find only one person who said yes. This person, moreover, was an aid post orderly with basic medical training (*ibid.*: 116), whose outlook could have been corrupted by his training. Some others said that Wambilipi "was possessed by a supernatural force, the implication being that it was little wonder his acts were sometimes difficult to understand or that occasionally he [...] behaved strangely" (*ibid.*). My guess is that Wambilipi's people continued to see him as a visionary, as indeed "possessed by a supernatural force" (*ibid.*), long after the cult had ended.

Most ethnohistorians of the Cult of Ain have observed that participants and their descendants consider the cult to have been successful in the long (if not the short) run (Biersack 1991; 1996: 100-101; 2005: 148-152; Gibbs 1977: 22-25; Golub 2006: 276-277; Jacka 2002: 207-210; Reithofer 2006: 2008-210; Wiessner and Tumu 2001: 317-318) because the transformations it promised have come true, at least to a degree. Although people are not immortal, with the introduction of Western medicine, they are healthier and live longer. Cows and sheep have been introduced, every man owns a steel axe, there is wage labor and other sources of cash income, and the possibility of "eating, resting", as it were, by buying rather than producing food for a perceived net saving of labor, exists today. Roads, vehicles and planes "make the far near", reducing the effort required to travel distances. When viewed through an Ipili lens, development *is* a millenarian project. As Lapu told me in December 1976, "The white man came and we are good now [...]. Now that the white man has come, our cargo [he used the word *pinju*, one of two categories of traditional wealth; *pinju* was the non-pig category] is big, our pigs are big, we eat the good food of the white man, we receive the white man's medicine [and, by implication, are less sick], and [hyperbole!] we don't die."

Ipili speakers divide purposive activity into two stages: the first stage, a planning or otherwise preliminary stage of laying the groundwork, and a second stage of completion and consummation. The first stage is considered necessary for the second stage to occur. The first stage – referred to as "merely trying" (*me makande pi*): to merely "get ready; try" (Ingemann n.d.: n.p) – is a stage of conceptualization involving the use of symbols and language. The second stage actualizes or realizes what was prepared for or attempted in the first stage, the word *angini* or "body" referring to this actualization or realization. In assembling bridewealth, for example, the first stage is preoccupied with collecting pledges. These are verbal, and they will be symbolized by small sticks (*sia kai*) that bridewealth accumulators count as they prepare for the prestation. The second stage involves assembling the pledged pigs, tying them to stakes on the dance ground and giving and distributing them. Pledged pigs tied to stakes in a context of prestation (the dance ground) are the "body": the project's coming to fruition as an imagined event, depicted in the language of the pledge, gives way to the actual event (the "body") in all its tangibility. A more exotic example of these two stages lies in the realm of magic and ritual. These set the stage for a desired outcome but cannot themselves, as linguistic, symbolic performances, realize that outcome. Only the events that magical spells and ritual anticipate can do that – can "become body" (*angini gu la*).

Those with whom I discussed *mata kamo* spontaneously drew parallels between *mata kamo* and the discourses, ideologies and practices of colonialism and Christianity. In regard to Christianity: the "sky water" (*tawe ipa*) that was drunk in some places constituted the first communion, some say; the ritual bathing was the first baptism; the missionaries advocated, as had the "spellmen" of *mata kamo*, the abandonment of traditional ritual in favour of new rituals; Christianity, with its notion of a merit-based heavenly afterlife, has confirmed, at least for observant people of faith, the ascent to the sky that *mata kamo* participants believed possible; and Christian themes and imagery – from the notion of a "garden of Eden" paradise to the resurrection story to the theme of purity to the symbolism of water and light – strongly resonate with those of indigenous cosmology and the philosophical anthropology that underlay it. On the secular side: Ipili speakers see a connection between the Pax Australianis of the colonial period and the prohibition of warfare in *mata kamo*; the *mana* taught by the Engan cult leaders is now widely regarded as having been "the white person's *mana*" (*onena mana*); and, overall, there is a sense in which development broadly construed – the creation of roads, the introduction of money and wage labor, the building and staffing of Western-style schools – is thought to have a millenarian impact. In short, the agenda of *mata kamo*, from acquiring wealth – most notably these days through gold mining, with its promise of windfall wealth (see Golub 2006: 277-279; Macintyre Ch. 5; see also Biersack 1999: 79) – to improving one's health to achieving immortality – persists to this day, infusing the everyday with a millenarian significance (Biersack 1991: 276-283, 1996: 101-111, 2005: 146-152; cf. Robbins 2001, 2004: 251). *Mata kamo*, in short, is viewed as the prequel to the present-day sequel, as the first stage of a two-stage process, the second stage, the "body" stage, being the world the Ipili inhabit today.

I interviewed Lapu in 1976, the year that Sharp talked to Wambilipi. Their perspectives, I suspect, were the same. History had vindicated the sons of Ain, who had prepared the way for the cult's sequel: the transformations that have accompanied colonialism and missionization but viewed within this optic as the culmination of the *mata kamo* project. From this perspective there was nothing delusional about Wambilipi. He did indeed introduce baptism, the destruction of *kepele* paraphernalia and ancestral skulls, the practice of speaking in tongues. If the Baptists were now indulging in these practices, they were indeed joining Wambilipi, not the other way around! They were his "body", the actualization of what had only been conceptualized and symbolized in the ritual he had done so much to promote some thirty years before in making preparations for the triumphant final stage of the Cult of Ain: the contemporary Ipili and Enga world.

Acknowledgments

I am heavily indebted to several generous funding agencies: to the National Science Foundation, which funded my first and longest stay in the Paiela valley; Wenner-Gren, which funded research from July 1993 to winter 1995; to a Fulbright Scholar Research Award, for funding from July 1995-February 1996; to Wenner-Gren and the American Philosophical Society, for funding in fall 1999 and 2000; and to a Fulbright-Hays Faculty Research Abroad progam award, for research in 2003-2004. I have received excellent logistical support from the Society of the Divine Word, Enga diocese, and in particular from Father Edward Osiecki, Father Andrew Sobon, Father Anton Somhorst, Father Henry Adler, Father Peter Weo and Father Casimir Niezgoda. Graham Taylor, Stephen Hepworth and Sam Adam have also helped me logistically. Hans Reithofer's critique of another of my papers on *mata kamo* has proved most useful in the writing of this paper. Meggitt's "The Sun and the Shakers" has, of course, been crucial to this effort to interpret the Cult of Ain. While doing my research, I was affiliated, initially, with the Department of Sociology, Anthropology, and Social Work of the University of Papua New Guinea. More recently I have been affiliated with the National Research Institute, receiving assistance from Michael Laki, James Robins and Colin Filer. Terry Borchard and Frances Ingemann, who have studied the Ipili language, have graciously fielded questions I put to them. During summer 2010, I benefited from conversations I had about the Cult of Ain with Chris Ballard, Father Philip Gibbs and Hans Reithofer, although any mistakes of fact or interpretation here are necessarily my own. I am most grateful to the people of the Porgera and Paiela valleys, who have tolerated my many questions and my presence over many field seasons, and who have done so always with warmth and humour. For the purpose of this writing, Lapu, Mata, Pilato, Kauwambo, Luke Pakena, Muyu, Peter Muyu, Pimbisu, Kainu, Kaiya, Yakob, Nane Pasia, and Lewambo and his wife Tendi should be singled out.

Bibliography

Primary sources

Wabag Patrol Report 2, 1952-1953. Available at the Papua New Guinea National Archive.
Wabag Patrol Report 8, 1952-1953. Available at the Papua New Guinea National Archive.
Laiagam Patrol Report 3, 1956-1957.

Secondary sources

Allen, Bryant J., and Wood, Andrew
1980   "Legendary Volcanic Eruptions and the Huli, Papua New Guinea", *Journal of the Polynesian Society*, 89(3): 341-347.

Bashkow, Ira
2006   *The Meaning of Whitemen: Race & Modernity in the Orokaiva Cultural World*. Chicago: University of Chicago Press.

Biersack, Aletta
1987   "Moonlight: Negative Images of Transcendence in Paiela Pollution", *Oceania*, 57(3): 178-194.
1991   "Prisoners of Time: Millenarian Praxis in a Melanesian Valley". In A. Biersack (ed.), *Clio in Oceania: Toward a Historical Anthropology*. Washington, D.C.: Smithsonian University Press, pp. 231-296.
1995a   "Introduction: The Huli, Duna, and Ipili Peoples Yesterday and Today". In A. Biersack (ed.), *Papuan Borderlands: Huli, Duna, and Ipili Perpsectives on the Papua New Guinea Highlands*, Washington, D.C.: Smithsonian Institution Press, pp. 1-56.

1995b   "Heterosexual Meanings: Society, Economy, and Gender among Ipilis". In A. Biersack (ed.), *Papuan Borderlands*, Ann Arbor: The University of Michigan Press, pp. 229-261.

1996   "Word Made Flesh: Religion, the Body, and the Economy in the Paiela World", *History of Religions,* 36(2): 85-111.

1998   "Sacrifice and Regeneration among Ipilis: The View from Tipinini". In L. R. Goldman and C. Ballard (eds), *Fluid Ontologies: Myth, Ritual and Philosophy in the Highlands of Papua New Guinea,* Westport: Bergin & Garvey, pp. 43-66.

1999   "The Mount Kare Python and His Gold: Totemism and Ecology in the Papua New Guinea Highlands". In A. Biersack (ed.), *Ecologies for Tomorrow: Reading Rappaport Today*, a contemporary issue forum, *American Anthropologist,* 101(1): 68-87.

2001   "Reproducing Inequality: The Gender Politics of Male Cults in Melanesia and Amazonia". In T. Gregor and D. Tuzin (eds), *Gender in Amazonia and Melanesia: An Exploration of the Comparative Method,* Berkeley: University of California Press, pp. 69-90.

2004   "The Bachelors and Their Spirit Wife: Porgera and Paiela Perspectives on New Guinea Male Rituals". In P. Bonnemère (ed.), *The Unseen Characters: Women in Male Rituals of Papua New Guinea,* Philadelphia: University of Pennsylvania Press, pp. 98-119.

2005   "On the Life and Times of the Ipili Imagination". In J. Robbins and H. Wardlow (eds), *The Making of Global and Local Modernities in Melanesia: Humiliation, Transformation and the Nature of Cultural Change,* Burlington, VT: Ashgate, pp. 135-162.

2011a   "The Sun and the Shakers, Again: Enga, Ipili, and Somaip Perspectives on the Cult of Ain. Part One", *Oceania,* 81(2): 113-136.

2011b   "The Sun and the Shakers, Again: Enga Ipili, and Somaip Perspectives on the Cult of Ain. Part Two", *Oceania,* 81(3): 225-243.

Bloch, Maurice, and Parry, Jonathan (eds)
1982   *Death and the Regeneration of Life*. Cambridge: Cambridge University Press.

Brennan, Paul
1977   *Let Sleeping Snakes Lie*. Australian Association for the Study of Religions, Special Studies, No. 1. Bedford Park, South Australia: Sturt College of Advanced Education.

Buchbinder, Georgeda and Rappaport, Roy A
1976   "Fertility and Death among the Maring". In P. Brown and G. Buchbinder (eds), *Man and Woman in the New Guinea Highlands,* Washington, D. C.: The American Anthropological Association, pp. 1-35.

Burridge, Kenelm
1969   *New Heaven, New Earth: A Study of Millenarian Activities*. New York: Schocken Books.

1993   "Melanesian Cargo Cults". In V. Lockwood (ed.), *Contemporary Pacific Societies*. Englewood Cliffs, N. J.: Prentice-Hall, pp. 275-288.

Clark, Jeffrey
1992   "Madness and Colonisation: The Embodiment of Power in Pangia". In A. Lattas (ed.), *Alienating Mirrors: Christianity, Cargo Cults and Colonialism in Melanesia,* Special Issue of *Oceania* 63(1): 15-26.

Clifford, James
1986   "Partial Truths". In J. Clifford and G. E. Marcus (eds), *Writing Culture: The Poetics and Politics of Ethnography,* Berkeley: University of California Press, pp. 1-26.

Dalton, Doug

2000a   "Introduction". In D. Dalton (ed.), *A Critical Retrospective on 'Cargo Cult':*
         Western/Melanesian Intersections, Special Issue of *Oceania*, 70(4): 285-293.

2000b   "Cargo Cults and Discursive Madness". In D. Dalton (ed.), *A Critical Retrospective on*
         'Cargo Cult': Western/Melanesian Intersections, *Oceania*, 70(4): 345-361. [Special issue.]

2004   "Cargo and Cult: The Mimetic Critique of Capitalist Culture". In H. Jebens (ed.), *Cargo,*
         Cult, and Culture Critique, Honolulu: University of Hawaii Press, pp. 187-208.

Feil, Daryl

1983   "A World Without Exchange: Millennia and the Tee Ceremonial System in
         Tombema-Enga Society (New Guinea)", *Anthropos*, 78: 89-106.

Frankel, Stephen

1986   *The Huli Response to Illness*. Cambridge: Cambridge University Press.

Giay, Benny, and Godschalk, Jan A.

1993   "Cargoism in Irian Jaya Today", *Oceania*, 63(4): 330-344.

Gibbs, Philip J.

1977   "The Cult from Lyeimi and the Ipili", *Oceania*, 48(1): 1-25.

1978   "The *Kepele* Ritual of the Western Highlands of Papua New Guinea",
         Anthropos, 73: 434-448.

Glasse, Robert M.

1995   "Time Belong *Mbingi*: Religious Syncretism and the Pacification of the Huli". In
         A. Biersack (ed.), *Papuan Borderlands: Huli, Duna, and Ipili Perspectives on the Papua New*
         Guinea Highlands. Ann Arbor: University of Michigan Press, pp. 57-86.

Golub, Alex

2001   *Gold +ve: A Short History of Porgera 1930-1997*. Porgera Development Authority
         Monographs. Mt. Hagen: Porgera Development Authority.

2006   "Who Is the 'Original Affluent Society'?: Ipili Predatory expansion and the Porgera Gold
         Mine". In P. West and M. Macintyre (eds), *Melanesian Mining Modernities: Past, Present,*
         and Future, Special Issue of *The Contemporary Pacific*, 18(2): 265-292.

Goldman, Laurence

1983   *Talk Never Dies: The Language of Huli Disputes*. London: Tavistock.

Harding, Thomas

1967   "A History of Cargoism in Sio, North-East New Guinea", *Oceania*, 38(1):1-23.

Harkin, Michael

2004   "Introduction". In M. E. Harkin (ed.), *Revitalization Movements: Perspectives from North*
         America and the Pacific Islands, Lincoln and London: University of Nebraska Press.

Hermann, Elfriede

1992   "The Yali Movement in Retrospect: Rewriting History, Redefining 'Cargo Cult'". In
         A. Lattas (ed.), *Alienating Mirrors: Christianity, Cargo Cults and colonialism in Melanesia*,
         Oceania 63(1): 55-71. [Special issue.]

Ingemann Frances

         n.d. Ipili Dictionary. Typescript.

Jacka, Jerry
2002   "Cults and Christianity among the Enga and Ipili", *Oceania*, 72(3): 196-214.
2003   God, Gold, and the Ground: Place-Based Political Ecology in a New Guinea Borderlands.
        PhD thesis, University of Oregon.

Kamma, Freerk Ch.
1972   *Koreri: Messianic Movements in the Biak-Numfor Culture Area.*
        The Hague: Martinus Nijhoff.

Kaplan, Martha
1995   *Neither Cargo Nor Cult: Ritual Politics and the Colonial Imagination in Fiji.*
        Durham: Duke University Press.

Kyakas, Alome, and Wiessner, Polly
1992   *From Inside the Women's House: Enga Women's Lives and Traditions.*
        Buranda, Queensland: Robert Brown and Associates.

Lattas, Andrew
1992   "Hysteria, Anthropological Disclosure and the Concept of the Unconscious: Cargo Cults
        and the Scientisation of Race and Colonial Power". In A. Lattas (ed.), *Alienating Mirrors:
        Christianity, Cargo Cults and Colonialism in Melanesia*, Special Issue of *Oceania*, 63(1): 1-14.
2007   "Cargo Cults and the Politics of Alterity: A Review Article".
        Anthropological Forum, 17(2):149-161.

Leavitt, Stephen
2004   "From 'Cult' to Religious Conviction: The Case for Making Cargo Personal". In H. Jebens
        (ed.), *Cargo, Cult, and Culture Critique*. Honolulu: University of Hawaii Press, pp.170-186.

Lévi-Strauss, Claude
1963   *Totemism*. Boston: Beacon Press.

Lindstrom, Lamont
1993   *Cargo Cult: Strange Stories of Desire from Melanesia and Beyond.*
        Honolulu: University of Hawaii Press.
2000   "Cargo Cult Horror". *Oceania*, 70(4): 294-303.
2004   "Cargo Cult at the Third Millennium". In H. Jebens (ed.), *Cargo, Cult, and Culture Critique*.
        Honolulu: University of Hawaii Press.

Marcus, George E., and Fischer, Michael
1999   *Anthropology as Cultural Critique*. [2nd edition.] Chicago: University of Chicago Press.

McDowell, Nancy
1988   "A Note on Cargo Cults and Cultural Constructions of Change",
        Pacific Studies, 11(2): 121-134.
2000   "A Brief Comment on Difference and Rationality". In D. Dalton (ed.), *A Critical
        Retrospective on 'Cargo Cult': Western/Melanesian Intersections*, Special Issue of
        Oceania, 70(4): 373-380.

Meggitt, Mervyn J.
1956   "The Valleys of the Upper Wage and Lai Rivers, Western Highlands, New Guinea",
        Oceania 27(2): 90-135.

Meggitt, Mervyn J.

1965   "The Mae Enga of the Western Highlands". In P. Lawrence and M. J. Meggitt, *Gods Ghosts and Men in Melanesia: Some Religions of Australian New Guinea and the New Hebrides*, Melbourne: Oxford University Press, pp. 105-131.

1973   "The Sun and the Shakers: A Millenarian Cult and Its Transformations in the New Guinea Highlands", *Oceania*, 44(2): 1-37, 109-126.

1974   "The Sun and the Shakers: A Millenarian Cult and Its Transformations in the New Guinea Highlands". In *Studies in Enga History*, Oceania Monograph no. 21: 1-56. Sydney: University of Sydney Press.

Otto, Ton

1992   "Introduction: Imagining Cargo Cults". In T. Otto (ed.), *Imagining Cargo Cults*. Special Issue of *Canberra Anthropology*, 15(2): 1-10.

2004   "Work, Wealth, and Knowledge: Enigmas of Cargoist Identifications". In H. Jebens (ed.), *Cargo, Cult, and Culture Critique*, Honolulu: University of Hawaii Press, pp. 209-226.

2009   "What Happened to Cargo Cults? Material Religions in Melanesia and the West", *Social Analysis*, 53(1): 82-102.

Raich, H.

1967   "Ein weiteres Fruchtbarkeits Idol aus den westlichen Hochland von Neuguinea", *Anthropos*, 62: 938-939.

Reithofer, Hans

2006   *The Python Spirit and the Cross: Becoming Christian in a Highland Community of Papua New Guinea*. Berlin: Lit Verlag.

Robbins, Joel

2001   "Secrecy and the Sense of an Ending: Narrative, Time and Everyday Millenarianism in Papua New Guinea and in Christian Fundamentalism", *Comparative Studies in Society and History*, 43(3): 525-551.

2004   "On the Critique in Cargo and the Cargo in Critique: Toward a Comparative Anthropology of Critical Practice". In H. Jebens (ed.), *Cargo, Cult, and Culture Critique*. Honolulu: University of Hawaii Press, pp. 243-282.

Rutherford, Danilyn

2005   "Review of Clive Moore, New Guinea: Crossing Boundaries and History", *Journal of the Economic and Social History of the Orient*, 48(1): 136-138.

Sahlins, Marshall

1972   "On the Sociology of Primitive Exchange". In *Stone Age Economics*. New York: Aldine-Atherton, pp. 185-230.

Schwartz, Theodore

1962   "The Paliau Movement in the Admiralty Islands, 1946-1954". *Anthropological Papers of the American Museum of Natural History* 49, Part 2. New York: The American Museum of Natural History, pp. 211-421.

Sharp, Peter T.

1990   "The Searching Sun: The Lyeime Movement – Crisis, Tragic Events and Folie à Deux in the Papua New Guinea Highlands", *Papua New Guinea Medical Journal*, 33: 111-120.

Sillitoe, Paul

2000   "Cargo Cults and Millennial Politics". In *Social Change in Melanesia: Development and History*. Cambridge: Cambridge University Press, pp. 181-197.

Strathern, Andrew, and Stewart, Pamela J.

2002   "The South-West Pacific". In A. Strathern, P. Stewart, L. Carruci, L. Poyer, R. Feinberg, and C. Macpherson (eds), *Oceania: An Introduction to the Cultures and Identities of Pacific Islanders*. Durham: Carolina Academic Press, pp. 11-98.

Wiessner, Polly, and Tumu, Akii

1998   *Historical Vines: Enga Networks of Exchange, Ritual, and Warfare in Papua New Guinea*. Washington and London: Smithsonian Institution Press.

2001   "Averting the Bush Fire Day: Ain's Cult Revisited". In E. Messer and M. Lambek (eds), *Ecology and the Sacred: Engaging the Anthropology of Roy A. Rappaport*. Ann Arbor: University of Michigan Press, pp. 300-323.

Worsley, Peter

1968   *The Trumpet Shall Sound: A Study of "Cargo" Cults in Melanesia*. [2nd edition.] New York: Schocken Books.

Chapter 5

Instant Wealth: Visions of the Future on Lihir, New Ireland, Papua New Guinea

Martha Macintyre

'This is something really good for Lihirian people. It gives them the confidence they need to stop being dependent on the mine.' (M, Lihirian Businesswoman)

'Some things are very good, because we Lihirians are ignorant about business. PV teaches us how to make money and keep it.' (K, Lihirian mining company employee)

'It's just a course that teaches people how to have a work ethic and how to think about money and not throw it away. I don't think it tells us anything new about being Christian. It makes you think about how to build up your family.' (H, Villager from Niolam, Lihir)

'This will enable us to really develop our place. It has a strategic plan for development that will enable us to all be rich long after the mine has gone. We are concerned for our future and the future of Lihirian people for ever.' (F, Local Level Government Councilor)

'Petztorme [the women's organization] should organize Personal Viability training for all women. Because then we will find money.' (Lihirian village woman)

'Well, I don't know about this 'Personal Viability', it seems a bit (pauses, searching for word) 'cultic' to me.' (B, Local Government Councilor).

'There are lots of good things [about PV] but, it's a bit (pauses, searches for word) outrageous thinking you can do anything just by putting your mind to it.'(L, Lihirian Businessman)

'This is just another way of trying to get people to support his way, it's all trying to distract people from the broken promises he made. It is just politics. It is really MS's fault. He's the one who went around telling people that when the mine came there would be so much money they'd be using kina to shoot birds with. He created the unrealistic expectations about instant money.' (M, Lihirian woman – mine employee)

'It's the same as Nimamar and Society Reform – just another cargo cult.'(Mesulam Aisoli, New Irelander who had been working in Community Relations at the mine since 1986)

The variation in local responses to the emergent social movement on Lihir over the years echoes the range of interpretations that anthropologists have offered for cargo cults (Lindstrom 1993). The yearning for economic 'development'; for the new businesses it will generate and the prosperity it promises; for political self-determination and the chance to acquire the knowledge and skills that until now have been monopolized by white men, are all elements of the ideology that is being offered as 'Personal Viability'. But this movement is the latest in a sequence. While it is new in some respects, Personal Viability as it is now manifest has incorporated the ideas and many of the political and economic aims of its predecessors (see also Bainton 2006, 2008, 2010).

The Lihir island group in New Ireland Province has been the site of a large gold mine since 1996. The mine site is a caldera adjacent to a large harbor and initially required the relocation of three villages. It has transformed people's lives as the company has built roads, an airport, schools and a thriving township. People have employment now, in the mine and in numerous businesses that have emerged in its wake and over a thousand employees work there on a fly-in/fly-out basis (see Bainton 2010: 13-39). The wealth from the mine has meant that the Government of Papua New Guinea and New Ireland Province have gained material benefits and new infrastructure associated with economic development. Lihirian people are now materially richer than ever before, yet like its predecessors, this new social movement has been able to attract large numbers of followers. Many are disenchanted with the 'development' the mine has brought as some have benefited more than others; few have gained the wealth they dreamed of when the mining company was negotiating the lease on Niolam, the main island. Lihirians have been unable to control and manage the mining operation that they see as their own. Moreover, the relationship between white expatriates (who mainly work in managerial or senior positions) and black Lihirians (who are predominately unskilled workers or unemployed by the mining company) has perpetuated the old colonial hierarchy. The wealth has come, but it has not transformed society and Lihirians see themselves as having been duped by the government and the expatriate mine owners and managers.

The current organization is known by various names – its political manifestation in 2004 was the *Lihir Pawa Mekim Kamap Asosiesen*, perhaps best translated as the 'Lihir Development Association'. The use of the Tok Pisin term *pawa* (power) is significant of the relationship between knowledge, especially esoteric knowledge, and the capacity to exert control over people and things. Powerful knowledge (Lihirian *anitua*) is considered to be embodied and to constitute the basis for effective action. When applied to a sorcerer, for example, the knowledge of *words* that can cause something to happen is manifest in the sorcerer's capacity to change form (to become a snake or an insect, for instance). Spirit beings (Lihirian *tandal*; Tok Pisin *masalai*), epitomize this fusion of esoteric knowledge, shape-changing and the capacity to influence events and effect change.

The doctrinal basis of this new movement is a motivational course called *Personal Viability* offered by a Chinese businessman from Rabaul, Samuel Tan, who runs a franchise company that operates out of East Sepik Province. His training program has been taken up by many businesses, government departments and organizations throughout Papua New Guinea. On Lihir it has inspired a complex social movement that extends its scope beyond self-improvement and the development of entrepreneurial skills to encompass every aspect of people's existence. Its manifesto or vision for the future is known as the *Lihir Destiny* (Bainton 2010). Led by a group of influential, educated Lihirians who are members of the committee that formally negotiates with the mining company over benefits to Lihirians, this new movement represents the latest manifestation of a cultic movement that began in entirely different economic and political circumstances more than thirty years ago.

Lihirian people are familiar with 'cargo cults' – indeed it is about the only thing the island was known for prior to the discovery of gold – for at one local election in the 1970s the majority of people were persuaded by the cult leader to vote for Jesus Christ (see also Bainton 2010: 55-72). But as the comments cited above illustrate, people adhere or object to the cult ideologies for quite different reasons. Cargo cults have been analyzed and interpreted in ways that tend to smooth out the debates *within* communities in their attempts to explain the rise of cults and cultic adherence in broad social or cultural terms. Lihir fits many of the theoretical models. In some ways it conforms to Worsley's view that cults arise in situations of relative deprivation (Worsley 1957) and this explanation is often voiced by Lihirians. In the past the island people were a marginal rural community with a small population who saw themselves as excluded from the benefits enjoyed by New Irelanders who lived close to the provincial center, Kavieng. Lihirian political movements, in both their cultic and 'secular' manifestations, have consistently been anti-colonial, anti-State and exclusive. They have also been millenarian, looking to a utopian future when their deceased ancestors would return with the material goods that white people had unjustly kept to themselves.

The political and social changes that have been identified as catalysts for such movements affect everybody – but individuals and groups respond in a range of ways. Moreover, some of the people who are in similar social positions differ in their interpretation of the meaning of the movement and in their reasons for joining or keeping their distance.

The 'irrational', the puzzling and the strikingly 'exotic' or theatrical responses are those that attract attention – and make for more entertaining reading – but in foregrounding these, we obscure the range of adherents and homogenize the people involved. For on Lihir, as my brief collection of quotes reveals – there are skeptics, opponents, people who embrace one aspect of the movement and reject others, as well as the enthusiasts, the timid adherents, and the opportunists. In the search for explanations and analyses that produce typologies, anthropology perhaps has glossed over the internal dissent that accompanies cargo cults and homogenized the motivations of those who join. But as the history of these movements on Lihir demonstrates, the perduring element is that their adherents join in the hope that they will gain access to wealth. While there are some, like Bruno, who perceive this as access to jobs and to markets for their produce (who in effect accept Western ideas about the ways that wealth can be generated) and participate in the movements because they see them as vehicles for economic development; there are many who do not. They stress the access to capital as the starting point for wealth generation – and that capital, in the form of cash, is often conceptualized as suddenly appearing without having been 'earned'. It is, I maintain, a mystery that has to be tapped and mastered. Once this mastery is effected, then it will instantly appear.

TKA/Nimamar

In 1969 people all over Lihir were caught up in a social movement that began on the island of New Hanover. The New Hanover cult has been written about by Dorothy Billings, who followed its various manifestations from 1964 to the present (Billings 2002). Known initially as the Johnson Cult, the cult attained international fame, for one of its political objectives was to persuade President Johnson to take over the government of New Hanover (Lindstrom 1993: 155-6). To this end people collected money from members which was meant to be sent to the United States and pay for Johnson's fare. The aim was to oust the Australian government (who had done nothing to advance the economic development of New Hanoverians), and to attract wealth, support, and knowledge from America. As with many other such cults, some followers believed that Americans were ancestors. One of the catalysts had been the visit of several US military mappers, who had placed cement markers with brass plaques on them in various places. These objects, with the mysterious message "US Army – War Department – Corps of Engineers. Bench Mark. $250 fine or imprisonment for disturbing this mark." (Billings 2002: 80) were interpreted as signs from ancestors in the form of Americans.

In 1966 the Roman Catholic priest at Lavongai, Father Bernie Miller, effectively intervened in the Johnson Cult and was instrumental in 'converting' it into a social movement that drew people together through co-operative copra production projects. The membership was almost exactly the same, but the activities were directed to more mundane material ends. It was renamed TIA (Tutukuval Isukal Association – "Stand Up Together and Plant"). It was this organization that became the prototype for the TKA (the acronym for the same words in Lihirian) on Lihir.

A Lihirian, Theodore Arau, who had been living in a village near Kavieng moved back to Lihir in August 1969 and began to persuade people there to set up their own 'branches' of the organization. Within three months more than half the population (of 4500) had joined (Ramstandt: 1) and it continued to expand throughout the early 1970s. In many formal respects it was similar to the TKA as it was institutionalized on New Ireland. People paid membership fees of $12 (that were sent back to NI to be used to pay 'for the Americans to come'), they had regular meetings and bought plantations. By Ramstadt's estimations these were small and 'a rather poor foundation for economic development – averaging only 6 palms per member'[p1]. Arau's leadership rested not only on his being the originator but on his reputation as having magical knowledge and familiarity with the ways of white people. Stories of his travelling by submarine to New Ireland, communicating with ancestral spirits and being able to magically influence people and heal illness reinforced his reputation and were part of his 'charisma'. But Ramstadt observed that he '... represent[ed] an extreme example of a trait common to all charismatic leaders, namely that their followers attach to them qualities representing their own hopes and needs'(nd. 2).

In conversation with Ramstadt, Arau voiced the common belief that the 'real' secrets of European wealth and power were being withheld – 'they learn[ed] a little, but only 'about books' and not how to do the important things that made people rich'. (nd: 3) The idea that whites withhold the 'secrets of their success' by not teaching the critical knowledge that brings wealth has been observed in many cargo cults. Paradoxically this often generates activities that are imitative of schooling, such as reading and writing, at the same time as adherents refuse to accept institutional education (Swatridge 1985). The appropriation and cultic transformation of observed educational practices into rituals that will effectively redeem and empower people who have been disenfranchised and demeaned by being 'illiterate' or 'school dropouts' (*cf.* Lattas 1998: 79) has been a consistent feature of Lihirian cultic activity.

Nimamar, as the cult was renamed, encompassed many of the attributes of the classic 'cargo cult' – it held out the promise of access to wealth; it looked forward to a time when Lihirians would not have to work so hard for a living and incorporated activities that were imitative of the 'work' of white men who organized development cooperatives. It also involved ritualistic emulation of aspects of colonial or European collective behaviour (especially the creation of social groups that cut across or expanded traditional kin and clan ties) with strong rhetoric about economic self-determination, political independence and the commitment to Christian (Catholic) morality. While the majority of people were committed to its activities, some thought it irrational and irreligious. One man, who often ridiculed cultists and believed them to be gullible fools, climbed a tree above the ritual meeting place in his village one night, with bags of Twisties (cheese pops), biscuits and some kerosene. He sprayed the kerosene from his mouth and lit it with a match, creating a flash of fire above the crowd. He then threw down the food and people below scrambled to gather what were at that time luxury items. Many people believed that this was a sign of the efficacy of their rituals. He allowed the excitement to spread and the stories to be exaggerated and then he (and some of his fellow skeptics who had been in on the ruse) revealed his trickery. While it had the effect of humiliating people momentarily, it in no way dented their faith in the efficacy of their rituals.

Cargo Cults

Within the anthropological literature cargo cult became an embarrassment for anthropologists during the late 1960s and 1970s, mainly because it appeared to endorse some of the colonial (and often racist) assumptions about colonized people. Monty Lindstrom's study of the popular and academic representations of 'cargo cults' Cargo Cult: *Strange Stories of Desire from Melanesia and Beyond* (University of Hawaii Press 1993) is a history of the concept that documents its origins in colonial discourse that was both racist and paternalist. The emphasis in both administrative and anthropological writings was often placed on the bizarre and economically irrational elements and the ways that Melanesian people appeared to believe that 'economic development' and the attainment of equality with whites could be effected through novel rituals and communication with ancestral spirits. Writers of all persuasions recognized that the politics were usually anti-colonial, pro-independence and political autonomy as well as being directed towards the acquisition of wealth, status and goods associated with whites. But the ritualistic means for achieving these ends were perceived as irrational and indicative of the ignorance, lack of education and social deprivation that characterized Melanesians under colonial domination.

Attempts by anthropologists to retrieve the dignity and intellectual perspicacity of Melanesians have taken many forms. As Lindstrom (1993) and Lattas (1998) have observed the major way was to 'nativize cargo cults' by rendering cult adherence comprehensible and in keeping with deeply engrained traditions, beliefs and modes of action: "Cargo and cult emerge as standard operating procedures for Melanesians. Thanks to anthropology, Melanesians are now known to be cargo cultists even when they are not actively having a cult." (Lindstrom 1993: 62) Lindstrom and others have also drawn parallels with the irrational consumerist desires and 'cargo' fantasies of Westerners.

Lattas and, in a quite different way, Billings emphasize the ways that the mimetic appropriation of Western technologies or behaviours enable Melanesians to manage ways of being 'white' that are simultaneously novel and draw on their cultural traditions, thereby affirming adherents' agency and their moral integrity. In designating the Lavongai TIA as 'theatre' and characterizing the social activities as 'performances' Billings suggests that in some ways cults are self-conscious parodies of 'white' activities and behaviour.

In the case of Lihir – where involvement in TKA was enthusiastic and widespread, the image of activities as deliberate humorous parodies cannot be sustained. First, because as Ramstadt and others observed, the members who believed that their organization was nothing more than a communally organized development project were often acutely embarrassed by some of their fellows who spoke of Americans arriving and the triumphal return of ancestors with cargo. Some dismissed these ideas as backward and superstitious. I have no doubt that the unanimous vote for Jesus Christ was a deliberate protest and did not really entail millennial ideas about a new era. The voters wanted to show their contempt for the State and its neglect of their economic and social welfare. As criticism it was a deadly serious, even angry rejection of the false promises Lihirians believed had been made by successive administrations. As a demonstration of their righteousness and faith in the Catholic religion, it was done in earnest. But the chiliastic aims of the movement were to be realized through more complex processes – by consistent Christian practice and by creating wealth through their own endeavors in growing copra and cocoa.

Burridge (1969) stressed the cargo cult as the expression of a longing for moral equivalence and Ramstadt argued that on Lihir, the millennial element was inevitably tied to the longing for deliverance from the feelings of humiliation and shame that they associated with the colonial relationship. In 1995, when eleven of the people who had been members talked to me about their beliefs in the promise of a 'new life' free of work and dependence on Europeans, I was made very aware of this element.

At that time, a few thought that I was a returned ancestor called Apollonia Weskon and the substance of their conversation with me was directed towards gaining my approval by answering my enquiries 'correctly'. As I was then unaware of their motive for calling me to meet them and of the identity they attributed to me, much of the conversation was at cross purposes. But it did enable me to glimpse both the formality and seriousness with which meetings must have been held and the ways that tenets of the Association were held to be prophesies that were now being fulfilled – by the presence of the mining company and by my own visit.

As someone 'writing a report' and asking questions about Lihirian ways of living, I was perceived as enacting a prophecy. In asking questions about the reasons why they had joined Nimamar (as the organization was then called – the syllables being taken from the first letters of each island in the group – Niolam, Malie, Masahet and Mahur) I was deemed to be 'testing' their commitment. One elderly man explained that those who were members recognized that the treatment by white 'bosses', the humiliation they felt and the shame when they were exposed as ignorant was something that they had to overcome. This would be achieved by being moral, peaceful, not jealous and by 'being like white men' in joining together to achieve development through business enterprise and cooperation. Engagement in communal work, attendance at meetings, having a 'number' that marked you as a member (which some people tattooed on their arms) were simultaneously *demonstrations* of commitment and *rituals* that were thought to effect change and win ancestral approval.

The mining project, then under construction, was deemed to be the outcome of this work, the manifestation of their hopes and the opportunity to fulfill their desires for social changes that would usher in both moral and economic equivalence with the white men. In particular, compensation payments for loss of trees, access to land and other impacts were at that stage generally perceived as '*winmani*', money that was like a windfall or lottery prize. The emphasis was placed on the fact that it was not a payment for work. On the basis of interviews over the first decade of mining development I maintain that it is this notion of 'instant money', money that simply 'blows in' without being earned, that inspired and continues to inspire, many Lihirians to participate in the various cults as well as to invest money in fraudulent money schemes. It is also because many people believe that white people have access to sources of money and wealth that are kept secret from others. This is one reason why they place so much faith in people whom they see as having 'bridged' the gap by acquiring knowledge about how money works. I offer three examples of conversations about this:

"This money for compensation that I received is 'winmani'. It came from nothing, no work; the way that expatriates find their money. You see, you just go to the bank and get your money. You go to the store and buy your food – you don't have to work in your garden. You know the ways of money. That is what will happen here when we have Nimamar as our government." (Londolovit Villager, October 1996)

"I gave some money to M... P.... to put in U-Vistract [A money scam operated out of Bougainville] because that will make my money grow. You look at him, he wears good clothes and goes to America because he has learned the secret and little by little we will learn these ways. I know some of the words already because I gave him my money.
MM: What are the words?
ZP: Me, I'm a village man, but these words are "World Bank" and "Global Economy". These are big words.
MM: But you have put in money now for over three years and received nothing. You would have got more putting it in the bank and keeping it there.
ZP: No, it will come. Arau prophesied that the gold mine would come. It is here. MP knows these things and the way that money grows, he will lead me. I can wait." (Kapit villager, July 1999).

"We Lihirian people have always looked for money and ways to get the things that we see other people have. All of these ways, TKI and Nimamar and now PV push us along, because the people learned·the ways of white people. But first we have to find our winmani and then use it the ways that PV teaches us. Then it will grow and we will have plenty of money. That is why I want some compensation. It will be my winmani." (Kinami Villager, August 2002)

The idea of a world in which people do not have to work for their sustenance is common to many millenarian movements (see Cohn: 1970). In 1986, when I undertook a study of the social impact of mining on Misima, in Milne Bay Province, Papua New Guinea, one of the main reasons that people wanted to limit the employment of outsiders was to ensure that the people of the island would earn sufficient money to be able to buy all their food. It is clear then that working for wages was not seen as 'work', which is primarily defined as physical labour. On Lihir this distinction was very marked during the construction phase of the project. Their was a hierarchy of 'non-workers' with the category of 'landowner' as the highest – as the large amounts of compensation meant that people had money without any work at all. Employment on the mine, while it did involve physical labour for some, was viewed as much less tiring than gardening and buying food from a store was a luxurious option.

Nimamar's 'cultic' dimensions prior to the gold mine construction are undeniable. It was in many respects a millennial religious movement in which the attainment of economic development was an integral part of a moral transformation in preparation for the arrival of 'America', the ancestors and the cargo. When Colin Filer and Richard Jackson undertook the research for the social and economic impact study prior to the negotiation of the agreement with local people, the President of Nimamar presented Filer with an account of the movement's beliefs and objectives. He was insistent:

> "All this is not a dream or a manifesto. It is a form of knowledge or belief, but men still have to work at it. God put men on this earth, and men must work to follow his plan, to develop the earth in accordance with our Father's own will. To accord with the will of God the Father, God himself has a plan. It is the TEN Commandments. If men are going to change this earth and renew it, Jesus alone is the road and the law by which it can be done." (Filer and Jackson 1989, 369)

But in discussion with others who were members of Nimamar the religious and chiliastic elements were sometimes completely denied. Bruno from Mosoi village explained Nimamar to me thus in 1997:

> "It was not a cargo cult. It was simply a business development association. Lihir had been neglected for so many years. The Germans, the Australians – they did nothing to advance the economic situation of people on Lihir and we decided to do it ourselves. During that time plantations were established, cocoa and copra. There were two fermenteries on Niolam, people worked cooperatively and sold their produce. Many of us who had experience outside, educated working people, saw this as a way of gaining some money and improving our way of life. When people voted for Jesus Christ it was just a way of saying that we wanted nothing to do with government"

Opposition to the State has been a central tenet of the various manifestations of the organization since its inception and has increased since the mine was established. But this separatist stance is tied to the idea of Lihir as a place exclusively for Lihirians and to the *Las Kos* -'Final Course (or Cause?)' which is unambiguously religious and chiliastic in its promise. For most members of TKA/TIA/Nimamar their adherence was not to a 'business development organization' and the melding of religious and political aims and the promise of economic transformation brought about by the arisen dead was essential. In his written description in 1989, the President concluded:

> "We here make known a number of ideas or statements, but they all come from one basic belief. The association believes that the dead will return to life. The Bible strengthens us in this belief. Throughout the history of the TKA [which then became] the TSA, TFA, TIA, and now Nimamar, this belief has not changed. Only the name has changed, while the belief remains the same...

Here are some further points on which the Nimamar Association is United:

The Final Course:
The nature of money will change.
The State will be abolished.
The Association will become the government.
Lihir will become a city.
Schools will be abolished.
There will be universal literacy.
There will be two classes of people:
"Life forever"
"Summon Prize"

During the height of commitment to the Nimamar Association movement in the 1980s when mining exploration, feasibility studies and negotiations for a mining lease were happening, the majority of educated Lihirians and those who had businesses lived elsewhere. Some were involved in the negotiation process and others were not. Most of the leaders on Lihir were members of Nimamar and during that period they were elected to the Local Level Government. This was then named the Nimamar Development Authority and later Nimamar Local Level Government – thereby fulfilling the promise that 'the Association will become the government'.

Similarly, as the coming of the mining project was interpreted by many Lihirians as the dawning of the long-awaited new era – one that they had predicted would come – many of their demands were directly drawn from Nimamar's vision of the future. The building of a ring road, and the commitment of almost the entire village development fund budget to building houses were crucial to making Lihir 'a city'. While most people recognize that this transformative process requires human labour, some older people clearly thought that it would be in some respects a 'magical' instantaneous process.

In 1998 I spoke with a man who had just moved into a Village Development Scheme house in Londolovit. He was very happy with the house, but very disappointed that it did not come with a flower garden like those he had seen around the houses of some of the white people in the new township. He made it clear that he believed that whites had some special knowledge about making gardens appear in 'one day' that they were withholding from Lihirians in order to maintain status differences in housing. I attempted to explain that the maintenance of this status difference rested in differences between incomes (and that expatriate wives did not grow food and so had time to plant and look after flower gardens) which enabled expatriates to employ Papua New Guineans to make and maintain their gardens rather than on any secret knowledge. He rejected this entirely, insisting that the Nimamar had told them that Europeans had knowledge that could make gardens grow 'between sunset and sunrise in one day', that this knowledge would be given to Lihirians and he was angry that the mining company was not doing so. I use this simply to illustrate the ways that *some* people continued to believe the old ideas of magical transformation, even though most did not.

But it also reveals aspects of the notions of 'secret' knowledge that permeate the cult. Here knowledge is conceptualized in similar terms to the magical power of sorcerers and tandal. It is linked to mastery of an esoteric vocabulary, analogous to the effective use of spells used in other contexts. It is conceptualized as knowledge that is transformative in itself, a belief that often results in a dedication to rote learning and the view that obtaining proof of qualification (in the form of a certificate, for example) will lead automatically to the acquisition of a job. The failure of students who complete high school to obtain high-level employment is thus interpreted as indicative that the school curriculum has withheld crucial (Western-derived) knowledge and therefore issued 'false' papers.

While some of the members obviously held fast to the religious and supernatural nature of economic changes, by the late 1990s more of the highly educated Lihirians were returning to participate in Lihir's development, and their ideas of that process were not inspired by ideas of 'secret knowledge'. The leader of the Landowner's Association Mark Soipang (who was also the Lihirian representative member of the Lihir Gold Board of Directors) was the main negotiator with the mining company and government. He returned to Lihir part-way through a course at university in Lae and was instrumental in convincing Lihirian people to proceed with the lease agreement. His promise that 'They would be shooting birds with kina' was a hyperbolic statement about the wealth that he thought would flow to Lihirians rather than a restatement of the promise that 'the nature of money would change'.

Society Reform

At the time when the first Integrated Benefits Package (see Banks 1998 for a discussion of this on Lihir) was being prepared, a new organization arose, led by Soipang and another prominent educated Lihirian, Leo Glaglas – who had been one of Papua New Guinea's first airline pilots. It was called 'Society Reform' and its explicit aims were to ensure that Lihirian society adapted to the changes brought by the mine in ways that were consistent with 'tradition' and with the Christian religion. This organization was the transitional movement between the TIA/Nimamar and the new social movement that has arisen during the last couple of years around a program called Personal Viability.

The mining company gave, as part of the Integrated Benefits Package, an annual budget of several thousand dollars to Society Reform to operate, a vehicle for the purposes of promoting its political ideology around the island and the services of a member of the Community Relations department to assist in developing community projects under its aegis. The leaders wrote lengthy plans and diagrammatic illustrations of the ways that it would integrate modern 'development' with the customary practices and social organization of Lihir and with the spiritual values of Christianity.

Society Reform was a program that in many respects was less ritualistic, more secular and overtly political in its aims than its predecessor – but it failed to spark the interest of the majority of Lihirians. It was presented to people in terms of 'strengthening custom' so that Lihirians could respond to the negative effects of modernization by asserting their 'traditional' laws, ceremonies and social values. The verbose and often incomprehensible plans and programs prepared by Glaglas did not capture the imagination of villagers – who at that time were caught up in the dramatic changes associated with construction. Very often his speeches were dismissed as *'mauswara tasol'* (just blather) and his non-separatist arguments about the mine being the means of proper integration of Lihir into the nation of Papua New Guinea were treated with general skepticism – not least because they seemed at odds with the demand that all benefits should be enjoyed exclusively by Lihirians. Many of his neighbors dismissed his talk of 'sharing benefits with all Papua New Guineans' as thinly disguised self-interest – for he had a Tolai wife and many of his relatives from East New Britain province had arrived on Lihir already, hoping to find jobs. Glaglas was the only Lihirian whom I heard dispute the value of the "Lihirians First" policy that others had argued had to be the crux of employment and other benefits.

The rise and fall of Society Reform provides an instance of a movement that failed. Its demise was undramatic – it simply did not 'take off'. The four-wheel drive vehicle was used by relatives for their business enterprise. The villagers lost interest in starting their own 'community projects' that remained vague and unfunded. They wanted 'free money' as capital. They wanted paid employment. Enterprising individuals were availing themselves of the interest-free loans that the company was awarding to fledgling businesses. Ideas about codifying customary laws were abandoned in the heady period of construction when almost all Lihirian men were employed and the compensation money and beer were flowing freely. I suspect that there are many comparable cases in other parts of Papua New Guinea and the reasons for failure might provide insight into the success of others. People were interested at first, but the rhetoric, the use of complicated language, incomprehensible diagrams and vague high-minded objectives sounded too much like the talk of politicians – and Lihirians were mistrustful of it.

The negotiations of the first Integrated Benefits Package, which began in 2000, were conducted in terms that were much more pragmatic and with an emphasis on financial compensation. But underneath lay the grand vision of Lihir as a city and the separatist ideal of development that had been nurtured in Nimamar. These surfaced once again in the renegotiation of the benefits by the Joint Negotiating Committee, but this time an entirely new organization is involved. Nimamar became institutionalized as the local level government. As a socio-political movement, the Lihir Pawa Mekim Kamap Asosiesen, is as all-encompassing in its ideology as its predecessors, but its form and its aims reflect new economic forces and a familiarity with the language and *modus operandi* of the corporate sector. Whereas the Church and the colonial state provided the inspiration for Nimamar, the mining company and its plans for community benefits in the form of infrastructural, business and social welfare improvements, have supplied the blueprint for attaining Lihir's new destiny.

Once again the urge to see the manifestos, strategic plans and development strategy plans as self-conscious parodies is strong – but I think misguided, for 'development' remains a serious business for those involved. The flow charts, budget projections, legalistic vocabulary and complicated programs are now produced on computers. The plans often read like their models – mining company documents, NGO project designs and government programs. They are replete with the language of managerialism, but their vision of future prosperity is in essence the same as that of their forebears in its utopianism.

The leaders and protagonists are almost all Lihirians who have some tertiary education. One of their major political aims is the assertion of their sovereignty over the mineral resources of the island. They have revived some of the moral and religious elements of Nimamar, but in a framework that is mimetically modernist rather than mystical. They know where the white man gets his money – the campaigns for equity and payment of dividends have ensured that most Lihirians understand that the large shareholders in Lihir Gold are mostly investors outside PNG. Even if there are many who do not understand the workings of international money markets, fluctuating gold prices and the stock exchange, the leaders of the new movement are determined that Lihirians should play a role in the running of the mine on their land and receive a far greater share of its profits. Having had to accept that their equity is not going to be more than 5.2%, they decided to push for greater financial benefits. It is in this context that the socio-political movement based on 'Personal Viability' has arisen. The language for their proposals derives from a novel mélange of jargon from motivational courses, 'self-help' books, corporate managerialism, New Age ideas of 'spirituality' and 'holism', development critiques from institutions such as AusAID and the United Nations Development Program, the 'project planning' ideas of aid organizations and NGOs, from Christianity and Lihirian neo-traditionalism.

Personal Viability

Nicholas Bainton has written on the way that Lihirian people have embraced the ideologies of Personal Viability (Bainton 2005; 2010), an enterprise that offers motivational and self-help courses. Here I want to stress the ways that its apparent departures from 'cargo cult' activities have in fact incorporated earlier ideals and practices.

The main agents are members of the Joint Negotiating Committee for the revision of the benefits package, who pressed for the company to fund and support the proselytizing activities of Personal Viability and its objectives as part of renegotiating benefits. They have all undertaken courses run by the Entrepreneurial Development Training Centre (EDTC).

The EDTC program is a motivational human development program devised specifically to encourage economic self-reliance and self-determination among Papua New Guineans (www.edtc.ac.pg/PVPhilosophy.htm). Its entrepreneurial vision has been used in a range of government departments and community programs and has been endorsed by a number of prominent citizens. Its intellectual inspiration is an eclectic mix of popular 'self-improvement' psychology, broad socio-economic analysis drawn from such diverse sources as the United Nations Development Program, Non-Government Organization literature, popular psychology, Marxist critiques written in the 1980s by UPNG academics, nationalist rhetoric and the Bible. Its founder and main proponent is a businessman who operates the educational program as a franchising business. Participants pay to attend courses which are structured so that they progress through various levels. One of its major aims is the establishment of "grassroots universities". In PNG the idea of calling institutions and programs 'Grasruts Yuniversiti' appears to have originated in Bougainville as secessionists defined the post-war reconstruction in ways that were distinct and in accord with the ideals of cultural revivalism that emerged during the civil conflict. Given that many Papua New Guineans cannot go to university, and those who aspire to hold senior positions are told tertiary qualifications are required, the idea that these can be acquired locally, drawing on local experience and knowledge, is immensely attractive. So too is the idea of building a large institutional complex (funded by the mining company) that enshrines Lihirian achievements and knowledge. Indeed, the emphasis on the built infrastructure absorbed far more time and energy amongst adherents than did the education that was to be offered. The educational aims remained vague.

On Lihir PV has gained momentum and incorporated many elements that were formerly platforms of the Society Reform Program – specifically the aims of integrating aspects of 'traditional' social organization and customary values with a program for economic development and improvement in living standards, while strengthening Christian adherence. It shares characteristics with the TDK Movement of the 1970s in that its leader is an outsider whose organisation is directed towards quite different ends. Like TDK, it has been introduced to Lihir where it has its own charismatic leader (Soipang) who has, with the help of other adherents, developed a manifesto and strategic plan that encompasses every aspect of Lihirian people's lives. The new organization, The Lihir Grasruts Pawa Mekim Kamap Association (Lihir Grassroots Power Development Association) is in many ways far more political.

Like many similar grassroots movements in Melanesia it has a complex hierarchical structure and numerous committees. The leaders have produced several manifestos outlining their aims, which are encompassed by the idea of the 'Lihir Destiny' – notably the 'Strategic Development Concept' and two 'Development Action Plans' – one relating to mining and the other (presumably for the long term) to 'non-mining'. These plans entail management of projects and programs through the Personal Viability Coordination Unit which monitors the progress of people through the educational programs.

All the literature produced by EDTC stresses self-reliance, the avoidance of indebtedness and the need to eliminate dependence on external capital, by concentrating on small-scale enterprises and 'working up'. The presence of the mining operation obviates the gradual embrace of capitalism by individuals who 'pull themselves up by their bootstraps', as Lihirians now see their future security in a constant stream of 'external' capital in the form tens of billions of dollars 'rent'. In effect, it has developed its economic policies in the context of increasing demands for money, infrastructure and services to be funded through the Integrated Benefits Package. The plans are highly elaborated and in many respects assume that the Local Level Government and the Special Purpose Authority will operate under the umbrella and in accordance with the doctrines and organizational structure proposed by the Lihir Grasruts Pawa Mekim Kamap Association. In this sense then it is in fact a political organization and might be seen as having evolved in the ways that Worsley predicted, from a magico-religious cult to one that is primarily political in its aims and ideology. Certainly, unlike its predecessors, the current movement looks to the future rather than concerning itself with any 'return' of ancestral beings.

The modernist assumption of earlier analysts (Worsley, Lawrence) that there will be a natural, progressive trajectory whereby the cultic, 'irrational' elements in these social movements will be rationally discarded as people gain more (Western) education and knowledge have not proven true. In many instances, the political aims have been primary from the beginning of the cult – indeed the perception of disadvantage is often rooted in the recognition of race relations as *politically* oppressive. The mechanisms of colonial or white domination are perceived to reside in the institutions that discipline and regulate the lives of Melanesians. Overt resistance has been relatively rare, but as Lattas has demonstrated, the mimetic appropriation of 'disciplinary' regimes, whether these are schools or military drills, is a way of asserting an alternate view of power, entitlement and resistance (1998, 37-40).

On Lihir, where there have been constant elements in the cults in varying political circumstances, each new phase has allowed for the continuity of earlier features of the cult. Thus the call for the establishment of a "grassroots university" is new and has arisen in other areas of the country in quite different contexts, but older adherents link it back to the Nimamar promise of 'abolishing schools' and ensuring literacy by working through indigenous institutions. The arrival of two SIL linguists is linked to this aim and interpreted by many older Lihirians as confirmation of the accuracy of Arau's prophecies. But for those modernists who see PV as breaking with the past, the wealth from the mine also represents the means for obtaining educational institutions that will ensure that Lihirians receive an education commensurate with that of the expatriates (and the Papua New Guinean elite) at International Schools funded by the mining company rather than the government community and high schools.

The Grassroots University idea has taken off since Francis Ona appeared in an Australian-made television documentary and referred to the fact that on Bougainville, during the period of sanctions, people rediscovered their traditional knowledge and learned its value. It has great appeal as it connects with ideas about pride in tradition and celebration of custom, breaking 'dependency syndrome' and affirming traditional values over those introduced by whites. From its early manifestation as TKA and Nimamar, Lihirian cults have been nativist, celebratory of Lihirian 'tradition', with great emphasis on finding ways for economic development that are entrepreneurial, but maintain core traditional Lihirian values and ways of doing things. The codification of customary laws and opposition to some introduced 'customs' have been central to cultic political ideology. At each phase, adherents to the earlier cult are able to subsume the new as in some way fulfilling the prophecies of the past. The malleability of cultic ideas ensures that for many, the magico-religious elements remain crucial if submerged.

The political aims that are attached to this latest movement are clearly secessionist, in spite of some attempts to disguise this. But a central tenet is that the era of *Peketon* (a Lihirian term that appears to refer to the transformative millennial moment, which I believe is a Lihirianisation of 'eschaton'; see also Bainton 2010: 59-60) is at hand – when Lihir will become the centre of wealth and the agent for economic transformation of Papua New Guinea. At one stage demands for company funding of their Sustainable Development Plan reached 3 billion kina (roughly equivalent to the national budget) and there are still plans for a bank and a financial institution linked to PV and located on Lihir. One stated objective of the leaders is to subordinate all government functions and management of funds to the authority of the leaders of the Central Coordinating Clearing & Monitoring Agency (CC-CMA) – which comprises those converts to PV who have received training to a high level. While at present the leaders are careful to avoid presentations of their aims as explicitly anti-State, the specific aims are based on a vision of a political system (which is designated 'The Lihirian Destiny') which gives the legitimate government very little authority over political and financial matters on Lihir, no authority at all over money from the mine and implicitly subverts the authority of elected representatives.

The EDTC program has some of the classic elements of a 'cargo cult' – whereby commitment (both financial and moral) to an ideology of self-determination and attainment of particular achievements (certificates that show that the individual has completed 'levels' of training and degrees from the proposed Grassroots University) will bring prosperity and self-reliance to the adherents. The ideological component is similar to many that have preceded it in Papua New Guinea – its mix of Christian principles and entrepreneurial values are reminiscent of the Moral Rearmament Movement's campaign in the 1970s. The progression through various levels, each time being awarded credentials, fetishize the educative process and are viewed in analogous ways to the former system of allotting numbers to ensure that members could 'win' their money.

Like other personal development and motivational courses, it attempts to inspire and direct people. It teaches strategies, behaviours and attitudes that can assist individuals in achieving their personal economic goals. Personal Viability (like Moral

Rearmament) ideology incorporates Christian morality and so promotes principles of cooperative enterprise, ethical dealings with others and concern for the common good. While these are all commendable aims that could have very positive social effects, realistically only a few will be able to attain their goals (especially those for economic advancement) as so many other factors determine their success or failure. As corporations and institutions in advanced industrial countries find, such courses (whether they are for team-building, personal development or to assist people in adjusting to structural change) work well for some people and not others, and often have a limited period of impact.

In the Papua New Guinea context, the tendency of such programs to incorporate other elements such as religious cultism and 'get-rich-quick' schemes, or to become the vehicle for political advancement of charismatic leaders, makes them far more complex. Within many cultures in PNG, the desire for development and political power is often expressed in cults and ritualistic adherence to codes of behaviour and conduct that people believe will *in themselves* generate the desired outcomes. Thus, learning precepts by rote, wearing 'uniforms' and engaging in activities that emphasize special status are often the drawcards for adherents. The Nimamar cult on Lihir had many of these elements and it appears that for many ordinary Lihirians the Personal Viability program represents a revision and 'upgrading' of the cult so that it deals with ideals of modernization derived from their new economic circumstances.

The cultic dimension of Personal Viability is not in the foreground at present – in fact it has operated mainly as straightforward personal development course. The organization of activities in the villages does have elements familiar from other so-called 'cults' – ritual singing and meetings of 'cells', overtones of secrecy about the 'superior, exclusive knowledge' of adherents, formal levels of enlightenment and meetings that enable people to air their views, hopes and plans for the future. Mark Soipang has assumed a leadership role and has indicated that he believes that the landowners' association (his former power base) should be subordinated to the new organization and become a vehicle for implementation of its objectives. His self-defined role now includes ideas of divine purpose. Prior to this Soipang presented himself as the hard-headed modernist – recently he has declared that the abandonment of his academic studies and return to Lihir was inspired by a dream or vision in which God told him to return and lead his people and revitalize traditional activities. The exclusionist aims have been most elaborated in a 'Sengseng (Outsiders) Policy' aimed at restricting the influx of migrants from other parts of Papua New Guinea and ensuring that they do not have access to any of the material benefits (such as housing, employment or businesses). The mistrust and hostility towards outsiders has been a component of all previous movements on Lihir and is in some ways the most likely 'rallying call' that would draw others behind the Lihir Pawa Mekim Kamap Asosiesen.

The members of Personal Viability reject the idea of State sovereignty over minerals and in 2002 one of them fraudulently attempted to sell gold to a foreign company. In recent negotiations they have proposed the establishment of the Lihir Surveillance Company that would monitor gold production and enable them to subtract a percentage of the product at source, rather than waiting for royalties and grants to be paid. Assuming management of the mining operations is an objective that has been voiced constantly – both to government officials and to the current management company. There is no doubt that most Lihirians believe that the gold reserves are theirs by right and that Lihir's continued neglect by the state legitimates their views about political autonomy and the exclusion of other Papua New Guinean citizens from any economic benefits.

Technocratic and economic vocabulary are used in the plans, documents and PowerPoint presentations in ways that simultaneously convey familiarity with the language of the corporate world while revealing confusion about its meanings and disciplinary foundations. For example, the Joint Negotiating Committee presented a complex development plan which they believed offered an alternative to the company's plans for economic development. Phrased in terms of the 'Lihir Destiny', it promised to fulfill the 'Lihir Dream' and 'Lihir becoming a City' by implementing the 'Ultimate Success Formula'. This involves policies that are 'self-reliant', dispense with ' the handout mentality' and 'based on converting "people" as liabilities to becoming assets (sic)'. (JNC n.d., 4). Terms such as 'supply and demand' are given a metaphorical twist so that they become modes of planning that are either company-inspired (Supply) or PV/Community-inspired (Demand). The language of foreign aid – 'empowerment', 'capacity building', 'institutional strengthening' - is sprinkled throughout documents; and terminology from environmental science is used (usually inaccurately) in place of ordinary words about the natural environment. Cryptic aphorisms such as 'Openness disqualifies negotiating with reservations' jostle with clichés of self-help books and managerialism such 'adding value', 'win-win situations' and 'guesstimates'. After three years of negotiating, the committee called for a speedy conclusion thus: '…it is time to align all stakeholders involved in the Lihir IBP Review and mobilize them into not only using the same thinking cap but responsibly walking the talk momentarily to concluding the review process.'

The novel use of language, mystification of concepts and appropriation of English words are recognizably strategies to convince the mining company that the JNC and Local government have a 'better' way of dealing with the development needs of Lihirians that draws on understandings of the business world. In displaying familiarity with what they perceive to be the shared jargon of the global business community they are engaging in mimesis that in many ways is analogous to the activities that characterize cargo cults of the past.

But in bandying around such vocabularies they are also engaged in a familiar Melanesian political game of words. Knowledge and use of esoteric (usually magic) words and claims of 'ownership' of language that facilitates access to sources of power over wealth, productivity and people have long been crucial elements of Lihirian political authority. The garbled flow charts, spread sheets and often incomprehensible documents produced in the context of negotiating benefits from the mine are aimed in part at convincing ordinary Lihirians (many of whom cannot read English, although increasingly English is spoken in daily life because it is the language of the mining company) that their destiny is in the hands of '*save*' (Tok Pisin – knowledgeable, educated, intelligent) men who understand the language of business, economics and development and can so represent their interests better than traditional leaders. The plans, documents and meetings are their armoury in a political struggle *within* the Lihirian community. This is between generations of men, the older, less-educated men whose power derives from traditional exchanges and cycles of feasting and the generation of men who have been educated and locate their power in control over the wealth generated by the mining project.

These grand plans of the leaders and their aspirations for Lihir's destiny are only partially accepted (or understood) by the majority of Lihirians, whose support for PV derives from their discontent and present disappointments rather than visions of a glorious future. While the JNC talks of Lihir's need to 'position itself to enter the global market by connecting the Lihir Economy with the global economy" (JNC n.d, 15) the majority of Lihirians have the more modest objective of getting a job that will allow them to participate in the national consumer economy. For the mine has not brought mass employment. Most of the highly-skilled employees come from elsewhere in Papua New Guinea. Nor have the infrastructural improvements transformed Lihir into the city that was envisaged – with sealed roads, reticulated water and electricity to houses that would all be built of milled timber with iron roofs. The training and educational programs instituted by the mining company have not transformed all Lihirian men into managers and successful businessmen who can buy beer, cars and flash clothes. After almost a decade, all but one managerial position were held by expatriates. The wages of Lihirians do not allow them to live like the senior staff in the township. Even those with jobs still have to grow the bulk of their food, as prices at the supermarket (which had been optimistically called Ataniom – the local word for garden – as many Lihirians expected that they would all be able to buy all their food) are too high for employed men to be 'breadwinners'. Besides, expenditure of money on food would mean that it could not be devoted to buying beer, motor vehicles and other goods that are valued as markers of status.

While ordinary villagers resent their continued economic marginality, their aspirations are comparatively realistic. They want to have small business projects that will generate income and they want their children to get good jobs at the mine. If any group is consumed by feelings of relative deprivation, it is the educated Lihirians who are PV leaders – most of whom are relatively rich (see Bainton 2008b). They aspire to the status and wealth of the senior expatriate managers and the rich shareholders. It is the wealthy Lihirians, those who have received large sums in compensation and royalties as well as contracts with the mining company, who have optimistically 'invested' thousands of kina in various fraudulent money-making schemes. It is they who send large sums to confidence tricksters who send them emails from Asia and Nigeria promising millions in return for their 'investment'. It is this group who harbour the most paranoid convictions that the company is concealing its true financial situation and withholding information that would enable Lihirians to become wealthy.

In this respect then, we might argue that it is the educated elite who are now the cultists while the Lihirians who are unemployed or working for low wages are the pragmatists, waverers and sceptics. The high cost of attending PV courses, the obscurantist language and the fact that some of the leaders gained great personal wealth from compensation, royalties and contracts with the mining company, rather than hard work and personal initiative, are regularly cited as reasons for *not* wholeheartedly supporting the JNC and its Strategic Plans or visions of a glorious future. For those who have undertaken the courses and participated in the IBP negotiation process, planning and politicking for the 'Lihir destiny' – the dream of Peketon – the wealth from mining is merely the means to a utopian future.

References

Bainton N, and Cox J.
2009   Parallel States, Parallel Economies: Legitimacy and Prosperity in Papua New Guinea.
        State Society and Governance in Melanesia Discussion Paper 2009/5 Research School of
        Pacific and Asian Studies, Australian National University

Bainton, N.
2006   '*Are You Viable?* Personal avarice, collective antagonism and grassroots development in
        Papua New Guinea'. SAGES Working Papers in Development, working paper 5.
2008a   "The genesis and the escalation of desire in Lihir, Papua New Guinea".
        Journal of Pacific History 43: 3, 289-312.
2008b   "Men of Kastom and the Customs of Men: Status, Legitimacy and Persistent Values in
        Lihir, Papua New Guinea." *Australian Journal of Anthropology* 19: 195-213.
2010   *The Lihir Destiny: Cultural Responses to Mining in Melanesia*. Canberra ANU e-press.

Banks, Glenn
1998   "Compensation for communities affected by mining and oil developments in Melanesia".
        The Malaysian Journal of Tropical Geography 29(1): 53-67.

Billings, Dorothy
2002   *Cargo Cult as Theater: Political Performance in the Pacific*. Lanham: Lexington Books.

Burridge, Kenelm
1969   *New Heaven, New Earth*. Oxford, Basil Blackwell.

Cohn, Norman
1970   *The Pursuit of the Millennium: Revolutionary Millenarians and Mystical Anarchists of the
        Middle Ages*. London and New York: Oxford University Press

Filer, Colin and Richard Jackson
1989   Social and Economic Impact Study for Lihir. Unpublished in Two volumes.

Lattas, Andrew
1998   *Cultures of Secrecy: Reinventing Race in Bush Kaliai Cargo Cults*.
        University of Wisconsin Press

Lawrence, Peter
1964   *Road Belong Cargo*. Manchester, Manchester University Press

Lindstrom, Lamont
1993   *Cargo Cult: Strange stories of desire from Melanesia and beyond*. Honolulu, University of
        Hawaii Press.

Macintyre, Martha and Simon Foale
2004   "Global imperatives and local desires: competing economic and environmental interests
        in Melanesian communities". In Victoria S. Lockwood (ed), *Globalization and Culture
        Change in the Pacific Islands*, Upper Saddle River New Jersey, Pearson Prentice Hall,
        pp. 149-164

Swatridge, Colin
1985   *Delivering the Goods: education as cargo in Papua New Guinea*. Carlton, Melbourne University Press.

Worsley, Peter
1970   *The Trumpet Shall Sound*. London, Paladin

Chapter 6

The Yali Movement of Papua New Guinea: the Dialogics of Representation

Elfriede Hermann

The Yali movement of Papua New Guinea was one of those indigenous initiatives in parts of south-west Oceania [1] which, coming in the wake of colonization and Christian missionization, made a serious effort to transform the living conditions of the people living there. So great was their concern to change society that these movements indeed merit the name of "social movement" (cf. Paula Brown 1966: 150). They meet the definition of social movements, formulated by Joachim Raschke (1987[1985]: 11), as "both product and producer of social change"[2]. Cultural activities exhibiting the character of such movements were chiefly concentrated in colonies later awarded to the now sovereign states of Fiji, Papua New Guinea, the Solomon Islands and Vanuatu. From the exogenous perspective of Western researchers, two aspects of these movements predominate: 1) a demand for industrial goods, i.e. what came to be called "cargo"; and 2) ritual practices for the purposes of acquiring the goods, i.e. what came to be called "cults". Thus, from the mid-1940s on, the term "cargo cult" was used to represent social movements of this kind.

In his study of two movements documented in colonial Papua New Guinea, the historian John Waiko (1973: 418-420) pointed out that what chiefly concerned the indigenous actors, in performing their rites, was alleviating the "disasters" inflicted by colonization and missionization. Their reaction to contact with Europeans had been to amass spiritual force. The "white man" proclaimed and demonstrated power outstripping that of the Melanesians. The indigenous peoples countered this demonstration of power by mobilizing their own sources of power, which they saw as represented in their ancestors. The fact that members of social movements in south-west Oceania focused on power relationships and were less interested in receiving goods than in

---

1. Given that partitioning into cultural areas is now controversial in anthropological debate, I have taken geographical description as my benchmark, as have also Strathern, Stewart, Carucci et. al. 2002.

2. Translated from the original German by Elfriede Hermann.

acquiring knowledge about how to produce them (Lindstrom 1981, 1984: 303-304) has long seemed to researchers less important than the material aspect of "cargo" promotion. The bulk of exogenous representations described the acquisition of Western goods as the core concern of the movements. Therefore they seized on the "cargo" components, extrapolating from "cargo" to "cult".

Papua New Guineans pointed out to me that designating cultural activities as "cargo cult" is quite problematic. As Pacific Islanders have done in other parts of south-west Oceania, they have kept a close eye on how the term "cargo cult" has fared from colonial times to today's post-colonial era. They took over the term itself, investing their own concept with meanings they could not help hearing in the exogenous discourses. In the course of interacting with exogenous perspectives, they developed perspectives of their own in respect of those activities designated as "cargo cult". In these indigenous perspectives, "cargo cult" is loaded with negative connotations; indeed, one thing is perfectly clear – no one identifies at all with "cargo cult".

In the following pages, I shall acquaint you with these indigenous perspectives. The representations by the Papua New Guineans to which I have referred to all concern the Yali movement – which sprang up in the latter half of the 1940s in the north-east of what at the time was New Guinea. It took its name from Yali, the man who spearheaded the movement. After loyally serving in the Australian army in World War II, he returned after the war to his home region on the Rai Coast, where he soon acquired considerable popularity with the local people. With the permission of the Australian administration, he embarked on consciousness-raising tours to many parts of Madang District, urging his compatriots to participate actively in developing their region. In the speeches he gave on these tours, he dwelt on the high standard of living he had witnessed during his three trips to Australia, calling on New Guineans to work towards achieving the same for themselves[3]. He laid down rules for village life, exhorted his countrymen to plant cash crops, encouraged them to get some education and dangled the prospect of them one day winning political independence for Papua New Guinea. With his rule-making and his visions Yali made a deep impression on the people of his home region. New Guineans from various parts of Madang District, and even beyond, were led to take numerous initiatives in a variety of areas – social, economic, political and religious – all with a

3. It often happened that indigenous men who had visited Australia during World War II would then, upon returning home, launch initiatives designed to bring about a socioeconomic transformation of conditions on the ground. One interesting case is Tom Kabu, as Joshua Bell made clear in his contribution to our session.

view to preparing themselves for the transformation. Because they regarded Yali as one who embodied the power and knowledge needed to alter their lives radically, he was able, in next to no time, to establish himself as a powerful and charismatic leader. From the indigenous perspective, he performed what they called "*wok bilong Yali*", or "Yali's work" – i.e. work in the sense that he was seeking to bring about social change in Papua New Guinea. The Australian administration, for its part, first acknowledged Yali's initiatives and supported him. However, by the end of the 1940s, the Yali movement had come under attack from the Lutheran mission and European settlers, as a result of which the authorities moved in and denounced the movement as a "cargo cult".

In the humanities and social sciences, "cargo cult" was long thought of as an objective scientific concept. One need only examine the bulk of earlier anthropological writings on the subject to see that their authors thought they were merely stating a fact in describing this or that social movement as a "cargo cult". It is this apparent "fact" that I will be placing in question here. My approach is indebted to discourse analysis as developed by Michel Foucault (1980[1977], 1991[1972]), but also to Lamont Lindstrom's application of Foucault to a particular South Pacific society (1990a). Drawing on this perspective, I shall review the historical record to show how social movements continually came to be described as "cargo cults" – and with such virulence that what *seemed* to be the case came, over time, to be a matter of steadfast *belief* (cf. Kaplan 1990). In the course of my treatment I hope to show, with regard to this construction of "cargo cults", that for a long time too little attention was paid to links existing between the discourses of the indigenous people and those of exogenous observers.

Links of this kind between exogenous and indigenous representations will be analyzed from the theoretical perspective of dialogics. This analysis owes much to studies by Martha Kaplan and John Kelly (1994; cf. Kelly and Kaplan 2001), and Francesca Merlan (2005). Drawing on earlier works by Bakhtin and Voloshinov, Kaplan, Kelly and Merlan conceive the formation of cultural discourses and practices as a process triggered when cultures enter into dialogic relationships with each other. On this view, dialogic relationships embrace social interactions in their entirety, i.e. more is at stake than merely linguistic relationships (Kaplan and Kelly 1994: 129; cf. Merlan 2005: 179). Merlan argues that when investigating the (re)production of sociocultural patterns, centrality must be given to how those speaking and/or acting are oriented toward others (Merlan 2005: 176-179). It is from just such a dialogic perspective that I consider how indigenous and exogenous discourses on social movements (as well as the practices that accompany these) take their bearings from each other. Such mutual alignment I construe as a form of linking. Based on this, I argue that taking such links seriously would be a great epistemological step forward. For then we would better understand the indigenous perspectives and grasp why the term "cargo cult" is by no means unproblematic for anthropological use.

In view of these problems, I suggested (2004), together with Vincent Crapanzano (2004: 227), that it was time to write "cargo cult" *sous rature* (after the French philosopher Jacques Derrida)[4]. Basically this means that a word is crossed out yet printed in order to show that, for all its inaccuracy, it is still indispensable[5]. The term is indispensable, in the sense that we must refer to it in our critical reflections. But in my view it is unsuitable as an objective scientific concept for analyzing social movements. It is in this context, therefore, that I use distancing inverted commas for "cargo cult" in my work[6].

Early exogenous perspectives I: colonial representations

First I shall look at early popular, missionary and administrative statements about social movements in south-west Oceania, for it is in such colonial descriptions that we first encounter the term "cargo cult". Studies of the genesis of the term "cargo cult", which Lamont Lindstrom (1993) and I (e.g. 1992, 1995, 2004) conducted independently of each other, reveal that from the mid-1940s on colonial discourses take to talking of "cargo cult" – before the anthropological discourses do.

The first documented mention of "cargo cult" is by N. M. Bird, a settler in what was then the territory of New Guinea. In an article in the *Pacific Islands Monthly* (PIM), a periodical widely read throughout the south Pacific, he introduced the term thus:

> "Stemming directly from religious teaching of equality, and its resulting sense of injustice, is what is generally known as 'Vailala Madness,' or 'Cargo Cult.' [...] In all cases the 'Madness' takes the same form: A native, infected with the disorder, states that he has been visited by a relative long dead, who stated that a great number of ships loaded with 'cargo' had been sent by the ancestor of the native for the benefit of the natives of a particular village or area." (Bird 1945: 69)

---

4. See Spivak 1976: XIV-XVIII for an explanation of Derrida's writing *sous rature*.
5. A similar observation was made by James Clifford at the session we held in 2009.
6. This article draws together a number of thoughts and passages taken from earlier, more exhaustive treatments of mine (Hermann 1992, 1995, 1997, 2004, 2009).

When Bird talks of "Vailala Madness", he is referring to a text by F. E. Williams, sometime assistant government anthropologist, who coined the expression for a certain movement that had arisen in 1919 in the vicinity of Papua's Vailala River (1976a, b [orig. 1923, 1934]). Bird warned that such "madness" in the local people constituted a potential military threat. And if there was a show-down, they would then reveal their true face, opined Bird:

> "His discipline and training will be discarded at a moment's notice and he will, emerge, as he is, a primitive savage with all a primitive savage's instincts." (Bird 1945: 70)

Bird's article must have touched a nerve, and soon the pages of the *Pacific Islands Monthly* were the venue for a vigorous debate on the reasons for the emergence of "cargo cults". The periodical published, among other things, an English summary (PIM, November 1946: 16,70) of a German article by G. Höltker (1946), a Catholic missionary with the Societas Verbi Divini (SVD), who possessed first-hand knowledge of the situation in New Guinea's Madang District. In this summary, the social movements were referred to as "Cargo-cult", "religious madness" and "mania", and their "characteristic features" were described thus:

> "The main characteristics of this mania are the following: A great confusion of old paganism with newly imported, half-understood Christianity; overemphasised local patriotism; arrogant consciousness of being a distinct race; and aspiration to political and religious independence." (PIM, November 1946: 16)

This notion that "old paganism" lay behind the evil of "cargo cult" was shared by both Catholic and Lutheran missions. Thus in a 1947 annual report written by the Lutheran missionary Wagner, who from where he was stationed in Ulap collaborated with Hofmann in Biliau for purposes of missionizing those parts of the Rai Coast hinterland as yet unoccupied by the Catholics, we read:

> "Outwardly the cargo-cult is a result of the war and its confusion caused in those primitives, who, a few generations ago, lived still in the 'stone age'. As for the inward reasons it is the result of the growing materialistic thinking which already had set in before the war, but now, seems to have seized their confused minds completely. Connected with it is, and was, a growing loosening from the gospel. The inward apostasy resulted in an open reversion into heathenism." (Wagner 1947: 4)

More or less simultaneously with these first references in popular and missionary sources, "cargo cult" begins appearing in documents of the Australian administration in New Guinea – for instance, from 1946 we find the term cropping up in patrol reports for parts of what was then Madang District. If we peruse these sources, it is clear the officers held a negative view of "cargo cult" and sought to proscribe it.

It was in this discursive climate that the colonial institutions on the Rai Coast began to cast a quizzical eye on Yali's activities, especially with regard to "cargo cult". The Australian administration initially decided that the rumours swirling around Yali here were baseless. Well aware of his popularity with the indigenous population, the administration wanted Yali to press ahead with propagating their development program. The officer charged with monitoring Yali's activities wrote: "One of his greatest claims for this is his denunciation of the 'cargo cult'" (Prowse 1946: Appendix E). But from 1947 the Lutheran mission had Yali in its sights, promoting a form of discourse about "cargo cult" that was to his detriment. Writing of the area to which he had been assigned in the south-east part of the Rai Coast, Wagner saw Yali as some kind of hero surrounded by devotees, adding:

> "The Yali-cult is the counterpart of the coastal-people to the more clumsy cargo-cult of the more backward mountain-people" (Wagner 1947: 4).

In the following years Yali himself turned away from the missions, calling for a return to indigenous religious practices. At the same time, the Lutheran mission stepped up its efforts to discredit him. In 1950 they finally succeeded in hauling him before a court. By now the Australian administration, too, had withdrawn their support. As it happens, Yali was not charged with "cargo cult" – though this, at the time, was an offence under law. Instead the charges related to kidnapping and rape, for which the court sent him down for a period of six and a half years. Yali himself, the members of his social movement (who came from various regions in north-east New Guinea) and also the local people from his home region shared a common fate: that of being stereotyped by European observers as followers of "cargo cult". In the course of this stereotyping, the administration took to characterizing the local people as "lazy" and "very backward" (Reitano 1949/1950: 4).

While it is true that, during the 1940s, discourses of popular, missionary or administrative provenance did not share the same agenda when it came to describing and judging indigenous activities, nevertheless, common to all of them was their propensity for associating "cargo cult" with pejorative ideas, as for example when they spoke of "madness", "primitiveness", "heathendom" and "backwardness". All of them referred to the fact that aspects of Western discourses had been adopted by the social movements. Thus popular and administrative discourses stressed that the social movements had borrowed parts of Christian teaching. Missionary discourses, in turn, complained that participants in the movements were taking their lead from the materialistic attitudes of the colonists. What none of these discourses did, however, was recognize the existence of links that might have promoted a dialogue between the indigenous people and the Europeans.

Early exogenous perspectives II: anthropological representations

The anthropological "cargo cult" discourse arose against a background of earlier popular discourses by missionaries and administrators concerning "cargo cult". Early anthropological representations differ in form and content from the colonial ones, but even they did not avoid the pitfall of slipping into the pejorative and the dismissive. Thus Lucy Mair (1948) introduced the concept by alluding to a movement that F. E. Williams (1976a, b [orig. 1923, 1934]) had documented only to dismiss it as "Vailala madness":

> "A notable feature of the reaction of the peoples of New Guinea to white rule is the occurrence at different times in almost every part of the Australian territories of a manifestation which used to be known as the 'Vailala madness', but is now more commonly described as the 'cargo cult.'" (Mair 1948: 64)

In her stock-taking of "cargo cult" manifestations, Lucy Mair stressed the element of "cargo" (1948: 66). Though she did refer to political agendas being pursued by the movements, it would be fair to say that in her classification she played down the importance of these for the movements.

Soon social and cultural anthropology was producing an anthropological discourse on "cargo cult". This discourse was thoroughly heterogeneous and contained analyses reflecting various schools of theory. Studies of social movements in south-west Oceania published between the late 1940s and the early 1970s placed their primary focus on traditional social structures and religious systems of belief, though they did allow for the impact of missionization and colonization on the indigenous cultures. They were therefore able to find room in their analyses for the indigenous adoption of Christian discursive formations as well as Western discourses relating to material goods and development. As a result, we can state that such studies were able to perceive the links between Western and indigenous discourses concerning these movements. But though their authors were alive to the existence of such links, what we largely miss in these studies, and the analyses they contained, is any sense of what the Western and indigenous discourses had in common, much less any readiness to question the practice of dubbing indigenous activities "cargoist" or "cultic". Given that the bulk of anthropological explanations of the "cargo cult" complex were based, at the time, on Western rationality discourse, the activities of movement members were adjudged more or less clearly to be "irrational".

Structural-functionalist studies in those years, according to Mondher Kilani (1983: 41-46), were particularly inclined to judge the ritual activities of the movements in terms of the extent to which they shored up social stability; accordingly, they applied their own (Western) benchmark of rationality versus irrationality (e.g. Firth 1951, 1955; Stanner 1953, 1958; Hogbin 1970 [orig. 1958]; Inglis 1957). Although the Marxist-leaning studies of Tibor Bodrogi (1951) and Peter Worsley (1957) did construe the movements as anti-colonial articulations by subjugated societies, it would be fair to say that their arguments contain formulations that amount to a certain discrediting of movements of the "cargo cult" type. In his psychological interpretation, Weston La Barre (1971) made no bones about claiming irrationality (again) as a characteristic of "cargo cults". His conclusion: "'cargo' ideology was not rational-economic but irrational-religious" (La Barre 1971: 17).

Peter Lawrence (1954, 1955, 1964), who worked on the social movements and, in particular, on the Yali movement in Madang District of what was then New Guinea, stood apart from the structural-functionalist interpretations of the time. By approaching the epistemology of indigenous societies from a classical historical perspective, he was able to uncover the logic of the systems of belief underlying the "cargo-complex". But because Lawrence was locked into the development discourse of the Australian administration, he condemned the "cargo" ideology as underlying the scant acceptance in the district of the administration-backed development programs, and wrote of the "... continuing native interest in cargo ideology, which is still a force to be combated" (1964: 264). The Yali movement was described by Lawrence (1964) as being part of a comprehensive "cargo" movement. On the one hand, Lawrence claimed that Yali's compatriots, given the "cargo" rumours that were then in circulation, saw his programs as containing a "cargo" message. On the other hand, he considered that even Yali had himself been inducted into a "cargo cult" for a certain time by a "cargo" prophet.

We will soon see how the inhabitants of Yali's home village, the members of the Yali movement and its successor organization entered into dialogue with early colonial and anthropological representations. But before hearing their voices, I will give a brief overview of recent studies that deal with the term "cargo cult" from a critical point of view.

Emerging critical perspectives on "cargo cult" in anthropology

In recent years, several historians and anthropologists have come to see the term "cargo cult" as unsuited for describing social movements in south-west Oceania. Certainly it was not mere chance that scholars from Oceania were among the first to express their unease at the use made of the "cargo cult" concept. Back in the 1970s, Waiko (1973: 420) rehabilitated the "Taro cult", and also the "Baigona cult", as movements that were not of the "cargo cult" type. Willington Jojoga Opeba (1981 [1977]: 128) confirmed this insight. Epeli Hau`ofa pointed out that the "cargo cult" label was understood in Melanesia as a negative stereotype, and joked that we anthropologists were "wearing dark glasses, through our fascination with cargo cults" (Hau`ofa 1975: 286). These early voices were soon joined by others. Louise Morauta (1974: 154) observed that Yali's supporters in the greater Madang area dissociate themselves from any activities labelled "cargo cult". Roger Keesing (1978: 243, 70), writing of the Maasina Rule movement in the Solomon Islands, was adamant that it could not be classified as "cargo cult". Peter Hempenstall condemned the "cargo cult" concept as a demeaning colonial label (1981: 1; Hempenstall and Rutherford 1984: 120). Kilani in his insightful study (1983) pointed up the interconnectivity between Western rationality-vs-irrationality discourse and the "cargo cult" discourse of the anthropologists. Entering a plea for researchers to give more attention to the contextual parameters underlying social change in Melanesia, instead of viewing such change as an isolated phenomenon, Nancy McDowell (1988) announced serious doubts as to the utility of such a category as "cargo cult". Taking account of ideological aspects, Pem Buck (1988) criticized that Western "cargo cult" discourses had been used to rationalize the exploitation of Papua New Guineans by Europeans.

Since the 1990s, the critique of academic discourse on "cargo cult" has gathered pace. Martha Kaplan (1990, 1995, 2004) focused on the historical agency of members of the erstwhile Tuka movement in Fiji, and in so doing has provided a valuable critical analysis of the colonial constructions of "cargo cult". Lamont Lindstrom (1990b: 240, 241; 1993; 2004), building on his research into the John Frum movement of Tanna, Vanuatu, trained a subtly critical eye on the multifarious "cargo cult" discourses propagated in south-west Oceania and in "the West". His essay (this volume) on the online face of Western cargo imagery demonstrates yet again the fascination that "cargo cult" clearly evokes in Western cultural circles. Based on a study of the indigenous reception of the Western concept of "cargo cult" (as well as its colonial baggage), I have myself called for a thorough rethinking of the issue (1992, 1995, 1997, 2004). Wolfgang Kempf (1992) too, citing his investigations into indigenous conceptions of change, questioned how an early millenarian movement among the Ngaing came to be classified as "cargo cult", and spoke of the "cargo cult" concept as already having the status of an historical "monument in the landscape of anthropological enquiry and discourse" (1992: 84). Writing in his introduction to the volume "Imagining Cargo Cults", Ton Otto (1992: 1) formulated doubts as to the analytic value of the concept. Max and Eleanor Rimoldi (1992) drew attention to the stigmatizing effects of ascriptions of "cargo cult" in connection with the Hahalis movement on Buka Island. Michele Stephen (1997: 335) noted that "cargo cults" were so constructed as to make them the most exotic of exotic beliefs – "the most other", as Stephen puts it. In view of this growing chorus of critical voices, Sjoerd Jaarsma (1997: 85) made the point that the academic "cargo cult" discourse might well founder on the rocks of its own critique of the concept. Critically resisting interpretation of Melanesian religion in terms of "cargo cult", Joel Robbins (1998) suggested instead an examination of the indigenous model of the role of desire. Vincent Crapanzano (2004) injected an innovative perspective into the debate, entering a plea that the role of hope be investigated in connection with these social movements. What also proved especially important in the critical debate was the insight that construction of the other in Western "cargo cult" discourses is closely linked to the construction of the self (see on this point Buck 1988: 158; Kaplan 1990: 4; Lindstrom 1990b: 241; Hermann 1995: 169; Stephen 1997: 335-336; Lattas 1992: 1; Jebens and Kohl 1999). Nancy McDowell (2000), too, seized on to this aspect, critiquing constructions invoking a false polarity: "them", the so-called cultists, versus "us", the observers. Finally, the essays in this volume shed new light on earlier movements. Hence Marcellin Abong (this volume) characterizes the Nagriamel movement of Santo, Vanuatu, as political, thereby contributing to that movement's rehabilitation.

If these authors declined to categorize the movements under investigation as "cargo cult", preferring alternative concepts instead, if some of these authors even went so far as to deconstruct the concept per se, this may indicate that some of them, at least, were acting out of an awareness that the indigenous actors felt themselves to have been misrepresented by exogenous representations. Let us therefore turn to the indigenous representations of Yali's work, which strongly suggest that indigenous actors developed a critical stance towards "cargo cult" from interacting with messages whose ultimate provenance was early colonial and anthropological representations.

Indigenous representations I: how Yali's work is seen by his home village

The people of Yali's home village Yasaburing [7] are well aware of the notoriety they gained through both Yali and the book by Peter Lawrence (1964). Thus two women from Yali's clan told me that all the villagers were ashamed of the allegations of "cargo cult" directed against them at the time:

> Kabak: He [Lawrence] twisted [what happened], and then ruined our name by saying: "They practised 'kago kalt'!"
> Thalia: That's why we're ashamed!
> Kabak: Yes!
> Thalia: That really hurt! That ruined our village's reputation! [8]

The sense of shame these two women expressed suggests the tenor of the local emotional discourse surrounding the Yali movement which is insistent that the Yasaburing were held in derision for years on account of alleged "cargo cult" activities. This, it must be said, was certainly not Peter Lawrence's intention. What is clear from what the Yasaburing say is that, rather than Lawrence himself, it was the representatives of the missions and the administration who, for decades, kept up their allegations of "cargo cult", sometimes backing these up by citing his book. Since the charge went hand in hand with insinuations of primitiveness, heathendom and irrationality, the Yasaburing, not surprisingly, felt degraded. They were firmly told to distance themselves from all and any "cargo" ideas and they were forbidden to participate in rites that were in any way linked to such notions.

In dialogue with colonial "cargo cult" discourses, the indigenous people devised a matching one of their own. In an act of transculturation, they took over the English term "cargo cult", fashioning from it their own concept "*kago kalt*", which they wove into both the Ngaing vernacular and Tok Pisin, the lingua franca of Papua New Guinea. They endowed "*kago kalt*" with meanings they derived from what they heard in the colonial discourses. Among the definitions of "*kago kalt*" communicated to me by the Yasaburing are the following:

> "*Kago kalt*, that means: people are waiting for money, hoping that money will come up out of nothing. People say the Yasaburing are waiting for money to come up out of nothing, for *kago* to come up out of very nothing." [9]

---

7. At their request, I refer to their village under a pseudonym.

8. Kabak and Thalia 22 September 1985. All of the Yasaburings' quotes have been translated from the original Tok Pisin by Elfriede Hermann.

9. S. 25 May 1989.

The idea that "money" or "*kago*" will "come up out of nothing" strikes the Yasaburing as nothing short of absurd. Moreover, they condemn any attitude of just waiting and sitting idly by, which in a subsistence economy such as theirs is bound to lead nowhere. For them it is clear that work is the key to getting anything at all. But in the perspective they develop, "*kago kalt*" is the diametrical opposite of work:

> "Kago kalt means: Somebody is not able to work his business. Somebody is not able to work his garden. He will sit there doing nothing and he will be waiting." [10]

"*Kago kalt*" in Yasaburing discourse stands for an attitude of muddled thinking, one that does not obey the logic of action in their world and which leads to laziness, indeed incapacity. For that reason, "*kago kalt*" is something to be condemned.

The people of Yali's home village are quick to protest when his work is described by such a pejorative term as "*kago kalt*" or "cargo cult". Witnesses who remember Yali's appearances after coming back from the war abruptly dismiss any suggestions of that kind. A highly respected elder, who had as a young man accompanied Yali on several of his tours through Madang District, offered this testimony:

> "Before [Yali was put into prison] he did not say, 'The *kago* will come or anything like that will come up! Only through our hard labour will anything come up, it's not possible for anything to come into existence out of nothing! [...]' That is what he told us. And I really believe in this, actually, all of us do. [...] Because we heard his speeches and his teachings." [11]

When talk turns to Yali and to his deeds, the Yasaburing dwell mostly on the teachings Yali strove to get across in his speeches. Among his teachings, which the Yasaburing refer to as "school" (or in Tok Pisin, "*skul*"), are the following points, as described to me by a man of great influence from Yali's clan:

> "Now Yali gave his '*skul*' [...]. He said: 'Earlier we Papua New Guineans practised a number of bad customs. But from now on we are going to change. [...]' And he went on to add: 'You yourselves are to plant a row of coconut-palms! And then you will plant coffee! And on top of that, you will plant cocoa! You will also sow rice, cabbage and onions! The experts in charge of agriculture will give us all these things, so that we can sow them. From now on we will stand on our own feet.' This he urged on everyone." [12]

These teachings the Yasaburing refer to as Yali's "good work". They allowed him to inspire his countrymen and also draw in a number of supporters from the outside,

---

10. P. 9 September 1990.
11. G. 27 May 1989.
12. L. 17 March 1989.

who took to visiting him in his home village. Scrutiny of local oral history shows that Yali's positive deeds fall in the period between his return from the war in 1945 and his arrest in 1950. The Yasaburing distinguish this early phase of Yali's initiatives from a later phase after 1955, the year when he returned home from prison. In this post-prison phase Yali was a broken man, they insist. From that time on, not only was he saddled down by "cargo cult" reproaches, he was also led astray by the actions of some of his followers. These were followers who had come from other parts of Madang District to Yasaburing and who had indeed, the villagers state, performed questionable deeds – for example, they had stood flowers in bottles and invoked the ancestors to create money in their place, and they had called upon Yali to deploy magical practices in order to harm others. It was these outsiders – the Yasaburing know – who were behind "*kago kalt*" and any recourse to it, and it was they, too, who had supplied the pretext for Yali's work coming to be labelled "cargo cult".

The Yasaburing distance themselves from such machinations as these. They point out that they had, at the time, expelled these outside supporters of Yali's from the village. To refute the "cargo cult" charges levelled by the Europeans, as well as the "*kago kalt*" rumours and aspersions of their countrymen, they were driven to devise counter-discourses of their own. In one of these, work plays an important role, as is manifest in the following statement by a middle-aged woman:

> "We are not waiting for *kago kalt* or for somebody to produce money and to give it to us … No! I, in fact, all of us know very well how to take pains working our gardens and working our business in order to earn money." [13]

As these words clearly show, the Yasaburing point additionally to the effort they put into business ("*bisnis*" in Tok Pisin) and into development ("*developmen*"). These two keywords are central to two counter-discourses in which they engage in order to repudiate charges of "cargo cult". A third counter-discourse focuses on their identity as Roman Catholics, who wish to have nothing to do with heathen practices of any kind. In addition, they have crafted a discourse turning on local tradition ("*kastom*"), which they are forceful in mobilizing against ascriptions of "cargo cult". They deploy this discourse for the purpose of protecting the indigenous domain of ancestor worship ("*tambaran*" in Tok Pisin and "*gabu*" in the Ngaing vernacular) from the least hint of suspicion. Being a traditional practice serving the common good, ancestor worship has, they insist, nothing whatsoever to do with dubious ideas of more recent date.

---

13. P. 9 September 1990.

There is a final point that is worth raising: in a conversation I had with Bikmeri, Yali's widow, she robustly rejected the allegations of "cargo cult". She linked Yali's actions to recommendations by the Australian military and administrative officials on the one hand and missionaries of European origin on the other:

> "He [Yali] worked together with them [the whites]! So we thought: 'We'll just go on doing exactly the same, and things will get better'. [Bikmeri is incensed by now] But no! They cut down [Yali's career]! They threw him into prison. And I said to myself: 'It isn't as if we were the ones to invent it! It was what you people [the whites] had taught him [Yali] and got him to spread! So the people here will learn to take the initiative themselves and to do the work! And behind you, you hear talk from some people and you go off in the very opposite direction!' I was so angry [...]." [14]

Bikmeri's comments hold a mirror up to Europeans, reflecting the "cargo cult" focus back at them.

Indigenous representations II: how Yali's work is seen by the Dabsau Association

Following Yali's death in 1975, a successor organization to the Yali movement emerged. It was called the Dabsau Association and tasked with articulating many of the issues that had been central to the Yali movement. When exactly it was that the Dabsau Association came into being can no longer be reconstructed, yet there can be no doubt that it had its origins in the Madang hinterland. Then, in July 1985, Yali's son James – who had studied agronomy –, along with some of his university friends took over management of the Dabsau Association, intending to restructure it as an economic-cum-political body aligned to Western models. That same year – 1985 – I had the opportunity to document developments inside this body and noted that the Dabsau Association had taken to holding meetings in many different places – in Madang, in the Trans-Gogol region, on the north coast, on the island of Manam and in a beach village on the Rai Coast. Former followers of Yali from these regions now flocked to join the Dabsau Association [15]. Only the people of Yali's home village maintained a critical distance from this new organization and its various activities,

---

14. S. 24 August 1990.

15. The Dabsau Association still exists. Thus, in the *Weekend Courier* (16-17 August 2008: 15) it was reported that its members had attended the funeral of Yali's widow Sungum who was James' mother. Many members of the Dabsau Association have formed a "Yali church" in the last decade. I owe this information to anthropologist Nancy Sullivan, who has been studying the activities of the Yali church and its members.

although some of them subsequently relented, especially when James Yali assumed the leadership.

Right from the start the Dabsau Association pursued a variety of goals, all of them responses to a globalizing world. Development was to be prioritized throughout Madang Province. Along with such intended changes to the economic order, social changes were to be set in progress as well. The better to achieve these multiple goals, the Dabsau Association strove for political representation, on the provincial if not the national level. Here the Association's interests overlapped with those of James Yali, who had political ambitions of his own. Beginning in the late 1980s, he repeatedly ran for office. In 1987 he was a Madang regional candidate, and in both 1992 and 1997 he was a candidate for the Rai Coast Open constituency (*Post Courier*, 11 March 2003). In the national elections of July 2002, he won a seat for Rai Coast Open and was installed as Governor of Madang, a post he held until 2007 [16].

Preserving of elements of "*kastom*", or traditional culture, was another of the Association's goals. "In my view, our local culture ('*kaltsa bilong yumi long ples*') is both very good and very strong. So we mustn't turn our back on it," was the opinion expressed by one speaker for the Association [17]. Members were called upon to jettison those aspects that were seen as negative, e.g. sorcery, while retaining all those aspects that fostered peaceful and productive co-existence.

One of the Dabsau Association's goals – right from the start – was to clear Yali's name, and the Yali movement's as well, from the stigma of "cargo cult". To this end, its members spent much of their time talking about the history of the Yali movement and how the Dabsau Association had come to be formed. The topic they returned to time and again was that of Yali's many achievements in driving forward the economic, sociocultural and political development not only of Madang but of the country as a whole: as they saw it, Yali had paved the way for the very independence of Papua New Guinea. Indeed, the team of leaders (especially) insisted that millenarian thinking (along with the activities this gave rise to, which had sparked off the outcry against "cargo cult") had no place in their future and must be abandoned. James Yali was explicit:

---

16. In 2007, after being vigorously attacked by the opposition, he was brought before the court and charged with rape. But when the next elections were held, also in 2007, he managed to win back his Rai Coast seat, from a prison cell, where he awaited the result of an appeal he had filed against the conviction (*PNG Post-Courier* 27 – 29 July 2007). In February 2010 he was released on parole (*PNG Post-Courier* 22 February 2010). I thank Steffen Dalsgaard for sending me a copy of the 2007 *Post-Courier* articles.

17. B. E. 2 January 1986. Translated from the original Tok Pisin by Elfriede Hermann.

"That's my aim: first and foremost it is to get the people to believe in self-reliance. That is not to wait for the service [rendered by some state institution], not to believe that my father would come back from the dead and lead them like he used to." (3 October 1985)

But even as the team of leaders at the helm of the Dabsau Association were asking their followers to redouble their efforts at self-improvement, their political opponents were revisiting the old charges and adding more of their own devising. It wasn't long before the organization was being accused of egging its members on to practise a new variety of "cargo cult"[18]. Thus, several ministers from the provincial government in Madang, who came from the Rai Coast and had preconceived views on the Yali movement, made threatening statements in which they called the Dabsau Association one big "cargo cult". The then minister for provincial affairs and local government even went so far (this was at the beginning of December 1985) as to repeat the charge on Radio Madang. James Yali reacted by challenging the minister to a public debate, a challenge which the latter declined to accept. Launching a counter-discourse, members of the Association set out to demonstrate what the Yali movement had achieved on a variety of levels: economic, social and political. If its successor organization – and James Yali along with it – were to succeed, so the logic went, it would have to be apparent, with the vantage of hindsight, that the Yali movement had played a transformative role.

Counter-discourses and counter-strategies of this kind clearly show the members of the Dabsau Association engaging in a dialogue of their own with diverse "cargo cult"-inspired representations of the Yali movement. Among these representations are Western discourses, to cite one example; another would be the discourses promulgated by indigenous elites in post-colonial Papua New Guinea. Among these elites there circulated discourses modelled on exogenous representations and replete with negative connotations. The members of Dabsau Association had always expected that anything they said in their own defence would be drowned out by raucous cries of "cargo cult". Small wonder, then, that they chose to stock up on counter-arguments so that, when the time came, they would be able to fight back. And they also took the precaution of forming alliances with powerful politicians, e.g. from Pangu Pati[19].

18. That movements which are linked to political interests are disparagingly dubbed "cargo cult" in an effort to discredit them is a phenomenon we encounter as well in other parts of south-western Oceania. Marcellin Abong (this volume) describes this for the Nagriamel movement that originated in the mid-1960s on Santo, an island in today's Vanuatu. See Marc Tabani (2009 and this volume) for some valuable insights into the nexi between indigenous movements and politics in Melanesia.
19. Pangu Pati was for many years the ruling party in Papua New Guinea; it was brought down in November 1985 by a vote of no confidence.

Conclusion: linking the exogenous and indigenous perspectives

All these discourses – those of the people of Yali's home village and those of the members of the Dabsau Association – attest to dialogues between indigenous and exogenous discourse and practice. Papua New Guineans in (or on the fringes of) the Yali movement have found their ways of formulating "*kago kalt*", ways that involve orienting their actions toward discourses and measures put in place by representatives of colonial and then postcolonial institutions. Their anticipation of the discourses of others was instrumental in shaping what they said and what they did about "cargo cult" and "*kago kalt*".

Thus, from a dialogic perspective, it is possible to point to several links between indigenous and exogenous representations. One of these proceeds by way of the negative connotations of "cargo cult" discourses. The Yasaburing have struggled to come to terms particularly with the negative stereotypes ascribed to "cargo cults" in the early popular, missionary and administrative sources. In the counter-discourses they developed, we find such stereotypes as "madness", "primitiveness", "heathenness" and "backwardness" recurring – yet these figure as criteria they utterly repudiate, and rightly so. Yali's widow Bikmeri, as we saw, had clear words to say about a link between the indigenous actors and the Europeans: in her perspective, she herself, Yali and Yali's followers had only done what the Europeans had urged them to do.

And it is possible to discern yet another link, this time a genealogical one, linking the exogenous constructions to "cargo cults". Popular, missionary, administrative and anthropological discourses made "cargo cult" the focus of their concern, delineating it from other concerns, endowing "cargo cult" with particular properties and creating through the act of definition a reality that would not otherwise exist (cf. Foucault 1988 [1969]: 74). Using these properties, it was possible to isolate, name and generally pin down something that was then required to function as the object of "cargo cult". By means of such objectivization, the phenomenon of "cargo cult" was brought into existence (cf. McDowell 1988). "Cultic" practices performed in anticipation of "cargo" were made into a category of demarcation: "cargo cult" characterized the "others", from whom the Western self could safely distance itself.

By proceeding to a fundamental revision of the "cargo cult" concept, we may open our eyes to how much we participate in the phenomena we observe. By selecting certain characteristics of social movements, we have involved ourselves in their construction, thereby obscuring the links between what it is we have constructed and the indigenous activities in question. Owning up to these links will, however, let us see the social movements of south-west Oceania in a more useful way, not as a phenomenon that excludes those who construct it but, rather, includes them – and this from the very beginning.

Acknowledgments

Warmest thanks to the people of Yasaburing for their hospitality and generosity in sharing their dialogues with me. To the people of other Ngaing villages, to members of the Dabsau Association and to my Papua New Guinean friends elsewhere I wish to express my gratitude for many stimulating conversations. I am greatly indebted to various institutions of government, on both the national and provincial levels but particularly to the National Research Institute and the National Archives of Papua New Guinea. Grants from the post-graduate scholarship program of Baden-Württemberg and from the German Academic Exchange Service greatly facilitated my fieldwork. I wish especially to thank Marcellin Abong and Marc Tabani for organizing the session at which this paper was first presented; also my thanks to them, the participants of the session, Steffen Herrmann and three anonymous reviewers for their valuable comments, and to Wolfgang Kempf for critically discussing my ideas with me following our fieldwork. Dr Bruce Allen has kindly helped, as on so many earlier occasions, in preparing the English version of this article.

Bibliography

Bird, N.M.
1945   "Is There Danger of a Post-war Flare-up Among New Guinea Natives?",
        Pacific Islands Monthly, 16 (4): 69-70.

Bodrogi, Tibor
1951   "Colonization and Religious Movements in Melanesia",
        Acta Ethnographica, 2 (1-4): 259-290.

Brown, Paula
1966   "Social Change and Social Movements". In Ernest K. Fisk (ed.), *New-Guinea on the Threshold*. Canberra: Australian National University Press, pp. 149-165.

Buck, Pem Davidson
1988   "Cargo-Cult Discourse: Myth and the Rationalization of Labor Relations in Papua New Guinea", *Dialectical Anthropology*, 13 (2): 157-171.

Crapanzano, Vincent
2004   "Thoughts on Hope and Cargo". In H. Jebens (ed.), *Cargo, Cult, and Culture Critique*. Honolulu: University of Hawai'i Press, pp. 227-242.

Firth, Raymond

1951   *Elements of Social Organization.* London: Watts.

1955   "The Theory of "Cargo" Cults: A Note on Tikopia", *Man,* 55: 130-132.

Foucault, Michel

1980 [1977]   "Truth and Power". In C. Gordon (ed.), *Power/Knowledge. Selected Interviews and Other Writings 1972-1977.* New York: Pantheon Books, pp. 109-133.

1988 [1969]   *Archäologie des Wissens.* Frankfurt a. M.: Suhrkamp.

1991 [1972]   *Die Ordnung des Diskurses.* Frankfurt a. M.: Fischer.

Hau'ofa, Epeli

1975   "Anthropology and Pacific Islanders", *Oceania,* 45 (4): 283-289.

Hempenstall, Peter

1981   "Protest or Experiment? Theories of "Cargo Cults"", *Occasional Paper* No. 2: 1-10. Research Centre for Southwest Pacific Studies. La Trobe University.

Hempenstall, Peter and Rutherford, Noel

1984   *Protest and Dissent in the Colonial Pacific.* Suva, Fiji: Institute of Pacific Studies of the University of the South Pacific.

Hermann, Elfriede

1992   "The Yali Movement in Retrospect: Rewriting History, Redefining "Cargo Cult"". In A. Lattas (ed.), *Alienating Mirrors: Christianity, Cargo Cults and Colonialism in Melanesia,* Special Issue of *Oceania,* 63 (1): 55-71.

1995   *Emotionen und Historizität: Der emotionale Diskurs über die Yali-Bewegung in einer Dorfgemeinschaft der Ngaing, Papua New Guinea.* Berlin: Reimer.

1997   "Kastom versus Cargo Cult: Emotional Discourse on the Yali Movement in Madang Province, Papua New Guinea". In T. Otto and A. Borsboom (eds), *Cultural Dynamics of Religious Change in Oceania.* Leiden: KITLV Press, pp. 87-102.

2004   "Dissolving the Self-Other Dichotomy in Western "Cargo Cult" Constructions". In H. Jebens (ed.), *Cargo, Cult, and Culture Critique.* Honolulu: University of Hawai'i Press, pp. 36-58.

2009   "Rappresentazioni dei movimenti sociali nell'Oceania sudoccidentale: Tra prospettive esogene e indigene". In E. Gnecchi Ruscone and A. Paini (eds), *Antropologia dell'Oceania.* Milano: Raffaello Cortina Editore, pp. 103-123.

Höltker, Georg (SVD)

1946   "Schwarmgeister in Neuguinea während des letzten Krieges", *Neue Zeitschrift für Missionswissenschaft/*Nouvelle Revue de Science Missionaire, 2: 201-216.

Hogbin, Ian

1970 [1958]   *Social Change.* Carlton, Vic.: Melbourne University Press.

Inglis, Judy

1957   "Cargo Cults: The Problem of Explanation", *Oceania* 27: 249-263.

Jaarsma, Sjoerd R.

1997   "Ethnographic Perceptions of Cargo: Fragments of an Intermittent Discourse". In T. Otto and Ad. Borsboom (eds), *Cultural Dynamics of Religious Change in Oceania.* Leiden: KITLV Press, pp. 67-85.

Jebens, Holger, and Kohl, Karl-Heinz

1999   "Konstruktionen von "Cargo": Zur Dialektik von Fremd- und Selbstwahrnehmung in der Interpretation melanesischer Kultbewegungen", *Anthropos*, 94: 3-20.

Kaplan, Martha

1990   "Meaning, Agency and Colonial History: Navosavakadua and the Tuka Movement in Fiji", *American Ethnologist* 17: 1-20.

1995   *Neither Cargo nor Cult. Ritual Politics and the Colonial Imagination in Fiji*. Durham: Duke University Press.

2004   "Neither Traditional nor Foreign: Dialogics of Power and Agency in Fijian History". In H. Jebens (ed.), *Cargo, Cult, and Culture Critique*. Honolulu: University of Hawai'i Press, pp. 59-78.

Kaplan, Martha and Kelly, John D.

1994   "Rethinking Resistance: Dialogics of "Disaffection" in Colonial Fiji", *American Ethnologist*, 21 (1): 123-151.

Keesing, Roger M.

1978   "Politico-Religious Movements and Anticolonialism on Malaita: Maasina Rule in Historical Perspective", *Oceania* 48 (4): 241-261, 49 (1): 46-73.

Kelly, John D. and Kaplan, Martha

2001   *Represented Communities: Fiji and World Decolonization*. Chicago: The University of Chicago Press.

Kempf, Wolfgang

1992   ""The Second Coming of the Lord": Early Christianization, Episodic Time, and the Cultural Construction of Continuity in Sibog". In A. Lattas (ed.), *Alienating Mirrors: Christianity, Cargo Cults and Colonialism in Melanesia*, Special Issue of *Oceania*, 63(1): 72-86.

Kilani, Mondher

1983   *Les cultes du Cargo mélanésiens. Mythe et rationalité en anthropologie.* Lausanne: Éditions d'en bas.

La Barre, Weston

1971   "Materials for a History of Studies of Crisis Cults: A Bibliographic Essay", *Current Anthropology*, 12 (1): 3-27.

Lattas, Andrew

1992   "Introduction. Hysteria, Anthropological Discourse and the Concept of the Unconscious: Cargo Cults and the Scientisation of Race and Colonial Power". In A. Lattas (ed.), *Alienating Mirrors: Christianity, Cargo Cults and Colonialism in Melanesia*, Special Issue of *Oceania*, 63 (1): 1-14.

Lawrence, Peter

1954   "Cargo Cult and Religious Beliefs among the Garia", *International Archives of Ethnography*, 47: 1-20.

1955   "The Madang District Cargo Cult", *South Pacific* 8: 6-13.

1964   *Road Belong Cargo: A Study of the Cargo Movement in the Southern Madang District New Guinea*. Manchester, Melbourne: Manchester and Melbourne University Presses.

Lindstrom, Lamont

1981   "Cult and Culture: American Dreams in Vanuatu", *Pacific Studies,* 4 (2):101-123.

1984   "Doctor, Lawyer, Wise Man, Priest: Big-Men and Knowledge in Melanesia",
            Man (n.s.) 19: 291-309.

1990a   *Knowledge and Power in a South Pacific Society.* Washington: Smithsonian Institution
            Press.

1990b   "Knowledge of Cargo, Knowledge of Cult: Truth and Power on Tanna, Vanuatu".
            In G.W. Trompf (ed.), *Cargo Cults and Millenarian Movements: Transoceanic Comparisons
            of New Religious Movements.* Berlin, New York: Mouton de Gruyter, pp. 239-261.

1993   *Cargo Cult: Strange Stories of Desire from Melanesia and Beyond.* Honolulu: University of
            Hawai'i Press.

2004   "Cargo Cult at the Third Millennium". In H. Jebens (ed.), *Cargo, Cult, and Culture Critique.*
            Honolulu: University of Hawai'i Press, pp. 15-35.

Mair, Lucy P.

1948   *Australia in New Guinea.* London: Christophers.

McDowell, Nancy

1988   "A Note on Cargo Cults and Cultural Constructions of Change",
            Pacific Studies 11: 121-134.

2000   "A Brief Comment on Difference and Rationality", *Oceania,* 70(4): 373-380.

Merlan, Francesca

2005   "Explorations towards Intercultural Accounts of Socio-Cultural Reproduction and
            Change", *Oceania,* 75: 167-182.

Morauta, Louise

1974   *Beyond The Village. Local Politics in Madang, Papua New Guinea.* University of London:
            Athlone Press.

Opeba, Willington Jojoga

1981 [1977]   "The Peroveta of Buna". In G. Trompf (ed.), *Prophets of Melanesia.*
                   Port Moresby: Institute of Papua New Guinea Studies, pp. 127-142.

Otto, Ton

1992   "Introduction: Imagining Cargo Cults", *Canberra Anthropology* 15 (2): 1-10.

Pacific Islands Monthly

1946   "How "Cargo Cult" is Born: The Scientific Angle on an old subject". Translated and
            condensed from a paper written by G. Höltker in Neue Zeitschrift für Missionswissen-
            schaft/Nouvelle Revue de Science Missionaire, *Pacific Islands Monthly,* 17 (4): 16, 70.

Prowse, D. R.

1946   *Patrol Report No. 3/46, Saidor Sub-District, Madang District.* Waigani: National Archives
            of Papua New Guinea.

Raschke, Joachim

1987 [1985]   *Soziale Bewegungen: Ein historisch-systematischer Grundriss.* Frankfurt: Campus.

Reitano, F. V.

1949/50   *Patrol Report No. 4 of 1949/50, Saidor Sub-District, Madang District.* Waigani:
               National Archives of Papua New Guinea.

Rimoldi, Max and Rimoldi, Eleanor

1992   *Hahalis and the Labour of Love. A Social Movement on Buka Island.* Oxford: Berg.

Robbins, Joel

1998   "Becoming Sinners: Christianity and Desire among the Urapmin of Papua New Guinea",
          Ethnology, 37 (4): 299-316.

Spivak, Gayatri Chakravorty

1976   "Translator's Preface". In Jacques Derrida, *Of Grammatology,* Baltimore: The John
          Hopkins University Press, IX-LXXXVII.

Stanner, W.E.H.

1953   *The South Seas in Transition.* Sydney: Australian Publishing Company.
1958   "On the Interpretation of Cargo Cults", *Oceania,* 29:1-25.

Stephen, Michele

1997   "Cargo Cults, Cultural Creativity, and Autonomous Imagination", *Ethos,* 25 (3): 333-358.

Strathern, Andrew, Stewart, Pamela, Carucci, Laurence et. al.

2002   *Oceania: An Introduction to the Cultures and Identities of Pacific Islanders.*
          Durham: Carolina Academic Press.

Tabani, Marc

2009   "Dreams of Unity, Processes of Divisions and Indigenous Movements: Inter-manipulations
          as Cultural Heritage in Tanna (Vanuatu)", *Paideuma, Mitteilungen zur Kulturkunde,*
          55: 27-47.

Wagner, Hans

1947   Ulap-Station-Report 1947. Archiv der Evangelisch-Lutherischen Kirche in Bayern.
          Neuendettelsau. Unpublished Manuscript.

Waiko, John D.

1973   "European-Melanesian Contact in Melanesian Tradition and Literature". In R.J. May (ed.),
          Priorities in Melanesian Development. Port Moresby: University of Papua New Guinea,
          pp. 417-428.

Williams, Francis E.

1976a [1923]   "The Vailala Madness and the Destruction of Native Ceremonies in the Gulf
               Division". In E. Schwimmer (ed.): *Francis Edgar Williams "The Vailala Madness"
               and Other Essays.* London: Hurst & Co, pp.331-384.
1976b [1934]   "The Vailala Madness in Retrospect". In E. Schwimmer (ed.), *Francis Edgar
               Williams "The Vailala Madness" and Other Essays.* London: Hurst & Co,
               pp. 385-395.

Worsley, Peter

1957   *The Trumpet Shall Sound. A Study of "Cargo" Cults in Melanesia.*
          London: MacGibbon & Kee.

Chapter 7

Even More Strange Stories of Desire: Cargo Cult in Popular Media

Lamont Lindstrom

Here are a few recent (November 2009) popular references to "cargo cult": A *Boston Globe* movie reviewer bashes: "'Planet 51' is a cargo-cult movie — a piece of pop-culture flotsam that exists by scavenging pieces of other, better films" (Burr 2009:G8). A blogger, founder and CEO of a "cloud-based business intelligence startup headquartered in San Francisco," warns that the European hi-tech ecosystem "bears some signs of a Cargo Cult" (Stanek 2009:np). And a Botswana Member of Parliament grumbles: "We are creating a cargo cult mentality amongst our people" (Gabarone 2009:np).

Simple Internet trolling uncovers many similar pop-cultural references to cargo cults, only a few of these so-called cults today still located in Melanesia. Previously, in *Cargo Cult: Strange Stories of Desire from Melanesia and Beyond* (1993), I had some fun quoting glum colonial critics who bitterly complained that despite their best efforts, "cargo cult won't die quietly" (1993:163). And those old-time observers have certainly proved prescient, at least *a propos* the ongoing vigor and popularity of the term itself if not, perhaps, the actualities and concerns of active social movements within Melanesia today. In that book, I also traced some of the incursions that the term and concept "cargo cult" have made into discursive arenas far beyond academic anthropology and Pacific Studies, and specifically their presence in popular, pre-Internet media accounts and texts (journalism, music lyrics, art, novels, and the like). Western fascination with "cargo cult" has not abated in the years since my book was published. With the emergence of the Internet and increasing global tourist flows, cargo cult has become even more famous, or infamous, and even more celebrated, or denounced.

In this paper, I bring my survey of popular uses of the cargo cult story into the present, investigating again why many find that story so compelling. I sample various ways the term continues to be applied and I briefly consider how these now global treatments of cargo cult may feed back and influence Melanesian understandings of their own local island practice. Back in 1993, reading through popular stories about Tanna's John Frum movement, I suggested that these accounts "play out in two main keys. There is dark-toned parody or irony... And there is a brightly lit romantic heroism" (1993:112). As we shall see, these two themes – cargo cult as obloquy, and cargo cult as noble resistance – still continue to dominate the range of recent pop-cultural deployments of the label. Cargo cultists are misguided, even stupid nitwits who are deluded by irrational thinking and overblown desire; or cargo cultists are gallant rebels, cultural critics even, who scorn and reveal the dull, soul-numbing lesions of our consumerist modernity.

The Internet, since 1993, has exploded in scope and significance and this today spreads cargo cult talk even more widely than when this circulated mainly in text and film. Cargo cult, nowadays, has certainly gone global: As excerpted above, it rattles through Boston, Botswana, the Silicon Valley, and beyond. The Blogosphere is particularly fond of the term. I suspect that many of those canny enough to blog like to think of themselves as well-read, and their uses of quasi-esoteric terms such as cargo cult serve to decorate their writings thus to impress readers. And cargo cult, moreover, is a useful literary cudgel that serves many bloggers' elemental carping and critical style.

I stand by my earlier conclusion (Lindstrom 1993) that cargo cult's celebrity beyond anthropology *per se* has much to do with the fact that the term, as metaphor, functions as a barely-disguised model of Western desire itself, although a desire that is displaced onto Melanesia: Cargo cult is a just-so story about our peculiarly modern mode of desiring that is always ultimately unrequited, unquenchable, and never-ending. These underlying cultural currents of, and about, desire sustain the term's continuing popularity and use, despite the particularities of its deployment online and elsewhere. Moreover, because we unthinkingly discriminate between good desire and bad desire, so we discern good and bad cargo culting. Our judgment here mostly reflects the proper object of presumed universal desire. Good desire focuses on personal development, creativity, and individual freedom. Bad desire seeks material goods and fetishes, quick but ineffective fixes to life's problems, and tawdry political programs.

As cultural moderns, however, we take our desiring, no matter its good or bad objects, to be naturally unending. We rightly desire human perfectibility and freedom but we would be astonished should we one day actually achieve this. Self-development is, and should be, an infinite task. Cargo cultists, both good and bad, take desire naturally to be an unquenchable human condition. Cargo cults serve to phrase our desire in constant, universal form. We appreciate cargo culting, even the bad sort, and love to gossip about it. It is nirvana, however noble and unattainable a goal, that makes us nervous and suspicious. The bloggers' message is that an end of desire, should this one day happen, must mean death.

Cargo Cult for Beginners

Cargo cult is ubiquitous enough nowadays so that graphic artists and others can freely pun off the term. For example, we cultists, now moved online, worship at the altar of those cargo pants (Figure 1):

© Original Artist / www.CartoonStock.com

CARGO CULT

Figure 1: Cargo Worship

CONTEMPORARY CARGO CULTS

i got my first blowjob while Nixon was president... if i elect Republicans, maybe i'll get some more

transformers made me happy as a child... i'm gonna be super happy now that i can afford more of em

all the great artists died penniless... i'm not rich, so i must be a great artist

Or, we consumers get the joke when an artist pokes fun at our forlorn desire for sex, happiness, or wealth or at our irrational means to achieve, or understand, such desires (Figure 2):

Figure 2: Forlorn Desire

Just in case, however, slowpoke World-Wide-Websters or even old-fashioned literati have yet to encounter the notion of persistent cargo culting, or have not yet come to grasp its global significance, several comic artists have drawn helpful explanatory depictions of the term itself. These run through the basics. Ryan North, for instance, creator of *Dinosaur Comics* simplifies cargo cult for his fans (http://www.qwantz.com/index.php?comic=1100) (Figure 3):

Figure 3: Cargo Cult for Beginners

This comic clarification features one of the standard cargo cult origin myths – that forlorn Melanesian natives turned to culting after Pacific War cargo evaporated from their shores. North, thus, offers a graphic version of higher anthropological theories of post-colonial mimesis and he is kind to remark that cargo cults are crazy not so much because they are, well, *crazy* but because their desires are sublime.

Allysa Nassner, a second graphic artist, narrows her pedagogical focus down to one particular Melanesian cult, the John Frum movement of Tanna, Vanuatu (Figure 4):

Figure 4: John Frum for Beginners

Nassner obviously has studied John Frum photographs although her cultists –
and that volcano – do not much resemble island actuality. She does, however, nicely
sketch a panel of island cargo dreams so to blur and conflate islander and Western
desire: Cultists everywhere, so it seems (and so many presume), naturally share the
same sweet dreams of potato chips, mobile phones, athletic shoes, and pepperoni
pizza (http://awkwardcity.blogspot.com/ 2008_05_01_archive.html).

Both these graphic explications of the term are sympathetic in the anthropological sense. The artists explain away culting, rather than denouncing this, as a sort of rational irrationality – culting makes good sense given people's historic experience or given the inherent and natural desirability of those Western goods. Who doesn't, after all, lust for potato chips? Many others who use the term to condemn and deplore, however, are not so even-handed.

Bad Cargo Cults

Cargo cult as obloquy continues to dominate spreading usage of the label online. There are more ignoble, than noble, cultists prowling about, at least as apparent on the Internet. Back in 1993, I suggested that those who find cargo cult useful as a label which defames what they deprecate presume a tripartite lowest common denominator. Almost anything might be called cargo cult if it: 1) Affects desire (for wealth, or whatever); 2) involves some group or collectivity of the desirous; and if 3) such desires, or purported means to achieve them, can be discredited as irrational. Or, "the distilled essence of cargo cult, in this most simplified delineation of the term, is a tragic relationship between rational ends and irrational means – between genuine desire and ineffective practice" (Lindstrom 1993:185-186). In years since, popular detection of cargo cults seems to have become unhampered by even these slight definitional requirements. Nowadays, cargo culting might be almost anything that some critic depreciates.

Popular uses of the term spin about the Internet mocking, in particular, misguided politics, misguided economic policies or business plans and, oddly, misguided computer programs and systems. Such cargo computing perhaps reflects the enduring influence upon computer geeks of physicist Richard Feynman who was an early adopter and academic importer of the onetime anthropological term. Feynman deplored "cargo cult science" in his 1974 commencement address at the California Institute of Technology: "So I call these things Cargo Cult Science, because they follow all the apparent precepts and forms of scientific investigation, but they're missing something essential, because the planes don't land" (1974:11). Frequent Internet critique of imprudent computer code is phrased in a language of "cargo cult programming." Cargoist abuse of this sort has been common enough that "cargo cult programming" is now a Wikipedia entry: "**Cargo cult programming** is a style of computer programming that is characterized by the ritual inclusion of code or program structures that serve no real purpose" (http://en.wikipedia.org/wiki/Cargo_cult_programming; for an example, see http://compsci.ca/blog/not-cargo-cult-programming-source-control-communication-and-lack-of-it-all/). Wikipedia also remarks "cargo cult software engineering," referring its readers onwards to "magical thinking" and "voodoo programming."

Most popular uses of bad cargo culting, though, target irrational economic or political endeavor – and this makes sense given that non-anthropological devotees of the term generally take "cargo" to refer to riches or prosperity, and "cult" to presume some sort of religio-politically organized practices aiming to achieve such wealth. These popular uses of the term are too numerous to catalog in full, but one finds examples thrown about the American national elections of 2008 which provided an opportunity for supporters of one party or another to accuse their opponents of being cargo cultists. One jokester blogger, for example, decried Republican Party candidate "John Frum McCain," writing:

> Trailing by large margins in US national polls, Republicans are hoping for the miraculous return of a presidential candidate known to them as "John Frum" McCain. Activists say Frum-McCain, who bears striking similarities to saviour figures in 20th century Pacific Island cargo cults, will return one day bringing winning vote margins and financial aid. "John Frum 'im go come wi' lotsa cargo," says North Carolina Republican party chairman Linda Daves. Frum-McCain supporters are known for fanaticism, often scarring their faces, or spending huge amounts of money on ceremonial vestments to prove their devotion. Critics say there have been very few sightings of John Frum-McCain in states the Republicans need to win, and that party officials are being unrealistic about their election hopes" (http://ollysonions.blogspot.com/2008/10/republicans-put-faith-in-john-frum.html) (Figure 5).

Figure 5: John Frum McCain

Republicans, though, have turned the tables to likewise accuse Democrats of engaging in cargo cult. In 2004, so they said, Congressman Denis Kucinich was actually "Dennis The Menace, back again, to suck all the life out of the American peace cargo cult – uh, American peace movement" (http://www.indybay.org/newsitems/2007/02/17/18364864.php). More recently, some have accused the Obama administration of engaging in crazy cargo cult economics, a charge conveniently featured on a cap for sale on the Internet (http://www.zazzle.com/cargo+hats) depicting Obama, the cargo prophet (Figure 6).

Figure 6: Obama the Cargo Prophet

Australians, too, easily toss about political cargo cult accusations. Cartoonist Jonathan Bentley, for instance, lampooned former Queensland Premier Peter Beattie as a cargo worshipper in a cartoon featured in the 11 July 2003 *Courier-Mail* newspaper (Figure 7).

Figure 7: Cargo Cult Politics

Not just politicians, anyone with irrational economic desire or strategy might actually be a crypto cargo cultist. The Canadian International Development Research Centre plotted out four possible global futures in light of "new information and communication technologies" – one of the more unpleasant futures being "cargo cult":

> By 2010 the *Cargo Cult* mentality prevails. Most national governments not only lack financial resources and know-how but also political will. Having a national computing centre, like having a national airline and a national satellite system, is a matter of national pride, if in reality a loss to the treasury. Computers symbolize the new religion; even if they do not work well or have any useful software. Every country has a national campaign to put computers in schools, but many fail to train the teachers to operate the computers and some put computers in schools that do not have any electricity or connectivity. Very few education officials have the skills that are needed... The result is widespread frustration (http://www.idrc.ca/en/ev-28773-201-1-DO_TOPIC.html).

Bad mentality, lack of "know-how," skill, and political will, and useless symbols that take the place of real, practical means all lead inexorably to dreaded cargo cult.

If less grandly, other critics smell out more specific irruptions of cargo cult across the land. One blog, "The Cargo Cult of Business," offers regular comment on current economic irrationality: "The desperate need for redemption of the corporation as a beneficial social organism is why it is our mission with this blog to provide exposition of this clash between corporate, social, and government interests; a clash that forms the turbulent ocean defining the world of early twenty-first century America" (http://www.cargocult.biz) A misleading veneer of business stylishness conceals inadequate, primitive product.

Figure 8: Cargo Cult Business

Many other commentators launch similar jeremiads about the decay of once tough American rationality into cargo cult thinking. Peter Klauser fingers the four "Principles of the American Cargo Cult" for instance, as "Ignorance is innocence, Causality is selectable, It's not your fault, and Death is unnatural" (http://klausler.com/cargo.html). Such madness, of course, reflects "a worldview that is orthogonal to reality" and leads to "Corporate Cargo Cults" (http://equityprivate.typepad.com/ep/2006/06/ from_idea_froth.html). Such cults deify irrational "personal rapid transit" schemes, among many others, where the deluded faithful throw away good money after bad (as early John Frum supporters on Tanna reportedly cast off their hard-earned Australian dollars and French francs into the sea) (http://www.roadkillbill.com/PRT-Cult.html).

Such economic madness flows from "cargo cult innovation" (breakthroughinnovation.wordpress.com/2009/02/03/cargo-cult-innovation/), "cargo cult management," or maybe "cargo cult entrepreneurship" that "allow inefficiency and bad management to creep into the system" (http://gigaom.com/2009/06/21/cargo-cult-management/). Or perhaps feckless tourism is the ultimate cargo cult? "Tourism is the quintessence of Commodity Fetishism. It is the ultimate Cargo Cult – the worship of goods that never arrive, because they have been exalted beyond the stench of mortality – or morality" (http://www.hermetic.com/bey/tourism.html). Cargo cults have occurred even in the hallowed precincts of professional American baseball: "Baseball's worst Cargo Cult has been on the wane for about a decade, the religion built around the value/virtue of starting pitchers throwing complete games (sometimes also the value of having a pitcher be a 20-game winner, or throwing 250 innings for a season)" (http://cmdr-scott.blogspot.com/2008/09/corporate-cargo-cults-bruce-jenkins_25.html). Cargo cultists spread across the land. Is nothing, anymore, truly sacred?

Good Cargo Cults

But not everything is dark and foolish in the land of cargo cult. There are, in fact, noble cargo cultists who struggle to repel and reveal the onslaughts and faux rationality of modernity. Here, the goal is not to reform and save modernity with threats of scary cargo cult, but rather to demystify and impugn it. Just as John Frum people on Tanna have stood to criticize the invidiousness of colonial, and now post-colonial, economic and political structures, so too do global cargo cultists impeach modernity's false claims. Here, we deal not so much with deluded politicians or businessmen but with farsighted bards and wise artists. These cargo cultists are cool.

The one-time Austin, TX rock band (their one album: *Strange Men Bearing Gifts*) and the more recent electronic/triphop artist Allan Vilhan both call themselves Cargo Cult, emphasizing a critical stance and a desire to remake the world, and they share that name with other Indy bands including Cargo Cult Revival. Members of the Paris-based music group Ulan Bator have also performed as "Cargo Cult." Cargo Cult Records, an independent music producer located in Knoxville, TN, specializes in "forward-thinking rock & pop music produced, performed and distributed with a DIY ethos" (www.cargocultrecords.com) (Figure 9).

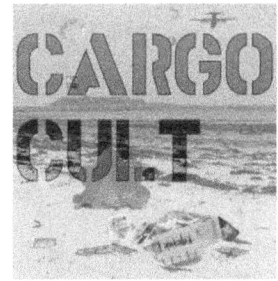

Figure 9: Cargo Cult Revivals

Our noble musical cultists, here, seek out do-it-yourself indy music that transcends today's commercialized schlock. Forward-thinking cargo culting is the future, not the past. Those Melanesian cultists, like the John Frum people, were prophets of post-modernity. And the spiritual savior John Frum, in fact, turns out to be ourselves. The cargo – the force – is already within us; just click your ruby slippers three times. We can scrape away modernity to locate good honest desire within. Devotees of one of the Cargo Cult groups sell t-shirts (wearecargocult.blogspot.com/) that proclaim "we are the ones we have been waiting for," featuring a spaceman John Frum walking out into the present (Figure 10).

Figure 10: Cargo Cult in Space

Other musicians, including Paris-based 7BZH (Frank Thorstein, www.7bzh.com) and Earl Reinhalter, have named albums or songs after cargo cult. Reinhalter's album *Cargo Cult* features a John Frum hymn, the first verse of which begins:

All of us are members
of the cargo cult,
waiting for the savior
that they call John Frumm.
If you are a member
of the cargo cult,
you will be rewarded
when the cargo comes.
We will be rewarded
when the cargo comes.
We will be rewarded
when the cargo comes.

The exact referent of "all of us" and "We will be rewarded" is blurred: who *are* the real cargo cultists, after all? Why, come to think of it, it's us!

Artists, too, celebrate cargo culting. Some, like Brisbane-based Ona Filloy, have depicted Melanesian cultists such as on her "John Frum Day" postcard that features planes flying over Tanna (http://onafilloy.blogspot.com/). Or, an anonymous artist offers a more fanciful depiction of a cargo plane pregnant with cargo (Figure 11).

Figure 11: Cargo Plane

Whereas Filloy's red cross and, perhaps, frangipani mark her cultists as Tannese, the generic cargo plane can pop up anywhere, and artists thus locate their cultists everywhere.

Carl Chew, for example, designed one cargoist homage to New York pop artist Ray Johnson: A facsimile sheet of postage stamps featuring twisted planes likewise pregnant with who-knows-what desirable (but dangerous?) cargo in their holds.

Australian sculptor Rudi Jass' cargo cult, on the other hand, features an older-fashion steel boat carrying, no surprise, mysterious cargo (http://www.axiamodernart.com.au/artists/sculpture/rudi-jass/index.html). Painter Robert Becraft (who has completed a cargo cult series "things belong to those who want them the most") is also now "working on a film animation loosely based around Melanesian cargo cults, how an adult film star and serial killer can loom larger in absence than in real life, among other things" (http://ucsdopenstudios.com/2007/artists. php?a=Robert_Becraft). Cargo prophets and transgressive porn stars and serial killers reveal the limitations of modern, "real life." And Seattle, WA artist Alden Mason's 1995 acrylic painting "Cargo Cult" is for sale on an online art gallery for only $7100 (www.foster-white.com/dynamic/artwork_display.asp?ArtworkID= 9287&Page=1). It is a pity that Melanesians, or even anthropologists, failed to copyright the now popular and ubiquitous term when we had the chance. "Well into his 70s, Mason traveled to New Guinea to live among native tribes (he still proudly displays in his Ballard studio an arrow he pulled from a tribesman struck in an inter-tribal war)" (www.cs.washington. edu/building/art/AldenMason/). Here, again, we find those favorite distorted cargo planes – an artistic comment, I think, about the psychological abrasions of materialism, or at least of modernist desire for material goods.

Literary cargo cultists also join with the artistic and the musical. Cargo Cult Press (where the "natives are notoriously slow"), for instance, is a "small press that will provide a home for the talented mid-list writer and celebrate fine boutique handcrafted binding" (www.cargocultpress.com) (Figure 12). Among its list one

Figure 12: Cargo Cult Press

finds *The Sound of Drums, Valley of the Dead* (deluxe edition), and other tales of modern, cargoist horror.

Writers, as I noted back in 1993, continue to stumble upon the cargo cult story and weave this into their work. Christopher Moore's comedy *Island of the Sequined Love Nun* (1998) most faithfully follows the cargo cult story, but the term also turns up in a flush of other recent popular novels.

Playwrights, too, have put cargo cult on stage, most often as modern tragedy of desire. I described a number of such plays in 1993 (Lindstrom 1993:170-172) and more have appeared in recent years. Writer and performer Mike Daisey, for instance, toured the USA with his one-man show, optimistically called "The Last Cargo Cult" (Figure 13). No surprise, this hammers the point that "the source of America's financial crisis and the faith of a group of islanders in the Vanuatu Islands don't look as different as you'd expect" (www.mikedaisey.com). The Tannese yearn for those cargo planes but we also worship financial hedge funds and the stock market. Lo and behold, we too are melancholy cargo cultists. Melanesian madness has conquered the rational West.

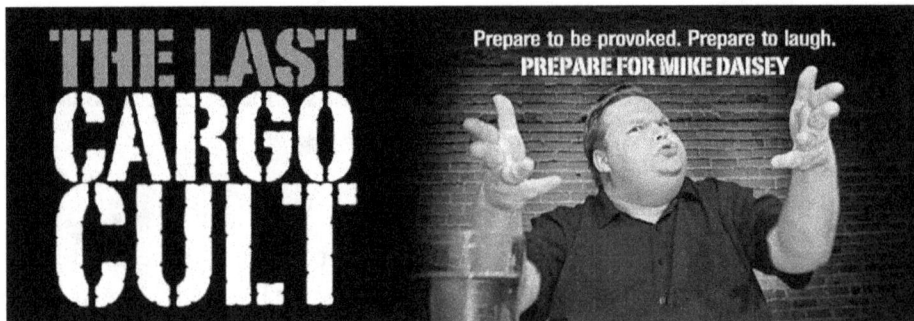

Figure 13: The Last Cargo Cult?

Cargo Cult for Sale

I could go on. The Internet is popping with cargo cults and Google makes it easy to seek these out. Instead, I conclude with a few thoughts about ways in which today's global exposures and images of cargo culting spill back into Melanesia. First, as I noted in 1993, cargo cult – the term – has always been one of opprobrium despite the fact that, for a time, it became part of standard anthropological jargon. Despite examples of good cargo culting, the majority of cargo cult branding today still carries a sting. Politically active Melanesians generally discount the term's local suitability, although within political tactics they sometimes apply it to one another – as did one blogger in criticism of recent plans to establish a free trade zone on Manus island, Papua New Guinea (www.benzinga.com/45597/the-vision-thing-papua-new-guinea%E2%80%99s-government-unveils-the-future). Bad cargo culting, worldwide, continues to tinge people back in Melanesia with feckless desire and irrational thinking insofar as they are identified with its origins.

But good cargo culting, too, may spill back into Melanesia insofar as the good cult experience, in the main, is for sale. One can buy into cargo cult in the form of CDs, DVDs, stage plays, edgy books, cool painting and sculpture, and more. And there is at least one Cargo Cult Shop (next to the Explorers Café-Bar) located in the UK's Cheddar Caves and Gorge (Figure 14):

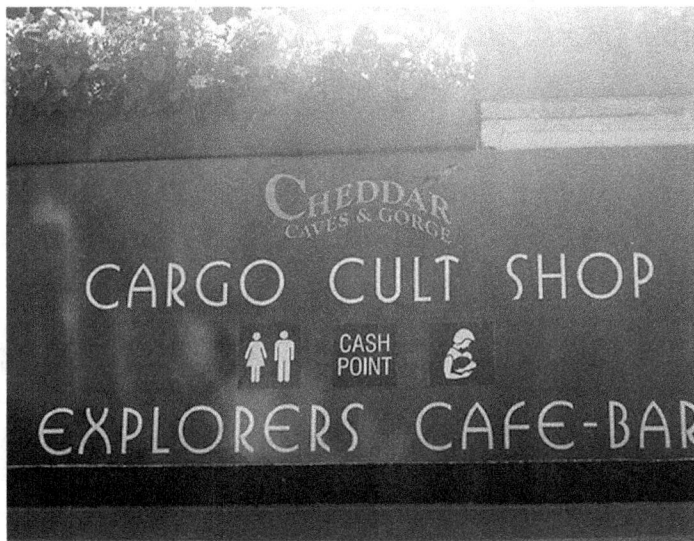

Figure 14: Cargo Cult Shopping

If shopping is your religion, Cargo Cult is named after a religious cult that sprang up amongst headhunters in the East Indies to explain the "magical" appearance of treasures brought to their islands by C18th sailing shops and later dropped by parachute to GIs in the jungle during WWII. Our Cargo Cult shop, situated beside Gough's Café entrance, has the perfect gift for you to buy for a friend or loved one, as well as that well deserved self indulgence just for you (www.cheddarcaves.co.uk/section.php/68/1/shops cafe_bar).

Cargo cult shopping comes back around to Melanesia, too, where the John Frum movement, among a few others, have become advertised and increasingly popular tourist attractions (Lindstrom 2013). Nowadays, one can buy the cargo cult experience on Tanna, too, as in the Cheddar Caves or on online bookstores and music sites anywhere. Cargo culting, now worth real money, brings in hard tourist dollars.

This global commercialization of cargo cult can transform local understanding and practice. Whereas a social movement was once just that – people organized in hopes of bringing about political and economic change – this now becomes touristic spectacle. In fact, as more-and-more people encounter global applications of the term online or elsewhere, be these so-called cargo cults noble or ignoble, they may eventually be drawn to visit cargo cult's Pacific sources (see Scott, 2012). Places like Tanna become cargo cult Mecca, Jerusalem, or Rome, gummed up with tourists. Outsiders appear to experience cargo cult as an amusing spectacle, as noble resistance to the evils of modernity, or merely as some undigested and poorly understood oddity. Whichever, Melanesians under tourist gaze have come to understand that they can sell certain local events if these can be packaged up as cargo cult. Nowadays, John Frum as cargo cult is bought and sold on Tanna just as it is in American theaters or on the Internet. Spreading global awareness of cargo cults and promiscuous use of the term unsettles its original Melanesian referents.

It is certainly piquant that some American cargo cultists, like performing artist Mike Daisey, are daring or foolish enough to offer up "the last" cargo cult. Cargo's secret – which is also the secret of modern desire itself – is that it is always unrequited, undying, and never-ending. I previously dared to reveal the true secret of the cargo cult: That "our metadiscourse of desire makes cargo cult for us both believable and emotionally compelling... The unrequited desire of cargo/love is undending" (Lindstrom 1993:210). Cargo cults, for us at least, are parables of modern desire and our particular mode of desire "seems even more real insofar as Melanesians appear to suffer it, too" (2004:32). Modernist unrequited desire, however, spreads powerfully within global economic structures and by now it has washed back everywhere including onto Pacific islands where people today confront the mysteries of late capitalism (Dalton, this volume; see also Hermann this volume). Daisey's title is too optimistic. Cargo cults now gone wild on the Internet will continue to erupt everywhere.

References

Burr, Ty
2009   Movie Review: 'Planet 51' Is Hardly Worth the Visit. Boston Globe (20 November): G8.

Feynman, Richard
1974   "Cargo Cult Science: Some Remarks on Science, Pseudoscience, and Learning How to Not Fool Yourself", *Engineering and Science*, 37(7):10-13.

Gabarone, Obebile
2009   "State of the National – A Response", *Mmegi Online* 26(175, 20 November), http://www.mmegi.bw/index.php?sid=1&aid=57&dir=2009/November/Friday20.

Lindstrom, Lamont
1993   *Cargo Cult: Strange Stories of Desire from Melanesia and Beyond.* Honolulu: University of Hawaii Press.
2004   "Cargo Cult at the Third Millennium". In Holger Jebens (ed.), *Cargo, Cult and Culture Critique*. Honolulu: University of Hawaii Press.
2013   "Cultural Heritage, Politics, and Tourism on Tanna (Vanuatu)". In E. Hviding and G. White (eds), *Cultural Heritage and Political Innovation in the Pacific Islands*. Honolulu: University of Hawai'i Press.

Moore, Christopher
1998   *Island of the Sequined Love Nun.* New York: Harper.

Scott, Michael W.
2012   "The Matter of Makira: Colonisation, Competition, and the Production of Gendered Peoples in Contemporary Solomon Islands and Medieval Britain", *History and Anthropology*, 23(1): 115-148.

Stanek, Roman
2009   "Avoiding the Cargo Cult and Getting the Trans-Atlantic Startup Model Right". TechCrunch (1 November). http://www.techcrunch.com/2009/11/01/avoiding-the-cargo-cult-and-getting-the-trans-atlantic-startup-model-right/

Agreeing to Disagree about *Kago*

Margaret Jolly

This volume emerges from a scintillating panel held as part of the meetings of the Association for Social Anthropology in Oceania in Santa Cruz and Alexandria. There was an extraordinary polyphony of voices in the papers presented at Santa Cruz in February 2009 and that polyphony, not without harmony, has been sustained in this volume. I was intrigued and impressed that the co-organizers and now co-editors, Marcellin Abong and Marc Tabani, agreed to disagree about the central concept: 'cargo cults'.

This reflects the extensive epistemological and ethical debate about the validity and value of the moniker 'cargo cults' in the vast literature to date. I am more of a critic than a celebrant, concurring with much in the successive critiques of Roger Keesing, Martha Kaplan and Nancy McDowell articulated for the Solomons, Fiji and Papua New Guinea (Keesing 1978, Kaplan 1995, McDowell 2000). There is much definitional, typological, political and ethical debate in the pages of this volume. Readers will doubtless judge for themselves whether Tabani's preference for 'retaining the concept at the same time as we are beginning to relinquish it' and 'using it even though it is "under erasure"' (Chs 1 and 6) is justified. I rather focus on three dimensions of the chapters assembled here. First, I consider the way in which the relation between the material and the spiritual is perceived in analyses of these movements and the effects of a tendency to split and dichotomize 'Melanesian' versus 'western' ontologies. Second, I ponder how the dialogical relation between insiders and outsiders, indigenes and whites, proximate participants and distant observers is constructed. Third, I highlight a rather neglected feature of such movements, their gendered character, and the significance of radical reconfigurations of gender relations in several movements.

The Dialectics of Matter and Spirit, Nature and Culture

In her superb chapter on *mata kamo* of the New Guinea Highlands, Aletta Biersack suggests that this cult was ultimately not so much about the acquisition of new wealth or 'cargo', but a ritual reorientation from earth to sky and a 'concerted, often exuberant, effort to escape the human condition' (Ch. 4), a life of work, suffering and eventual death, by instantiating a millennium. 'To interpret *mata kamo* in cargoistic terms, as evidence of indigenous materialism, is to miss the point of *mata kamo*, which was to transcend the material conditions of terrestrial life by celestializing human life' (Ch. 4). Through a searching and rigorous review of the ethnographic materials across several regions, amongst Ipili peoples of the Paiela and Porgera valleys as well as among Enga, Somaip and Huli, Biersack consummately argues that despite visions of new wealth – variously pearlshells imported by Europeans from the coast, steel axes, metal houses, cars, planes and new foods such as cows (perceived as huge pigs) – millennial abundance would especially be manifest in pigs raining down from the sky and the immortality of people as they ascended on pythons or 'sky bridges' to dwell on high with the eternal sun (and his 'wife', the moon).

The millennium was to be secured through novel ritual devotion to the sun rather than terrestrial ancestors, staring at the sun along the shaft of a spear, sacrificing pigs (and eating their kidneys), scraping sweet potatoes with pearlshells, purification through bathing and new dietary and sexual regimes (variously abstinence and promiscuity). She perceives a gradient from an emphasis on wealth acquisition for Ipili speakers at Tipini in the far east to its absence as a goal for Paiela in the west and connects this to their differential exposure to the material culture of whites. But she concludes that since cargo was not a focus in all variants, *mata kamo* was fundamentally 'not a craving for riches but the desire to enter the sky' (Ch. 4), a realm of 'workless bliss, free of horticulture and reproduction, fertility and regeneration, and thus death' (Ch. 4). Now, it may be that whites were first seen by many in this region as 'sky travellers' (Gammage 1998) but this does not diminish the force of Biersack's core argument. And, in my view, an undue focus on the material and on the novel wealth of Europeans in some manifestations of *mata kamo* rips apart the way in which indigenous cosmologies inexorably connected matter and spirit, seeing material abundance *and* immortality as a result of spiritual devotion, sacrificial exchange and ritual efficacy (see Tabani on Tannese conceptions of wealth, *nauta*, as not just material objects but the product of supernatural powers, and the slow process whereby novel goods were perceived as 'modern' or 'western') (Ch. 1).

This of course is not a peculiarly Melanesian conception. The prospect of an ascent to a divine heaven, of immortality after death for the faithful is a key promise of all denominations of Christianity while in some Protestant and Pentecostal variants proclaiming a 'prosperity gospel', an immortal afterlife is prefigured by wealth and health in this life on earth. Indigenous Ipili and Paiela constructions of the axis of earth and sky are different from the Christianity they would ultimately embrace. But, Biersack heard many compare the ritual bathing of these cults to Christian baptism and their skyworld to heaven while several people suggested that peace, development and especially the promise of 'windfall wealth' from gold mining is evidence that *mata kamo*'s millennium has been realized, at least in part. Like Biersack, I think we need to acknowledge the similarities and continuities between some Melanesian and some Western knowledge systems to get beyond the us/them dichotomy, the 'nativization' inherent in much cargo cult discourse and to break out of the 'savage slot' or 'metonymic prison' (Appadurai 1988: 37) to which Michael W. Scott (2010)[1] suggests 'Melanesia' has been confined (cited in Ch. 1)[2].

Doug Dalton persuasively argues that there is a need to move beyond reductive explanations of cargo cults which deploy a functionalist sociology of 'social movements'[3] or posit a teleology of proto-nationalisms moving inexorably towards secular western forms. He insists that the ontology of cargo cults is but one manifestation of the religious ontology of Inner Oceania, which makes no separation of nature and culture and which underlies less 'millennial', more quotidian religious beliefs and practices (Ch. 2). Taking his Rawa interlocutors as exemplary, he suggests that the '"outside" appearance of things in nature possess an unseen interior living subjectivity which is continuous with human intelligence' (Ch. 2). This he claims is radically different from the European view of a 'disenchanted' world whereby humans are knowing subjects of an impersonal, unaware and objectified nature which they aspire to control. He characterizes the encounter between 'Western civilization and cultures of inner Oceania' as a 'meeting between "materialist" and "religious" views of

---

1. Scott's paper (2010) presented at the ASAO panels in 2009 and 2010 is unfortunately not included in this volume.

2. I have problems with the regional name given the long European genealogy whereby, since Dumont d'Urville's formulation, 'Melanesia' has condensed region and race in negative ways. Despite its persistence in contemporary scholarship in naming a culture area and its reclamation by Pacific peoples, including (for example in the writings of Bernard Narokobi) I prefer to use the more expansive concept of Oceania, as articulated by Epeli Hau'ofa in a number of visionary essays (Jolly 2007, Hau'ofa 2008).

3. But to name the phenomena 'social movements' does not perforce equate them with western movements nor dictate an approach emanating from a functionalist sociology. See Hermann's use of the term to denote both products and producers of social change and her espousal of a dialogical approach (Ch. 6).

reality' (Ch. 2) [4]. These 'contrasting world views' he suggests configure 'neural patterns, somatic experiences and ways of sensing, knowing and interacting with the world' in divergent ways (Ch. 2).

The hegemonic view of science now dominant in the West may be materialist and objectivist, policing the separation of nature and culture, subjects and objects, human agents and non-human entities, but as Bruno Latour persuasively argues (1993 [1991]), such modernist rituals of 'purification' are rarely successful and hybrids are proliferating in the 'natural' sciences (psychotropic drugs, hybrid crops, frozen human embryos) [5]. Just as Dalton allows for diverse views rather than a homogenous 'shared' Rawa culture so we must allow for them elsewhere. It seems odd to perpetuate a clichéd view of a thoroughly secular West, especially from a country like the contemporary United States where Christianity is so pervasive and millennial and Pentecostal forms are resurgent. It may be that many Christians have assimilated ideas about humans as semi-divine beings 'above' nature and above irra-tional 'natives', 'cargo cultists' whom they must guide. But their world is hardly 'disenchanted' since Christians often subscribe to ontologies which fail to separate material from spiritual efficacy and which see the nature of the world not as an evolutionary outcome but as a divine creation, animated by God. In the recent BBC television series, *The History of the Bible*, novelist Howard Jakobsen interviewed a Cambridge don who was both a practising scientist and a Christian and who strenuously resisted charges of a contradiction between his conjoint beliefs as he espoused the creation story (or rather stories) in Genesis.

It may be as Viveiros de Castro (2004) has argued for AmerIndian peoples that, in an animist cosmology, 'an object' is an incompletely interpreted subject. It may also be that Rawan people first saw white men as uncertain, dangerous and immortal subjects. It may also be that ultimately 'cargo cultists' were not so much seeking material goods as opposing materialism, 'the cataclysmic and emotionally devastating impact of living in a religiously alive universe that is overwhelmed by a dead materialist one' (Ch. 2). It may also be, as Webb Keane (2004) has argued, that certain Protestant, Calvinist forms of Christianity encouraged a strong distinction

---

4. He speculatively traces Rawa arboreal concepts of 'roots' as the 'inside hidden, mystical forces' and 'fruit' as the visible manifestations as akin to that of their Polynesian seafaring ancestors' concept of *mana*, as the 'transcendental signifier'. There are doubtless ancient Austronesian linkages but this speculation is not referenced to the extensive prehistorical or linguistic research on such questions (e.g. Spriggs 1997, Keesing 1984 citing the linguistic research of Pawley).

5. See Keane (2004: 7, 23-4) for some excellent reflections on Latour in the context of his study of 'Christian moderns' in Sumba Indonesia.

between subjects and objects, nature and culture in the process of conversions to modernity. But Catholicism and other forms of Christianity were not so zealous about purging the idolatry of animated objects, of objects which were personified like subjects, like the sacra of saints and icons of the Virgin Mary (see Anna-Karina Hermkens 2012). And many Christians in the Pacific still sustain views of an animated and enchanted world rather than of an inert 'nature'. So there are surely some continuities between the ontologies of Christianity as practised by many in the West, past and present, and the ancestral and contemporary religious ontologies of inner Oceania.

This then brings us to the related question of how we construct the relation between the 'West' and inner Oceania, between 'us' and 'them'. Dalton riles against the double bind created by the simultaneous critiques of 'ethnocentrism' and 'othering' in anthropology, suggesting these are logical opposites. I prefer those other Greek ancestors, the proximate twin dangers of Scylla and Charybdis as a depiction of the anthropological predicament. To dwell between these poles does not negate anthropology nor render it impossible since the best ethnographic accounts are in my view those which are not trapped by the either/or logic of sameness or difference, which allows the possibility of continuity as well as rupture in our translations of the lives of other peoples. This is what I discern in persuasive ethnographic accounts such as Biersack's (Ch. 4) which is attentive to the compelling particularities of the Highlands of PNG and the universality of human quests for immortality, the continuities between indigenous constructs of the skyworld and the historical irruptions of the 'skytravellers' and the eternal Christian God in His Heaven.

The Dialogics of Insiders and Outsiders: Mimetic Resistance

This leads me to the second dimension of these chapters which I highlight here. How do we construct the relation between insiders and outsiders in looking anew at these Melanesian movements which have been called 'cargo cults'? There is a powerful paradox, long appreciated, namely that many of these movements although strongly 'anti-colonial' and 'nativistic' seek and emulate the power and knowledge which *waetman* are seen to possess unjustly or to have stolen or secreted. Similar paradoxes have been explored elsewhere in studies of India and Africa, whereby resistance to colonizers is effected through a process of mimesis: 'almost white but not quite' (see for example Dipesh Chakrabarty (2000) and Homi Bhabha (1994) on India and Fanon (1967) and Jean and John Comaroff (1991, 1997 and 2001 on Africa). I dub these paradoxical practices not derivative discourses but mimetic resistances.

The John Frum movement on Tanna, the subject of many fine analyses, including by Lamont Lindstrom (1990) and Marc Tabani (2008a) offers a powerful demonstration of this paradox. Early manifestations of John Frum from c. 1937 were intent on removing the tyranny of Tanna Law imposed by theocratically inclined Presbyterians and the Condominium authorities of Britain and France and sought the eventual eradication of the whites. But early and later manifestations also sought western commodities and powers and through emulating some of the practices of the strangers (and especially Americans encountered during World War Two) – drilling like soldiers, communicating through liana field telephones, and building air strips – sought to acquire goods, power and knowledge. Now, it may be true, as Keesing (1978) argued long ago in his analysis of Maasina Rule on Malaita in the Solomon Islands, that there has been a tendency to parody this as a naïve imitation of American soldiers, as 'Marching Rule' and to fail to recognize the profound anti-colonial resistance of such movements, distilled in the indigenous concept of Maasina or brotherhood. It may also be that colonial hegemony of certain kinds of *waetman* (British, French, Germans, Australians) was contrasted with the novel *waetman*, the Americans, seen as far more wealthy and powerful in the context of military campaigns in the Pacific during World War Two. White American soldiers were often, and perhaps unduly, seen as intimate compatriots of African-Americans[6]. The latter were frequently seen as relatives of long dead, departed ancestors.

Tabani (Ch. 1) depicts the powerful recent re-emergence of John Frum on Tanna, in the movement of the prophet Fred who, in the millennial year 2000, predicted the end of the world, enjoined the creation of a new village at Yenkahi and the rebuilding of Noah's Ark. His faithful followers were promised eternal life, by changing their old skins for new, like crabs. His visions, creolizing Christian and ancestral meanings, attracted thousands of followers who abandoned their gardens and sacrificed hundreds of pigs in expectation of billions of dollars and the resurrection of the dead. Like its colonial precursors Fred's movement was opposed with armed force by the independent Vanuatu government.

Tabani (Ch. 1) offers a useful articulation of the concept of *kago* with that of both *kastom* and *kalja*. Clearly in the Vanuatu context the latter two concepts avow the values of indigenous ways of the place as against introduced ways, in contemporary

---

6. The recent conferring of a belated military award on an elderly African-American veteran who survived a naval battle in World War Two near Okinawa, reveals the reality. African Americans in the US Navy could only be employed as stewards although in the heat of battle, they fought alongside whites. While heroic white soldiers were decorated during or soon after the war, it took more than six decades to confer similar decorations on African-Americans.

discourses and practices of *kastom ekonomi* for instance. *Kastom* as many have argued is a labile and dynamic term of legitimation (and, more rarely, denigration by evangelical Christians), as much an ideology directed towards the future as the past (see Jolly 1992, Jolly 2012, Curtis 2002, Rousseau 2004). It arguably condenses ideas of place and race, if in complex and diverse ways. *Kastom* signifies representations of self, of indigeneity; *kago* rather signals otherness, whites, even if in intimate complex relations with the indigenous self. And whereas *kastom* celebrates more of a quotidian continuity and creativity in indigenous culture, *kago* projects a radical upheaval or reversal of values (Ch. 1). *Kago* projects often manifest a revolutionary, even modernist developmentalist ethos, even though there may be powerful persistences, for example in the conjunction of the material and spiritual in pursuit of a future destiny (see Macintyre Ch. 5 on Lihir). For Tanna, Tabani notes how missionaries and colonial officials vilified both *kastom* and John Frum as alike incompatible with Christianity and the Condominium's colonial order (Ch. 1). 'Cargo cult' is, as Tabani suggests, similarly semantically vague [7], admitting both celebratory and denigratory uses and being used not just to critique some indigenous movements but the totality of western capitalism as materialistic, as *kago kalja*.

This is certainly the sense in which Tabani's co-editor Marcellin Abong uses the concept of *kago*. In his consummate and original analysis of the Nagriamel movement, Abong (Ch. 3) eschews the moniker of 'cargo cult', applied to it by both foreign and indigenous opponents. His aim is to retrieve the history of the movement and in particular its charismatic leaders, Chief Paul Tari Buluk of Santo and Jimmy Stevens [8], as an integral part of Vanuatu's movement towards independence:

> This paper seeks to rehabilitate Nagriamel, a political movement of which our elders should no longer feel ashamed and from which our youngsters should draw inspiration [...]. Let us remember, with great respect, our ancestors' travels along the sad path of humiliation [...]. Their mistake was being Melanesian, being black – and claiming their rights (Ch. 3).

Abong remembers the blows, the kicks, the whips of a repressive colonial order as part of a struggle for rights and freedom for this and future generations. And yet in recuperating the history of Nagriamel (see also Abong 2008) he also reveals the

---

7. Although during the conference in Santa Cruz in 2009 James Clifford noted that the panel members' conversation was predicated on some shared understandings and Macintyre offered some defining characteristics (see Ch. 1).

8. Jimmy's surname is variously spelt, Stephens, Stevens and Steven. Mary Patterson (2011) prefers the latter which, according to his eldest son Franky, was Jimmy's preference. I rather follow that adopted by Marcellin Abong which is the far more common one in written material both in English and Bislama.

paradoxical and even contradictory relation to *ol waetman* that was inherent in it. He demonstrates that Nagriamel was, from its inception in 1965, a movement aimed at the restoration of Indigenous land rights in the context of renewed incursions by foreign companies into the undeveloped *dak bus*. It also encouraged a return to *kastom*, distilled in its creolized name derived from two indigenous words for croton and cycas, potent symbols in rituals of alliance and peace. More than John Frum it rejected Christianity at first, which in Abong's view 'force[d] us to hide our nudity by means of rags' (Ch. 3). Abong alludes to powerful precursors of Nagriamel in prophetic, anti-colonial movements on Santo, Malakula and Ambae in the early twentieth century. Its early credentials as an independence movement were as great as those of the Vanuaku Pati which eventually brought the country to independence. It attracted a huge number of followers, estimated at 15,000 from many northern islands of the archipelago, and especially from Ambae. Many came to live at Vanafo and participated there in the economic modernization of agriculture and infrastructure and the development of a complex political federation.

Yet as Abong makes clear the 'foreign relations' of the movement and its racial cosmography were complex and fluid. He stresses how seeing many African-American soldiers amongst the US troops 'offered proof that potential equality between Whites and Blacks was possible; that we were not eternally condemned to being the simple boys of the *masta*' (Ch. 3). He sees the war as precipitating a movement for racial liberation and notes how on Ambae, as on many islands of Vanuatu, African-Americans were linked to departed ancestors. Moltare, the guardian of wisdom and knowledge on Ambae, was said to have been kidnapped by the Americans and his powerful knowledge stolen. Jimmy Stevens sought such power. But, according to Abong, for Jimmy

> America was not a mythical country where cargo comes from, but rather represented the awakening of a political conscience spurred by the presence of the US military in the New Hebrides during World War II. America had become the imagined source of equality and fraternity (Ch. 3).

Jimmy Stevens' own ancestry was mixed: his grandfather was an English naval officer, his grandmother came from the Tongan royal family and his mother from the Banks Islands. His conversion to the Church of Christ in 1967, along with that of Chief Paul Tari Buluk and many local Santo people likely catalyzed a major migration from the Indigenous Church of Christ stronghold Nduindui in West Ambae. But, as Abong notes, Jimmy's ardent pursuit of polygamy (at one point he had 25 wives) was problematic for many Ambae elders, who were affronted by this local manifestation of 'big love'[9], his many progeny and the way he combined *kastom* and Christianity. Despite his detractors Jimmy's messianic status as 'Moses'[10] grew. And increasingly his power was amplified by alliances with a series of whites, some American, some French, either 'foreign speculators and land sharks' (Ch. 3): Eugene Peacock, Jean-Jacques Henin, Leconte and especially the millennial neoliberalism of Michael Oliver of the Phoenix Foundation (see Patterson 2011)[11]. But the Nagriamel logo of 'a black hand shaking a white hand' belied the reality that each of these deals between Stevens and foreign investors further compromised the ideals of indigenous land rights in the interests of cash and constructing the modern infrastructure of capitalism: concrete buildings, roads, water, electricity.

Although Stevens disparaged the idea that Nagriamel was a political party and, especially after December 1975, pursued independence through secessionism rather than nationalism, in its committee structure, passion for written documents, declarations and constitutions and the icons of the state (coins, flags and passports), the movement clearly emulated the structures and processes of an emergent state. As Abong wryly avers (Ch. 2), the Vemarana government structure proposed was hardly a neoliberal's minimalist state since it combined a Prime Minister, a Cabinet, a Supreme Court, and an Assembly based on a 'popular vote in accordance with custom' with the avowedly masculinist customs of the *nakamal* and customary chiefs assembled as a High Court. Jimmy as Chief President Moses and later in his hopes to create a royal dynasty had 'growing delusions of grandeur' (Ch. 3), as much fuelled by local adulation as foreign chicanery. The movement was ultimately quashed in the context of the attainment of national independence in 1980: a failed blockade, the massing of British Marines and French police and finally the armed intervention

---

9. Michael Allen recalls Ambae elders complaining that he 'threw his sex in their faces' (personal communication, 2012).
10. Note this was the name with which he was baptized on converting to the Church of Christ.
11. Patterson suggests that in the New Hebrides of the 1960s there was 'an extraordinary crossing of paths... Between two apparently divergent utopian visions, one indigenous, the other an exogenous precursor to world economic orthodoxy' (2011:62). She discerns affinities as well as complicities between Nagriamel and these several zealous foreign libertarian capitalists, but cogently observes that the myth-dreams of the latter, although satirized were not characterized as 'cargo cults'. She argues that their anti-socialist libertarianism was a precursor to the neoliberalism of Thatcher and Reagan which ultimately became hegemonic in the West and powerfully pervaded aid and development policies in the Pacific, including Vanuatu. She sees the present spread of expatriate land speculation on Efate and the continuing engagement between Franky Stevens (Jimmy's eldest son) and Michael Oliver, in the context of plans to establish a free-trade zone in Big Bay in the north of Santo and the leasing of parcels of 80,000 hectares of proximate land to Israelis, as the re-emergence of a desirous 'phoenix' in the 'post-colony' (2011: 74-78).

by Papua New Guinea's Kumul force supported by the Vanuatu Mobile Force and the Royal Australian Air Force. Stevens' son was killed, several others were brutalized and an estimated 2774 rebels were violently arrested. Stevens was sentenced to fourteen and a half years in prison but was released after eleven years. He was at this point generous about the achievements of his enemies, the victors of the Vanuaku Pati in the decade since independence and still hopeful of an act of reconciliation from the President of the Republic when he died in 1994. But, as Abong suggests, after his death (and his immolation in a mausoleum at Vanafo), Nagriamel continued to have political aspirations, if now as a party in the *politik* of the independent state of Vanuatu.

The example of Nagriamel shows the complexity of the race politics of many such movements, combining powerful anti-colonial resistance with alliances with whites and the emulation of western models. It also graphically shows how the spectre of 'cargo cult', despite its racist colonial origins can be used by indigenous people against others. The Vanuaku Pati was able to discredit its rivals Nagriamel and John Frum because, despite the Christian commitments of its many Anglophone followers, it presented itself in more modernist guise as a secular political party committed to nationalist ends, led by educated men, and without unfortunate associations with the 'irrationality' of cargo cults and the *dak bus*. In Abong's view the portrayal of Stevens as a borderline schizophrenic by foreign researchers (Kolig 1981, 1987, see also Hours 1974, 1976 and Patterson's 2011 critique) only reinforces such denigration. Of Stevens he adjudges: 'He deserves more respect even if he did make mistakes' (Ch. 3). He recuperates Nagriamel as a movement asserting island rights and the legitimacy of *kastom*, values which he sees as newly urgent in Vanuatu given the contemporary alienation of land by expatriate speculators 'who come to plant dollars instead of coconut trees, with the approval of state authorities' (Ch. 3).

Martha Macintyre's excellent chapter (Ch. 5) similarly situates contemporary 'cultic social movements' on Lihir, New Ireland in the history of earlier movements described as 'cargo cults', such as the 'Johnson Cult' of New Hanover which in the 1970s asked President Johnson to take over their government. The indelible racial imprint of World War Two was evident here too: the wealth and power of America was opposed to the aporia of Australian colonial rule while some believed Americans were their departed ancestors. Macintyre observes how this early cult was, at the instigation of a Catholic priest, converted into a cooperative copra project, 'Stand Together and Plant', the precursor of the TKA on Lihir. The local TKA was led by Theodore Arau who was credited with talking with the ancestors, travelling in a submarine and communing with whites. He reiterated the common view that whites withheld the true secrets of their knowledge which gave them wealth and power. While it imitated the 'work' of white men in schools for reading and writing it foresaw a time when hard work would be eclipsed by heavenly bliss (Ch. 5). But contra Dorothy Billings (2002), Macintyre argues the Lihirian mimesis of white practices was never a self-conscious parody but a deadly serious hope that by both Catholic devotion and the work of making copra and cocoa that vast wealth would be theirs (Ch. 5).

Macintyre shows how through successive manifestations and movements with diverse names – TKA, Nimamar, Society Reform and most recently from 2004 the *Lihir Pawa Mekim Kanap Asosiesen* (the Lihir Development Association) – there has been a perduring tendency to conflate notions of money and modern commodities with 'earlier ideas that stress the ritualistic and esoteric management of wealth generation' (Ch. 5). Notions of *bisnis* and *winmani* (windfalls, like lottery prizes) are she suggests 'hybrid ideologies' in which cultic ideas of the creation and control of wealth persist. The Personal Viability movement, a motivational course run by a franchise company headed by a Chinese businessman from Rabaul grounds the latest local vision: the 'Lihir Destiny' (see Bainton 2011). As Macintyre shows, this has had a tremendous success nationally with government, corporations and NGOs in PNG but in Lihir its particular stress on material success through self-motivation articulates with a historical sense of relative deprivation, of being marginal, neglected and thus consistently 'anti-colonial, anti-State and exclusive' (Ch. 5). She suggests that the notorious unanimous vote for Jesus Christ in a local election in the 1970s was not the act of naïve cultic Christians but an angry and deliberate protest against the State's neglect of their economic and social welfare and a righteous expression of contempt (Ch. 5).

In her chapter Macintyre consummately demonstrates the local currency of the concept of 'cargo cult' and indeed the diversity of opinions as to whether the former or the latest manifestations of such movements are cargo cults or not. Apropos Nimamar, many interlocutors in the 1980s and the 1990s were adamant in denying the chiliastic elements: e.g. 'It was not a cargo cult. It was simply a business development association' (Ch. 5). The President of Nimamar in 1989 denied it was a 'dream' but still openly acknowledged its religious, Christian vision and welcomed not just the abolition of the State but the economic transformation of Lihir into a city, a conjoint miracle to be effected both by the arisen Dead and the work of the association. Later when Nimamar morphed into Society Reform some of its highly educated leaders tried to distance themselves from their predecessors proclaiming that there was no secret knowledge entailed in their combination of *kastom* and Christianity in development. Yet this more avowedly secular political movement failed to ignite support among most Lihirians, partly because it espoused sharing with other Papua New Guineans rather than advancing the particular, exclusivist visions of Lihirians (Ch. 5).

But what of the *winmani* occasioned by the gold mine on Lihir? In the construction phase of the mine, during the 1990s, the compensation monies were seen as being like a lottery prize, coming to those landowners, who received money without work. Even working for the mine and buying food from the store was seen as a luxury compared to real 'work', the arduous labour of gardening. Yet, as the mine developed, the sense of relative deprivation intensified. Macintyre sees the latest manifestation of the movement as fuelled by ideas that the dreamed 'development' from the gold mine has not materialized, but has benefitted some rather than others. The old colonial hierarchy is perpetuated in the extreme differences between white expatriate managers in senior positions and the black Lihirians who are unskilled workers or unemployed (Ch. 5). But such grievances are now also directed at non-Lihirian workers as well as whites. Opposition to the PNG State is thus a claim for Lihirian separatism.

This is clear in contemporary blueprints for Lihir's destiny, developed by educated leaders, which assert sovereignty over the island's mineral resources. The contemporary discourse is in Macintyre's words more 'mimetically modernist rather than mystical' (Ch. 5). The Lihir Development Association's documents are saturated with the new language of managerialism – flow charts, budget projections and legalistic vocabulary – in ways akin to reports of corporations, governments and NGOs. Its leaders understand the structure of global capital and the fact that their equity in Lihir Gold (at present 5.2%) will always be small compared to foreign investors. Yet, they still envisage greater benefits as the inevitable outcome of the movement for Personal Viability, a mélange of self-help, spirituality and corporate managerialism. The evangelical fervour of these contemporary movements for individualist self-reliance and collective entrepreneurial visions has a very mixed genealogy as Macintyre attests (Ch. 5). But she highlights important continuities with TKA, Nimamar and Society Reform. The seeming secularization of successive movements is for her an illusion. Mark Sopiang, the local leader of Personal Viability has moved from a self-presentation as a 'hard-headed modernist' to a leader inspired by divine purpose communicated in a vision from God (Ch. 5).

Just as mimetic appropriation of colonial disciplinary regimes was a way in which 'cargo cultists' simultaneously resisted and appropriated foreign powers, so contemporary movements imitate and appropriate foreign knowledge and power through visions of grassroots universities, a literacy which is inherently Lihirian and engaging capitalism in a way which is consonant with codified *kastom*. The present discourse advocates dispensing with dependency, empowerment through self-reliance and the development of people as assets not liabilities. But the local use of the 'shared jargon of the global business community' (Ch. 5) is, Macintyre asserts, a mystifying mimemis akin to past cargo cults. And in seeming to embrace global development, contemporary movements also occlude their separatist morality. As in the past, contemporary movements are 'clearly secessionist' (Ch. 5). The *gavman* may no longer be white but it is still equally foreign for Lihirians. Macintyre observes that ordinary villagers resent their continued marginality but advance realistic visions. Educated, middle-class Lihirians in contrast rather entertain fantastic aspirations of equality with the status and wealth of expatriate managers and rich foreign shareholders. In her view it is the educated elite who are now the cultists while grassroots Lihirians are more likely 'pragmatists, waverers and sceptics' (Ch. 5).

Macintyre's compelling ethnography of Lihir raises the question of what is seen as 'inside' and 'outside' to such movements. The colonial antinomies of white and black are perpetuated in the context of mining development, but complicated by class and ethnic differences and inequalities between blacks, between elites and grassroots, between Lihirians and other Papua New Guineans. This exploration of the significance of 'inside' and 'outside' is further explored in the final chapters by Elfriede Hermann and Lamont Lindstrom.

Continuing her forensic deconstruction of the portrait of Yali's movement in Madang as a 'cargo cult', Hermann envisions the interaction between indigenous and exogenous discourses as dialogical, as modes of speaking and action between cultures which are oriented towards each other (Ch. 6). She shows how denigratory colonial discourses of 'cargo cults' fashioned by missionaries, administrators and settlers and even anthropologists in Papua New Guinea are challenged by local counter discourses, originating in Yali's home village of Yasaburing, which refuse the label and its negative connotations of backwardness, naïveté, confusion or irrationality. Like Lindstrom, Hermann locates the birth of the concept in an article by the white expatriate planter N.M. Bird published in the *Pacific Island Monthly* (PIM) in 1945, in which the concatenation of madness and disorder in the native mind is yoked to the fear that 'the sense of injustice' will erupt in a military threat from primitive, instinctual savages (Ch. 6). Significantly, although Bird implicated Christian missions by blaming 'the religious teaching of equality', Catholic and Lutheran missionaries soon joined the dialogue, but preferred to blame the materialism of white settlers for the pervasive hope for cargo and resurgent heathenism for the certain trust in an ancestral source of wealth and knowledge. Many administrative reports on cargo cults from 1946 are clearly persuaded of the facts of cargo cults, and the necessity of quashing them, with force if necessary.

The combined if somewhat discordant voices of settlers, missionaries and administrators created the extraordinary vilification of Yali's movement. As scholars from Peter Lawrence (1964) to Hermann have clearly demonstrated, Yali's initial 'work', stemming from his experiences serving in the Australian forces during World War Two and his first hand experience of the wealth and power of Australia, was a modernist, development project, encouraging literacy and schooling, the cultivation of cash crops and ultimately forms of self-reliance leading to political independence. Early support for Yali by the administration transmuted into denigration and violent repression as the Lutheran mission sustained its attacks and intensified them when he called for the reanimation of indigenous religion. Yali was sentenced to six and a half years in prison on charges of kidnapping and rape. In local perceptions his time in prison left him a 'broken man' on his return in 1955 (Ch. 6).

Hermann persuasively argues that many earlier anthropological representations perpetuated this belief in the facticity of cargo cults and their vilification. She is right that the prevailing structural functionalist vision of anthropology from the 1940s to the 1960s likely promoted a view of such movements as disruptive 'social change'. But equally important, as she acknowledges, is how many anthropologists writing about 'cargo cults' in this period were in the direct employ of the Australian administration or working as advisors to it (e.g. Lucy Mair, Ian Hogbin and Peter Lawrence). Despite the alternative views of Marxist scholars like Peter Worsley who stressed the anti-colonial elements, (he was denied research access to PNG by the Australian administration), the perception of the irrationality and backwardness of 'cargo cults' was shared by anthropologists of most theoretical persuasions. Peter Lawrence's study of Yali's movement (1964) was historical and empathetic but yielded to the view that cargo ideologies should be eradicated in the interests of true development.

Indigenous interrogation and challenge of the 'cargo cult' discourse perhaps preceded its anthropological deconstruction. Many of Hermann's interlocutors from Yasaburing, including Yali's widow Bikmeri, defy the harm done to them by the label, insisting that it has brought them shame, hurt and anger (Ch. 6). Unlike the situation Macintyre depicts for Lihir, it seems no one here accepts the moniker of 'kago kalt' either for Yali's movement (describing Yali's teachings as *skul* and his practice as 'good work') or its successor, the Dabsau Association led by his son, James Yali, a member of Parliament and for a period Governor of Madang Province [12].

They resist allegations of backwardness, confusion and heathenism, and especially the idea that *kago* will come from nothing. They celebrate their hard work in subsistence, cash cropping and *bisnis*, their faithful Catholicism and their perpetuating of ancestor worship as *kastom* as keys to their future development.

But the label of cargo cult *is* deployed by some to distinguish the authentic insiders of Yali's movement and those followers who came from outside and some say distorted his movement towards more cargoistic ends after his return from prison in 1955 (Ch. 6). And, in the political terrain of provincial and national politics in the 1980s and 1990s, some rivals and opponents (including ministers from the provincial government in Madang) critiqued the Dabsau Association and its leader James Yali of reviving *kago* hopes. He and his followers strenuously resisted such allegations and tried to distance themselves from the vilifications of the past. But such processes show how 'cargo cult' has become an othering discourse within PNG, applied to those seen as outsiders, and to critique other Papua New Guineans.

It would be interesting to chart the later dialogical relations between these indigenous challenges, including those by scholars like John Waiko (1973) and reinscriptions of the cargo cult discourse and the anthropological genealogy witnessed in successive critiques by Epeli Hau'ofa (1975, 2008), Keesing (1978), Peter Hempenstall and Noel Rutherford (1984), McDowell (1988, 2000), Kaplan (1995) and of course Lindstrom (1993) and Hermann herself (1992, 1997, 2004). Hermann consummately charts this genealogy and thereby shows how, regardless of whether we accept or reject the label 'cargo cults', whether we use inverted commas or simultaneously inscribe and erase cargo cults, anthropologists are hardly objective impartial scientific observers, but instead create their objects of study dialogically with their interlocutors.

In the culminating chapter of this book Lindstrom moves his previous critique of cargo cult discourse into the blogosphere. His earlier work (1993) persuasively argued that cargo cult discourse was fundamentally a displaced projection of the materialist fantasies of the West, the untrammeled desire for commodities onto others, and in particular Melanesia. '[C]argo cult does not exist per se; rather it appears in the dirty mirror of the European self – a cultic other as a reflection of the imperial self' (1993: 7). As he demonstrated the concept broke free of its earlier uses to describe

---

12. According to Jean Zorn writing in our ANU-EPress volume (2012), James Yali was, like his father, also tried for rape, of the sister of the woman he then lived with, in a much debated case in 2006. There was discussion as to whether this was an 'aggravated' rape due to the position of trust and responsibility he held as either a de-facto affine or a powerful politician.

'the actualities and concerns of active social movements within Melanesia' (Ch. 7) within the scholarly discourses of anthropology and Pacific Studies, being transplanted to other regions of the world and sprouting up in popular media, literature, art and music. He suggested that the very promiscuous 'celebrity' of the cargo cult concept derives from its being both model and metaphor for western desire itself, 'unrequited, unquenchable and never-ending' (Ch. 7). The end of desire spells death.

In this chapter, with pungent humour, he extends that analysis on the semantic ground of the clouds, the Internet. The sequence of extraordinary examples he offers here are testament to the dominant twin themes of cargo cults as obloquy and cargo cults as noble resistance: 'Cargo cultists are misguided, even stupid nitwits who are deluded by irrational thinking and overblown desire; or cargo cultists are gallant rebels, cultural critics even, who scorn and reveal the dull, soul-numbing lesions of our consumerist modernity' (Ch. 7). These twin tropes are at play in a series of comic cartoons, some of which are loosely based on stories about John Frum and other movements. Some universalize and empathize with consumer desire, blurring the boundaries of Tannese and American dreams (Ch. 1). Others portray bad cultists: misguided politicians, financiers and CEOs, computer wizards etc., all of whom promise impossible, useless, dreams (e.g. Frum McCain, Prophet Obama, Ch. 7). Some of the most interesting examples are those who deploy the label, not as an othering discourse but as self-branding, in the naming of products and performances by musicians, poets, artists, sculptors and dramatists (Ch. 7), promoted as cool prophets of post-modernity. This is nicely captured in the proclamation: 'We are the ones we have been waiting for' (Ch. 7).

Lindstrom wonders about the dialogical effects of this globalizing consumer culture on the Internet. How might all this (as with earlier dialogical encounters in the colonial era) be occasioning self-reflections and changes in the very places where 'cargo cults' allegedly originated. Indeed, how far can we clearly distinguish in this contemporary epoch (if we ever could) between the 'real thing' in its 'ethnographic accuracy' and 'the stories which we tell about them' (Ch. 1)? Outsiders' stories have surely constituted that reality not just in colonial and ethnographic representations but in the changing self-conscious reflections and practices of Oceanic peoples. As a discerning and faithful long-term ethnographer of the John Frum movement on Tanna, Lindstrom is rightly concerned that Tanna is becoming a cargo cult Mecca 'gummed up with tourists' (Ch 7). Tannese people are already framing certain local events as cargo cult practices and negotiating the presence of diverse tourists, some seeing 'an amusing spectacle', others 'a noble resistance to the evils of modernity' and yet other others 'a poorly understood oddity' (Ch. 7). As Lindstrom strongly concludes 'John Frum as cargo cult is bought and sold on Tanna just as it is in American theaters or on the Internet' and 'Cargo cults now gone wild on the Internet will continue to erupt everywhere' (Ch. 7).

Engendering Modernity, Masculinity and the Millenium

Finally, I want to highlight a dimension of these movements which is not focal in this volume nor indeed in much of the literature to date, that is the gendered character of the experience of modernity and the gendered character of these movements which we might depict as 'millennial' to different degrees and in different ways.

I am struck not just by the fact that most of the charismatic leaders of these movements are male but often men who have had distinctive experiences of outsiders and indeed of the concatenation of diverse processes which we designate as 'modernity'. This is not to deny the fact that some precursor movements, as Peter Worsley (1957) and others acknowledged long ago, emerged in regions which were remote from centers of white power and colonial development. Moreover, the social change envisaged by such movements is as much an internal revolution as it is an engagement with powerful outsiders. So, in Biersack's example from Highlands PNG, *mata kamo* spreads in different forms across a wide terrain in places which are unevenly engaged with colonial influences. The constant stress on an Indigenous ritual revolution to achieve immortality through an ascent to the skyworld is complemented by a stress on acquiring novel wealth and power in those regions rendered less 'remote' by European contact.

Yet throughout all the places discussed in this volume – in Highlands PNG, in the Madang region of Yali's movement, Lihir, island home of TKA and its successors, and Vanuatu's islands of Tanna and Santo, the sites of John Frum and Nagriamel respectively – there was a constant in that it was men rather than women who were at the forefront of engagement with outsiders, colonial influences and modernity. This has variously been interpreted as the result of male dominant structures in most 'Melanesian' societies (e.g. apropos the divergent experiences of European explorers in 'Polynesia' and 'Melanesia' see Jolly 2012b) or as the result of the patriarchal patterns of European colonizers, traders and settlers, administrative officials and perhaps slightly less, Christian missionaries. In my view both indigenous and exogenous forces were at work in configuring supremely masculinist dialogical encounters.

In the domain of the colonial state it was men rather than women who were designated as assistants to white *kiaps*, as 'native police', assessors or chiefs. In the sphere of Christian missions it was mainly men who attended mission schools to train as catechists, preachers, pastors and priests (even if women were crucial in early conversions, accompanied missionary husbands and were enthusiastic recruits to women's groups). In the different aspects of commodity economy and especially in the earliest phases of indentured and wage labour and local *bisnis*, men were patently dominant. Indeed, successive administrations in both PNG and Vanuatu (as elsewhere in the Pacific), tried to sequester women from the undue influences and effects of 'contact' with the economic dimensions of modernity.

This is nowhere clearer than in widespread policies excluding or restricting women's employment as indentured or wage labourers in plantations, ports or mines. In Papua and New Guinea (but not the New Hebrides) this extended to restrictions on domestic service: prescribing *hausbois* rather than *haosgels*. Such regulations were legitimated by recourse to arguments about the specter of depopulation if women engaged in such work, about the inherent promiscuity of mobile, migrant women (see Jolly 1987) and about the way in which migrant labour undermined the 'civilizing' message of Christian missions to refocus women away from hard work in gardens and plantations to their domestic lives as wives and mothers [13]. By women continuing to ensure the reproduction of the labour force back in home villages and by not having to provide accommodation beyond barracks for single male workers, Europeans employed such workers at very cheap costs. Although there was doubtless kidnapping and forcible persuasion in the period of the indentured labour trade, labelled 'blackbirding', Clive Moore (1985) and other historians insist on the fact that the majority of men who engaged in such labour did so voluntarily, although these were hardly acts of unfettered 'free will', given the pressures of colonial policies (such as taxes) and of older men who enjoined younger men to recruit. The younger men who formed the majority of early recruits to plantations of cotton, sugar and coconuts both internally and externally in Queensland, Fiji and New Caledonia, were likely enticed by the prospect of travel, the cash, novel commodities like steel axes and guns and access to foreign knowledge and power, including Christianity. Many recruits to Queensland and Fiji brought back the word of God before foreign missionaries succeeded in converting people in their home villages.

Keesing (1986) has stressed the centrality of this migrant labour experience in the emergence of the early forms of Pidgin and in the forming of a pan-Melanesian plantation culture. There were conflicts between men of different islands and regions (e.g. between man Tanna, man Ambrym, man Malaita, man Guadalcanal, often

---

13. There was a tiny minority of women who evaded these structures, e.g. about 5-7% of those recruited as indentured labourers to Queensland were women (Jolly 1987).

fuelled by white *mastas*) but there was also a development of a shared plantation culture of predominantly young unmarried men, paralleling in intriguing ways the congregations of boys and young men in indigenous 'male cults' and initiation ceremonies. These young men unlike young women in their home villages were exposed to the cash, the commodities and the knowledge and power of whites. Signing on for such labour also brought ill-health and death, oppression and humiliation as whites '*mastas*' treated '*bois*' to humiliating insults, cruel kicks and stinging whips as Marcellin Abong reminds us (Ch. 3). So perhaps it is unsurprising that the paradoxical ideas and practices of mimetic resistance might be born in such contexts. The history unfolded differently in different regions: migrant male labour culture developed in the coastal and insular parts of PNG, Solomons and Vanuatu far earlier than in the Highlands of PNG, from the mid-nineteenth century rather than the mid-twentieth century. Such divergent historical experiences of generations of Melanesian men might be worth exploring in future research.

Moreover, in those regions which were dramatically and often tragically drawn into World War Two, such as the islands of Vanuatu where 200,000 Americans were located at a forward base in the vicinity of Luganville town and numerous parts of PNG and the Solomons where brutal battles were fought (Kokoda, Milne Bay, Malaita, etc.), the relation between white men and indigenous men was radically reconfigured. Lamont Lindstrom, Geoffrey White, James Gwero and Hank Nelson have all written eloquently about the significance of World War Two in the histories of Vanuatu, the Solomons and PNG (White and Lindstrom 1989, Lindstrom 1989, Lindstrom and White 1990, Lindstrom and Gwero 1998, Nelson 2006). The sheer power and wealth of Americans was quickly contrasted with that of previous white men: British, Germans, French, Australians. Moreover, as is clear in Abong's chapter on Nagriamel, America became a place associated not just with *kago*, but with the prospect of racial liberty and fraternity. Lindstrom (1989: 412-3) is doubtless correct that the intimacy and equality which ni-Vanuatu discerned amongst the American troops was belied by the racism and the spatial segregation which suffused the military in that period. But he is also right to stress how differently ni-Vanuatu were treated by Americans: most oral histories of the war stress the generosity, the familiarity and even the respect they received from American forces. These were a different kind of *waetman* and indeed some of them were black!

It is in this context that we might better understand the crossings between the stories of the origins of death and long-departed ancestors and the fantastic histories of World War Two. The historical events at Million Dollar Point in Santo were telling: at the end of the war, when Americans dumped much of the mobile infrastructure into the sea (MacClancy 1980: 110) some was recovered by local divers, long before dive tourists descended! The events of 'history' often seem dangerously proximate to the 'myths' of cargo cultists. In many locales in different local languages, stories were told of how black Americans were descendants of their own departed ancestors. Others told of how local men had been taken by plane or submarine to America, as volunteers or, like Moltare of Ambae, as kidnapped conscripts. America became associated in the minds of many ni-Vanuatu besides Jimmy Stevens not just with wealth and power but as Abong insists with 'liberty and *fraternity*' (my emphasis and compare Keesing (1978) on 'brotherhood' in Maasina rule in the Solomons).

So I suggest that we might approach the history of these movements also in the light of historically changing and relational masculinities (see Jolly 2008 for an articulation of such an approach). The life history of Yali is symptomatic: a man who had close experience of Australian troops while serving in World War Two and whose first-hand experience of Australia ignited his ideas about development in Madang Province just as much as it fuelled his visions of the future independence of PNG. The various manifestations of John Frum, both before and after World War Two show the salience of relations not just with strangers but a particularly uneasy *masculine* form of mimetic resistance, both in emulating the knowledge and powers of white men but also in trying to rid the island of those white men who had cruelly and unjustly usurped the powers of indigenous men in *kastom*.

In stressing the dominance of male leaders and prophets and this masculine inter-cultural dialogue I am not wanting to disavow the strong engagement of women in such movements, and the fact that on occasion some women, often wives, sisters or mothers of male prophets rose to the status of charismatic leaders or prophets, like Yali's widow, aptly called Bikmeri. This is also clear in several variants of *mata kamo* described by Biersack. In the Paiela valley men such as Kau were the dominant cult leaders but a sister of one of them, Lauwe, appears focal in the account of one male participant. She is said to have straddled and defiled a stream in defiance of ideas of female pollution. In Kau's own account of the movement he led, his mother's participation is also stressed. The Engan male prophet and resistance fighter Kaiyamba described himself as the 'son of the sun' (Ch. 4), but in this case, there seems to have been no comparable 'daughter of the moon'. Amongst the Ipili by Phillip Gibbs's account, after an early phase dominated by Engan male cult leaders, a young single woman called Ipiyama emerged as a prophet promising white manufactured goods which would appear at the bottom of a pool on Mount Tongapipi (Ch. 4). Some followers were so ardent in their faith in her message that they entered the water and were drowned.

In several striking examples in the literature as well as female prophets or leaders there were attempts to subvert and eclipse the prevailing sexual and reproductive relations between men and women in the context of the cult. Apropos the Hahalis Welfare Society of Buka, the relaxation of sexual taboos, and the cultivation of 'baby gardens', described at several points in the ethnography of Max and Eleanor Rimoldi (1992) was important in campaigns against it by both missions and colonial administration. In the context of Nagriamel in Vanuatu radical sexual and reproductive experimentation was more confined to charismatic leaders like Jimmy Stevens (Ch. 3). But, as noted above, his ardent polygyny, embracing over twenty-five wives, was deemed by most, except his most faithful followers, to be excessive, even for a man who followed both Mormonism and *kastom*.

Biersack's chapter (Ch. 4) reveals even more extraordinary and thorough-going attempts to revolutionize relations between men and women in the context of *mata kamo*. In several variants of the cult, women and men were enjoined to bathe together in local streams, thereby violating the strict sexual segregation and taboos on pollution which characterized the region. In the Porgera valley there are reports of the wives of cult leaders using a stone to scrape pearlshells and 'the dust thus generated falling into the water and entering the vaginas of the bathing women so that they could not contaminate their husbands during intercourse. For greater purity copulation was suspended for a month' (Ch. 4). At Asiaputenga, Paiela cultists dislodged their aprons and grass skirts, exposing their genitals, and bathed together. Women who were menstruating or who had just given birth bathed with men and thus dispersed the dangerous pollution. In Ipiyama's variant of the cult, en route to Mount Tongapipi it was said that everyone had indiscriminate sex and even that siblings had intercourse, violating the foundational incest taboo, as if no penalties would be incurred in the future for such intimacies. (As we saw, several drowned when they entered that mountain pool, but it is unclear how this was locally interpreted). Biersack's commentary on this erotic abandon, especially among the Ipili is worth quoting:

> While considerations of space prevent me from developing this point at length suffice it to say that the organization of social networks through marriage [...] and sexual reproduction, all of which depended on the incest taboo, was the most important and pervasive category of 'work' that Ipili speakers undertook [...]. To overthrow the incest taboo was to relinquish the most important tool Ipili speakers wielded, effectively voiding a vast domain of effort, from precontact rituals to prepare male youth for marriage, to fattening, assembling and distributing bridewealth, to maintaining and repairing networks through future exchange, to bearing and rearing children.

In future scholarship perhaps the origins and consequences of such internal indigenous 'sexual revolutions' as a way of envisaging and instigating the millennium might deserve some more analytic treatment alongside the externally directed 'racial liberation' that many such movements doubtless aspired to deliver.

Bibliography

Abong, Marcellin
2008   *La pirogue du Dark Bush: aperçus critiques sur l'histoire du movement Nagriamel au temps des Nouvelles-Hébrides (Vanuatu)*. Port Vila: Centre Culturel du Vanuatu/ Vanuatu Cultural Centre.

Appadurai, Arjun
1988   "Putting hierarchy in its place", *Cultural Anthropology*, 3(1): 36-49.

Bainton, Nicholas
2010   *The Lihir Destiny: Cultural Responses to Mining in Melanesia*. Canberra: ANU E–Press. http://epress.anu.edu.au?p=30161

Bhabha, Homi
1994 [1985] *The Location of Culture*. London: Routledge.

Billings, Dorothy
2002   *Cargo Cult as Theater: Political Performance in the Pacific*. Lanham: Lexington Books.

Chakrabarty, Dipesh
2000   *Provincializing Europe: Postcolonial Thought and Historical Difference*. Princeton: Princeton University Press.

Comaroff, Jean and John Comaroff
1991   *Of Revelation and Revolution: Vol 1. Christianity, Colonialism and Consciousness in South Africa*. Chicago: University of Chicago Press.
1997   *Of Revelation and Revolution: Vol 2. The Dialectics of Modernity on a South African Frontier*. Chicago: University of Chicago Press.
2001   *Millenial Capitalism and the Culture of Neoliberalism*. Durham and London: Duke University Press.

Curtis, Tim
2002   "Talking about Place: Identities, Histories and Powers among the Na'hai Speakers of Malakula (Vanuatu)", PhD thesis. Canberra: Australian National University.

Fanon, Frantz
1967   *Black Skin, White Masks*. Trans C. L. Markmann. New York: Grove Press.

Gammage, Bill
1998   *The Sky Travellers: Journeys in New Guinea 1938-1939*. Melbourne: Melbourne University Press.

Hau'ofa, Epeli
1975   "Anthropology and Pacific Islanders", *Oceania* 45(4): 283-289.
2008   *We Are the Ocean: Selected Works*. Honolulu: University of Hawai'i Press.

Hempenstall, Peter and Rutherford, Noel
1984   *Protest and Dissent in the Colonial Pacific*. Suva: Institute of Pacific Studies, University of the South Pacific.

Hermann, Elfriede
1992   "The Yali Movement in Retrospect: Rewriting History, Redefining 'Cargo Cult'". In Andrew Lattas (ed.) *Alienating Mirrors: Christianity, Cargo Cults and Colonialism in Melanesia*, Special Issue of *Oceania*, 63 (1): 55-71.
1997   "*Kastom* versus Cargo Cult: Emotional Discourse on the Yali Movement in Madang Province, Papua New Guinea". In Ton Otto and Aard Borsboom (eds), *Cultural Dynamics of Religious Change in Oceania*. Leiden: KITLV Press, 87-102.
2004   "Dissolving the Self-Other Dichotomy in Western 'Cargo Cult' Constructions". In H. Jebens (ed.), *Cargo, Cult and Culture Critique*. Honolulu: University of Hawai'i Press, pp. 36-58.

Hermkens, Anna-Karina
2012   "Circulating Matters of Belief: Engendering Marian Movements during the Bougainville Crisis". In Lenore Manderson, Wendy Smith, & Matt Tomlinson (eds) *Flows of Faith: Religious Reach and Community in Asia and the Pacific.* New York: Springer, pp. 161-181.

Hours, Bernard
1974   "Un mouvement politico-religieux néo-Hébridais: le Nagriamel", *Cahiers ORSTOM*, 11(3-4): 227-242.
1976   "Leadership et cargo cult: l'irrésistible ascension de JTPS Moïse", *Journal de la Société des Océanistes*, 32(2): 207-231.

Jolly, Margaret
1987   "The Forgotten Women: A History of Migrant Labour and Gender Relations in Vanuatu", *Oceania*, 58(2):119-39.
1992   "Specters of Inauthenticity", *The Contemporary Pacific*, 4(1):49–72.
2007   "Imagining Oceania: Indigenous and Foreign Representations of a Sea of Islands", *The Contemporary Pacific*, 19(2): 508-545.
2008 (ed.) *Re-membering Oceanic Masculinities*, *The Contemporary Pacific*, 20(1). [Special issue].
2012a   "Material and Immaterial Relations: Gender, Rank and Christianity in Vanuatu". In Laurent Dousset and Serge Tcherkézoff (eds), *The Scope of Anthropology*. Oxford: Berghahn, pp. 100-154.
2012b   "Women of the East, Women of the West. Region and Race, Gender and Sexuality on Cook's Voyages". In Kate Fullagar (ed.), *The Atlantic World in the Antipodes: Effects and Transformations since the Eighteenth Century.* Newcastle upon Tyne, UK: Cambridge Scholars Publishing, pp. 2-32.

Kaplan, Martha
1995   *Neither Cargo nor Cult: Ritual Politics and the Colonial Imagination in Fiji*. Durham: Duke University Press.

Keane, Webb
2004   *Christian Moderns. Freedom and Fetish in the Mission Encounter*. Berkeley: University of California Press.

Keesing, Roger
1978   "Politico-Religious Movements and Anticolonialism on Malaita: Maasina Rule in Historical Perspective", *Oceania*, 48(4): 241-261 and 49(1): 46-73.
1984   "Rethinking Mana", *Journal of Anthropological Research*, 4(1): 137-156.
1986   "Plantation networks, plantation culture: the hidden side of colonial Melanesia", *Journal de la Société des Océanistes*, 82(42): 163-170.

Kolig, Erich
1981   "The Paradox of Santo, Vanuatu", *Pacific Perspective*, 10(1): 57-61.
1987   "Kastom, Cargo and the Construction of Utopia on Santo, Vanuatu: The Nagriamel Movement", *Journal de la Société des Océanistes*, 85(2): 181-204.

Latour, Bruno
1993 [1991]*We Have Never Been Modern*. Trans. Catherine Porter. Cambridge/Mas.: Harvard University Press.

Lawrence, Peter
1964   *Road Belong Cargo. A Study of the Cargo Movement in the Southern Madang District New Guinea*. Manchester and Melbourne: Manchester University Press and Melbourne University Press.

Lindstrom, Lamont
1989   "Working Encounters: Oral Histories of World War Two Labour Corps from Tanna, Vanuatu". In White, Geoffrey and Lamont Lindstrom (eds), *The Pacific Theatre: Island Representations of World War II*. Pacific Island Monograph Series, No 8. Honolulu: University of Hawai'i Press, Center for Pacific Island Studies, pp. 395-417.
1990   *Knowledge and Power in a South Pacific Society*. Washington and London: Smithsonian Institution Press.
1993   *Cargo Cult: Strange Stories of Desire from Melanesia and Beyond*. Honolulu: University of Hawai'i Press.

Lindstrom, Lamont and Geoffrey M. White
1990   *Island Encounters: Black and White Memories of the Pacific War*. Washington and London: Smithsonian Institution Press.

Lindstrom, Lamont and James Gwero (eds)
1998   *Big Wok: Storian blong Wol Wo Tu long Vanuatu*. Christchurch and Suva: Macmillan Brown Centre for Pacific Studies and Institute of Pacific Studies, University of the South Pacific.

MacClancy, Jeremy
1980   *To Kill a Bird with Two Stones: A Short History of Vanuatu*. Port Vila: Vanuatu Cultural Centre Publications No. 1.

McDowell, Nancy
1988   "A Note on Cargo and Cultural Constructions of Change", *Pacific Studies,* 11: 121-34.
2000   "A Brief Comment on Difference and Rationality", *Oceania*, 70(4): 373-380.

Moore, Clive
1985   *Kanaka: A History of Melanesian Mackay*. Port Moresby: Institute of Papua New Guinea
          Studies and University of Papua New Guinea Press.

Nelson, Hank
2006   *The Pacific War in Papua New Guinea. Memories and Realities*. Rikkyo University Japan:
          Centre for Asia Area Studies.

Patterson, Mary
2011   "Enchanted economies in the Pacific and beyond". In Mary Patterson and Martha
          Macintyre (eds), *Managing Modernity in the Southwest Pacific*. St Lucia: University of
          Queensland Press, pp. 90-120.

Rimoldi, Max and Rimoldi, Eleanor
1992   *Hahalis and the Labour of Love: A Social Movement on Buka Island*. Oxford: Berg.

Rousseau, Benedicta
2004   "The Achievement of Simultaneity: *Kastom* in Contemporary Vanuatu". PhD thesis.
          Cambridge: Cambridge University.

Scott, Michael W.
2012   "The Matter of Makira: Colonisation, Competition, and the Production of Gendered
          Peoples in Contemporary Solomon Islands and Medieval Britain", *History and
          Anthropology*, 23(1): 115-148.

Spriggs, Matthew
1997   *The Island Melanesians*. Oxford: Blackwell Publishers.

Tabani, Marc
2008a   *Une pirogue pour le paradis: le culte de John Frum à Tanna*. Paris: Maison des Sciences
          de L'Homme.
2008b   "A political history of Nagriamel on Santo, Vanuatu", *Oceania*, 78 (3): 332-357.

Vivieros de Castro, Eduardo
2004   "Exchanging Perspectives: The Transformation of Objects into Subjects in Amerindian
          Ontologies", *Common Knowledge*, 10(3): 463-484.

Waiko, John
1973   "European-Melanesian Contact in Melanesian Tradition and Literature". In Ron J. May
          (ed.), *Priorities in Melanesian Development*. Port Moresby: University of Papua New
          Guinea, pp. 417-428.

White, Geoffrey and Lamont Lindstrom (eds)
1989   *The Pacific Theatre: Island Representations of World War II*. Pacific Island Monograph
          Series, No 8. Honolulu: University of Hawai'i Press, Center for Pacific Island Studies.

Worsley, Peter
1970 [1957] *The Trumpet Shall Sound: A Study of "Cargo" Cults in Melanesia*. London: Paladin.

Zorn, Jean G.
2012   "Engendering Violence in the Papua New Guinea Courts: Sentencing in Rape Trials".

In Margaret Jolly and Christine Stewart (with Carolyn Brewer), *Engendering Violence in Papua New Guinea*. ANU E-Press, pp. 163-195.

Biographies

Marcellin ABONG is the Director of the Vanuatu Cultural Centre and of the Vanuatu National Cultural Council. He was trained at the University Paris-I-Sorbonne-Panthéon (Master degree in Ethno-Archeology) and at the University Paris-VI-Pierre et Marie-Curie (Fundamental Xylologie). He has published a book, *La pirogue du dark bush : apercus critiques sur l'histoire du Nagriamel* (Port-Vila, VKS publications); he has also co-edited two other books, *Oceanic Ancestors/Ancêtres Océaniens* (Paris, Somogy Editions d'Arts) and *101 mots pour comprendre le Vanuatu* (Nouméa, editions du GRHOC). In 2008, he received a chiefly title from his community in Lamap (south Malekula), "Gulgul Maingi Taridumlegh Baraghabat", which refers to the morning star and symbolize hope.

Aletta BIERSACK has conducted research on the Ipili speakers of Enga Province, Papua New Guinea, over several decades. Her publications have concentrated on indigenous ritual, its relation to gender ideologies (her several studies of *omatisia*, a ritual designed to grow boys in puberty), cosmology (her writings on *mata kamo*), Christianity (her *mata kamo* studies again as well as her writings on Paiela Christianity), and gold and its mining; gold mining in its impacts and politics; and gender, marriage, and the organization of reproduction and thus networks through marriage. Her special areas of interest are gender, social organization (but understood entirely through the organizational projects and strategies articulated by Ipili speakers themselves), and theorizing the history of Ipili speakers as involving forces for both the preservation and the alteration of culture in an era of globalization. She is the editor of four anthologies: *Clio in Oceania* (on historical anthropology), *Papuan Borderlands* (on Ipili, Huli, and Enga cultures), *Ecologies for Tomorrow* (on political ecology), and (with James Greenberg) *Reimagining Political Ecology*.

Doug DALTON teaches cultural anthropology at Longwood University in Farmville, Virginia. His research and scholarship is concerned with indigenous concepts and historical change employing ideas from symbolic anthropology, phenomenology, critical cultural studies, and chaos and complexity theory. Dalton has published several articles which consider the notion from several perspectives and edited one volume of *Oceania* on the idea of "cargo cult." He has also published articles on shell valuables and their meanings, money, economic spheres and card games in relation to "cargo cult," on concepts of self, memory, and "development," mythology, mortuary rites, and intellectual history in Melanesian anthropology. His teaching focuses on cultural research methods, the history of anthropological theory, religion, language and culture, and ethnographically focused courses in the Pacific region.

Elfriede HERMANN has conducted long-term research with the Ngaing of Papua New Guinea and the Banabans living on Rabi Island in Fiji, Banaba Island and Tarawa Atoll in Kiribati. Currently she is also engaged in research with various island communities in Kiribati. Her foci have been social movements, emotions, historicity, identifications, gender, migration, ethnicity, cultural transformations and transculturation, and, most recently, local perceptions of climate change. Since earning her PhD from the University of Tübingen in 1995, she has been with the University of Göttingen's Institute of Cultural and Social Anthropology, where she gained her venia legendi and currently has the responsibilities of a professor. From 2005 to 2011 she has also been a research fellow at the Honolulu Academy of Arts, Hawai`i. Among her publications are *Emotionen und Historizität: Der emotionale Diskurs über die Yali-Bewegung in einer Dorfgemeinschaft der Ngaing, Papua New Guinea* (the conclusion is in English) (1995); and "Emotions and the Relevance of the Past: Historicity and Ethnicity among the Banabans of Fiji," *History and Anthropology* 16 (3) (2005): 275–291; she is guest co-editor with Wolfgang Kempf of "Relations in Multicultural Fiji: Transformations, Positionings and Articulations," a special section in *Oceania* 75 (4) (2005), and edited *Changing Contexts – Shifting Meanings: Transformations of Cultural Traditions in Oceania* (2011).

Margaret JOLLY is an Australian Research Council Laureate Fellow and Professor in Gender and Cultural Studies and Pacific Studies in the School of Culture, History and Language, College of Asia and the Pacific at the Australian National University. She is an historical anthropologist who has written extensively on gender in the Pacific, on exploratory voyages and travel writing, missions and contemporary Christianity, maternity and sexuality, cinema and art. Her most recent book, co-edited with Serge Tcherkézoff and Darrell Tryon is *Oceanic Encounters: Exchange, Desire, Violence* with ANU E-Press.

Lamont LINDSTROM, Kendall Professor of Anthropology at the University of Tulsa, is the author of *Knowledge and Power in a South Pacific Society* (Smithsonian Institution Press, 1990), *Cargo Cult: Strange Stories of Desire from Melanesia and Beyond* (University of Hawaii Press, 1993), and has also published on cultural policy, kava, chiefs and governance, Pacific War ethnohistory, and adventurer-photographers Martin and Osa Johnson, and he has written a dictionary and grammar of the Kwamera language of southeast Tanna, Vanuatu. He is currently following the life stories of Tanna urban migrants who have moved up into the settlements surrounding Port Vila, Vanuatu's capital town, whose lives have spanned the eras of colonialism, national independence, and globalization.

Martha MACINTYRE is currently the editor of *The Australian Journal of Anthropology* and an honorary Research Fellow at the University of Melbourne. She gained her PhD from The Australian National University and has held positions at The Australian National University, Monash University, La Trobe University and The University of Melbourne. She has undertaken research in Papua New Guinea since 1979. Her research interests include historical ethnography, economic anthropology, gender, the social impacts of mining, medical anthropology, fisheries in Melanesia, environmental anthropology and human rights. Her publications include *Human Rights and Gender Politics: Perspectives on the Asia Pacific Region*, co-edited with A. Hildson, V. Mackie, and M. Stivens (2000), and *Women Miners in Developing Countries: Pit Women and Others*, co-edited with K. Lahiri-Dutt (2006) and *Managing Modernity in the Western Pacific* (2011), co-edited with Mary Patterson.

Marc TABANI is Senior Research Fellow at the Centre National de la Recherche Scientifique (CNRS) and affiliated to the Centre de Recherche et de Documentation sur l'Océanie (CREDO) and to the Vanuatu Cultural Centre as Honorary Curator. He has conducted research in many islands of Vanuatu since 20 years. His main topics have been politics of identity and tradition, cultural change, millenarianism. Many of his writings have focused on ni-vanuatu indigenous movements, especially the Nagriamel and the John Frum movements. After being based since over three years in Vanuatu he has extend his researches to such topics like commodification and commercialization of cultures, globalization and national politics, monetarization of domestic modes of production based economies. Among his different achievements in project managements, he became the cofounder with Marcellin Abong and Jacob Kapere of the TAFEA Kaljoral Senta. This branch of the Vanuatu Cultural Centre is located in Tanna and focused its cultural and artistic activities on the societies of the southern province of Vanuatu (islands of Tanna, Aneytium, Futuna, Eromango, Aniwa). Marc Tabani has published several articles in french and English and edited two volumes in French (2002, *Les pouvoirs de la coutume à Vanuatu : traditionalisme et édification nationale* and 2008, *Une pirogue pour le paradis : le culte de John Frum à Tanna*). He is also editor and co-author of the french version of Histri blong yumi : an history of Vanuatu in four volumes (2010-1012) and editor of a special issue of the *Journal de la Société des Océanistes* dedicated to the 30 years of Vanuatu's independence (2011).

www.ingramcontent.com/pod-product-compliance
Lightning Source LLC
Chambersburg PA
CBHW080610270326
41928CB00016B/2990